HARD FROST

Also by John Newton

Tales from the Angler's Eldorado (1985)

The Double Rainbow: James K. Baxter, Ngāti Hau and the Jerusalem Commune (2009)

Lives of the Poets (2010)

Family Songbook (2013)

HARD FROST

Structures of Feeling in New Zealand Literature 1908–1945

John Newton

Victoria University Press

TE WHARE WĀNANGA O TE ŪPOKO O TE IKA A MĀUI
VICTORIA
UNIVERSITY OF WELLINGTON

VICTORIA UNIVERSITY PRESS
Victoria University of Wellington
PO Box 600 Wellington
vup.victoria.ac.nz

First published 2017

A catalogue record is available at the National Library of New Zealand.

ISBN 9781776561629

Published with the assistance of a grant from

creative nz
ARTS COUNCIL OF NEW ZEALAND TOI AOTEAROA

Printed by Ligare, Auckland

. . . nothing changes from generation to generation except the composition in which we live and the composition in which we live makes the art which we see and hear.

—Gertrude Stein, 'Portraits and Repetition'

Contents

Preface

What was New Zealand Literature?

From my grad school days I remember the sting of that past tense conceit with its bullying subtext. 'What *was* the Novel?' 'What *was* Postmodernism?' 'What *was* Literary Studies?' Ambitious young folk would use titles like these and we all knew what they were trying to tell us: that the thing we were attached to, the thing we were comfortable with, or (most of all) the thing we were just beginning to get our heads around, was dead, shamed into obsolescence by the hungry time-consciousness of academic thought. So I hesitate now, on grounds of taste and good manners. But I'm going to forgive myself for using it. First, because it's not really news: that 'New Zealand literature' is effectively 'dead' has been thought and said often enough for it not to shock anyone. And second, because I'm not here to gloat about it. No one is more sad about this than I am.

New Zealand literature has been a very large part of my life. For me it's been a fundamental source of that language (what I've called elsewhere that 'family songbook') out of which each of us patches up our subjectivity. I have always wanted to be a writer—I can date the ambition from my early teens—and from as early as 1980, when as a 20-year-old I first encountered local writing in an academic context, I understood that this meant being a *New Zealand* writer. Behind this, of course, was a local feeling; New Zealand was where my reality was. But there was also, I would come to realise, a modernist assumption that writing accrued around other writing, and that to read or to write in a sophisticated way was to take up an ongoing conversation. When I read the writers of the 1970s I could hear them talking to the writers of the mid century; even when this meant avoiding those writers, this gesture, too, was addressed to a local audience. In 1985, when *The Penguin Book of New Zealand Verse* grabbed everyone's attention, I knew that its significance depended not just on the cultural politics of the 1980s but on its relationship to its predecessor of 1960. This was what it was to have arrived at a national literature; it was to be able to recognise the signs, to read and speak the language and to make oneself understood in it. Crucially there was an infrastructure. Today it's almost hard to believe that we once rushed out each week to buy the *Listener*, expecting to find the new Frame or Curnow reviewed at length by a well-credentialled critic, and more than likely argued over subsequently in letters to the editor. *Landfall* came out four times a year, nearly always with chunky essays on New Zealand writing. And in academic English programmes 'N.Z. Lit' was on the march. At the University of Canterbury, where I was teaching by the mid 1990s, undergrads could at one point choose between four different courses in New Zealand literature, with another two or three at Honours level. In a context like this it was no stretch at all to imagine oneself writing 'New Zealand literature'. The phrase meant something: a discourse, a home, a context in which to explore and develop an idiolect and a literary vocation.

Plainly it doesn't mean the same thing today. As best I can tell, millennial writers don't think like this at all. 'New Zealand literature' is barely on their radar: they find little incentive to read it, let alone attach themselves to it, or aspire self-consciously to write it. For them the world has turned on its axis. They locate themselves on a different grid. Where my generation identified with our local predecessors, even if they might be only 15 years older, today's smart young writers seem to think horizontally; they align themselves with admired international contemporaries, but just as importantly with their immediate peers. Ask a young writer today to name their favourite New Zealand poet or novelist and they are more likely to name one of their friends or teachers than a writer from the previous century. Their relationship to other writing, past and present, is mediated less by formal criticism than by social media, the blogosphere and the pedagogy of the creative writing schools. They are conscious, too, of different markets, institutions and rewards—from an energetic local reading scene, to global publication, international prizes and the festival circuit. In this setting, speaking to an inherited local context must (I imagine) appear as quaint as talking to your neighbour across the back fence. There are gifted young writers who happen to be New Zealanders, but seldom do I get the impression that any of them is trying to write 'New Zealand literature'.

The reader won't fail to hear a note of complaint. But I don't mean to write a jeremiad. No one is going to hell in a handcart. My aim here is simply to sketch the context in which this project has been conceived. That New Zealand literature is now a finite chapter, complete and increasingly remote, invites us to read it in different ways, and to feel about it differently, too.

I am not trying to turn back the tide of change, or insist that our writers should still think like regionalists. Rather, I am trying to make the best use I can of the view that begins to emerge as this history falls away from us.

Around the turn of the millennium an interruption takes place, of which a generation turning its back on local precedent is one expression. A break has occurred in what I will be calling, after Raymond Williams, the *structure of feeling*. Like a full stop nailing down the end of a sentence, this break confers a new, finite logic on the history leading up to it; the narrative arc of 20th-century writing is re-punctuated. Our accustomed sense of a national literature emerges, as we know, in the 1930s. While the dominance of the Caxton generation will be challenged by the younger writers of the Baxter cohort, what we can broadly call 'nationalist' thought sets the tone for a further two decades beyond World War II. A more decisive challenge comes with the Baby Boom. From the late 60s, and particularly in the 70s, the generation of *Freed* and *Islands* will remake the local literary scene in their own image. With their hippie insouciance, their pop culture and their Americanism, they are a group who seem indifferent to the struggles of literary nationalism. And yet, for all that was new, what becomes clear in retrospect is how strictly these writers were still working within a national framework. It may have been time to stop 'nam[ing] them hills', as Murray Edmond put it in a *Freed* editorial—national *identity* was off the agenda—but the assumed frame of reference was still *writing in New Zealand*. In this respect, *Islands* was as nationalist as *Landfall*. And even later, in the 80s and 90s, as both the mid-century nationalists and the *Freed* generation came under the microscope of 'theory' and postcolonialism, the discourse held its national shape. The critical armoury was threateningly new, but the conversation still addressed the question of writing *here*, and proceeded (as in the work of Roger Horrocks and Leigh Davis) by critical analysis of an established local tradition.

Here is one sense in which the view has now changed. It takes the turning away of the new millennial writers to make apparent what a long career the assumptions of literary nationalism previously enjoyed. Again and again we hear that nationalism is done with—in the 50s, in the 70s, in the supercilious 80s—but through each of these noisy interruptions the discourse retains its New Zealand parameters. At times the arguments are bloody, but even that intensity is evidence of a shared cultural memory. There *are* breaks, of course; I will talk about them constantly; shifts in the structure of feeling supply the backbone of my argument. But across them flows a residual consensus—an assent to the pertinence of a national conversation—that underwrites six or seven decades of coherent activity.

A second respect in which local writing of the previous century now reads and feels differently I can only describe in terms of *partisanship*. Is it only me who feels this? I miss New Zealand literature! I miss being able to talk about it, talk back to it, write into it. And if I can't resurrect it, then at least I want to remember it. I bring to this project a partiality, and for better or worse a certain nostalgia. I also bring, like any historian, a sense of unfinished business. Even where the critical traffic has been heaviest, we are far from having solved all the outstanding problems. Even more, perhaps, what we owe to the nationalist mid century is not merely critical attention to certain sticking points but a different *style* of attention, more appreciative, more tolerant. In the 80s and 90s, theoretically informed scholarship ruthlessly exposed the movement's limitations: its masculinism, its monoculturalism, its allegedly naïve representationalism. With this wave of critique came some highly productive insights. But along the way we have managed to forget the things that nationalist writing did well. As Roger Horrocks put it a few years ago, 'Surely enough time has been spent demystifying nationalism for us to be able to return to it in a secular spirit'. That such a 'return' has not yet taken place leaves our sense of mid-century writing depleted. Having proved that we can censure nationalist writing in complex ways, we still have not brought the equivalent sophistication to less anxious, more wide-ranging and curious ways of engaging with it.

So here is my curatorial wager: that as New Zealand literature slips over the horizon it's time to try to retell its history from beginning to end. This means, by my count, not one book but three, and if all goes to plan two more instalments will follow this one. *Hard Frost* begins with the break of the 1930s, loops back to take account of the nationalists' immediate predecessors, and extends as far the end of World War II. The second instalment coincides with the classic phase of *Landfall*, under the editorship of Charles Brasch, from 1947–66; post-war nationalism expands the movement's range, while it struggles with familiar limitations, particularly around sex and gender. The third begins with that massive shift in the structure of feeling that we know loosely as 'the 60s', signalled with increasing clarity by the handing-off of *Landfall* to Robin Dudding (1966), the emergence of *Freed* (1969), and then conclusively in 1972 by the establishment of *Islands*. This third stanza also needs to account for a twilight phase as this 'long' literary nationalism enters what will prove to be its death throes in the 80s and 90s: say, from *the bone people* (1983) to *The Vintner's Luck* (1998), or from *The Penguin Book of New Zealand Verse* (1985) to *An Anthology of New Zealand Poetry in English* (1997).

The further back we travel along this timeline, the more thoroughly the ground has been dug over. The inaugural period of nationalist writing—the one we are about to plunge back into—is not just the mostly studiously mythologised chapter in our literary history, but has also proved the most critically productive. Even so, it still harbours unresolved difficulties.

At this distance, two problems strike me as crucial. The first is the role of modernism. The 'modernist' character of the nationalist intervention has solidified into a given without ever passing through a systematic analysis. As a consequence, I don't believe we've paid enough heed to what may in fact be the most singular feature of our particular literary nationalism: namely that, unlike any other I can think of, it is formulated under the historical aegis, not of high or late Romanticism, but of modernist disenchantment. What does it mean to propose a discourse of settler nationalism *downstream of modernism*? What kind of modernism could this be, and more to the point, what kind of nationalism? Second, there is nationalism's gender, and its sex. It is far from being a secret, of course, that nationalist writing is a masculine affair. Nor is it news that in the 1930s writing by women seems to all but disappear. The literary demographics of this drama have become familiar, as have the nationalists' pervasive misogyny and the corresponding importance of (in particular) Robin Hyde. But *why* does our literary culture take this assertively masculine turn? Are we reading these events in a broad enough context? If the scene of 30s writing is a crime scene, have we correctly identified the perpetrators? The answers to these questions lead beyond 'New Zealand literature'. They also remind us how much goes to waste if we accept that our own literary history has nothing left to say to us.

They say it takes a village to raise a child and I feel something similar about specialised books. To produce a work like this you need to believe that a community, however small, wants to read it. It's the message you get, if you're lucky enough, from institutions, colleagues and friends. This book would not exist if I hadn't been so enviably supported by all three.

The Stout Research Centre at Victoria University hosted me as J.D. Stout Research Fellow in 2010, and has once more served as a second home since I returned to Wellington in 2015. I am deeply indebted to my friend Lydia Wevers, the outgoing director; to Louise Grenside and Debbie Levy; to the wonderful colleagues I have worked alongside; and of course to the generosity of the Stout Trustees. A New Zealandist simply couldn't wish for a more favourable environment.

I am deeply grateful, too, to Creative New Zealand and to the English Department at the University of Waikato, where I worked on this project as Writer in Residence in 2014. For her support and encouragement, my particular thanks to Sarah Shieff. I am happy to report that Little Bethel isn't nearly as frightening as Frank Sargeson had led me to anticipate.

New Zealand literary criticism has always been a boutique industry. Everything happens at close quarters and one's debts to other contributors feel more than usually personal. I won't say we stand on the shoulders of giants—it doesn't sound like the Kiwi way. So instead let me say that if this book does stand, it's on the shoulders of colleagues who as often as not are also personal friends. There's an urge to list and thank them by name but the text and the footnotes do the job more accurately. There is one critic, though, whom I don't reference often, even though his work is all over this book. My friend and mentor Patrick Evans has done so much to shape the way I think about New Zealand writing that if I started to itemise precisely what I owe him I wouldn't know where to stop.

A note on earlier versions. The argument of this book has taken a long time to settle; my first attempts to think through some of these problems are in articles that go back almost twenty years. As I indicate at one or two points in the text, initial conclusions haven't always survived. It has often been said but bears repeating: a critic is someone who conducts their education in public.

Victoria University Press do amazing things with remarkably few hands. Thank you to everyone in the building. In particular, a huge thanks to Fergus Barrowman for his confidence in the project and his patience with its endless mutations; and to Ashleigh Young for her skilled and tactful editing.

When a writing project marinates as long as this one has, inevitably debts get forgotten and kindnesses taken for granted. The friends, colleagues and fellow toilers named below will all know what I owe them. So will those whom I've managed to forget and whose names will return to me the moment this book goes to print. Ka nui te mihi ki a koutou katoa:

Philip Armstrong, Barry Barclay, Rachel Barrowman, Sarah Beaven, Cynthia Brophy, James Brown, Alex Calder, Hamish Cooper, Wystan Curnow, Kate De Goldi, John Dennison, Simon During, Murray Edmond, Cliff Fell, Bruce Foster, Mark Fryer, Alice Galletly, Olivia Galletly, Craig Gamble, Simon Garrett, Michael Gilchrist, Anna Green, Charlotte Handy, Dinah Hawken, Richard Hill, Jeffrey Paparoa Holman, Mark Houlahan, David Howard, Holly Hunter, Chris Jacomb, Anne Kennedy, The Last Chance Salon, Michele Leggott, Bernadette Macartney, Kirsten McDougall, Howard McNaughton, Paul Millar, Charles Macdonald, Kirstine Moffat, Gregory O'Brien, Vincent O'Sullivan, Tony Paine, Mary Paul, Bill Pearson, Emily Perkins, Chris Prentice, Chris Price, Alan Prosser, St Andrews Escape, Peter Simpson, Tracey Slaughter, Rachel Smith, Jane Stafford, Ray Toomath, Robyn Toomath, Linda Tyler, Ian Wedde, Lis Whyte, Damien Wilkins, Mark Williams, Nicholas Wright, Redmer Yska, Diane Zwimpfer.

Introduction

A hard frost

It was Charles Brasch who coined the phrase. In a memoir of his earlier life that concludes at the end of World War II, he recalls his impressions of New Zealand writing as he contemplated coming home from Britain to establish a literary journal:

> There was no such thing yet as a distinct New Zealand literature; but the small cloudy nucleus of one was already forming [. . .] Allen Curnow's *Book of New Zealand Verse 1923–45* [. . .] announced that New Zealand literature had begun, and put forward a first bold idea of it. In its combination of incisiveness, economy and generosity the anthology marked an epoch. Like a hard frost, it killed off weeds, and promoted sound growth; it set a standard not for poetry alone but for all the arts [. . .][1]

It's a moment encrusted with critical mythology, the birth of our modern literary tradition. We return to it habitually. But no one describes it more aptly than Brasch. His metaphor offers a pitch-perfect shorthand for the distinctive characteristics of his cohort's literary nationalism. It evokes at a glance its geographical orientation, its modernist severity, its stoicism, its hard-body vernacularism. If for Brasch it calls on memories of his beloved Central Otago, anchoring the national in the regional, this is appropriate too. And it underlines a willingness, particularly on the part of Allen Curnow, to think about the local outlook critically, even harshly. This negative disposition—creation through negation, the nurturing of culture with a kind of critical 'tough love'—will be the movement's most provocative characteristic, as well as its boldest innovation.

However, as we've seen since the mid 1980s, the values that this *hard frost* commemorates are readily revalued. Its virtues can be made to sound like vices. The appeal to geography becomes the colonial habit of 'landscape', precision is reduced to 'realism', hardness betrays a repressive and unrelenting masculinism. As for growth by critical weeding, the all-too-obvious correlative will be the systematic decimation of writing by women. By now, I think it's fair to say the negative implications of all this frostiness speak as loudly as the positive ones. Whenever I appeal to Brasch's metaphor in this book, then, I am counting on it to evoke both responses. It alludes to an 'ideal' reading of literary nationalism, as well as to a resistant reading; to the mood of nationalist writing as the nationalists saw it themselves, and to a later, revisionist temper that has viewed it with scepticism.

But in nailing that phrase to the masthead of this book I also mean it to indicate something more difficult, more elusive: not simply the tough talk of mid-century writing, but the wider emotional climate from which that idiom emerges.

The affective vocabulary of the literary nationalists, with its leanness, its meanness, its masculine belligerence, was not just their own perverse creation. Writers can only play the cards they are dealt: they can articulate feelings, refine them, formalise them, complicate them, but they don't invent them. It is this understanding of what it means to read contextually—the sense that we need to be reading these cards—that sends me to Raymond Williams and his focus on structure. When I'm reading nationalist writing, I am trying to tune my ear to what it felt *necessary* to write, and to what it was *possible* to write. Until we ask these questions, I would say that we are not yet thinking historically, and my ambitions for this project are nothing if not historical and contextual. At the same time, however, the style of attention these questions call for can only be, if not in a wholly familiar sense, *literary*. We are not going to reconstruct a context of feeling without knuckling down to some diligent close reading.

Structures of feeling

'Structure of feeling' is a slippery term, and it comes with a problematic pedigree. Williams first uses it first in 1954 (it's as old as the entrenched phase of nationalism itself); 25 years later he's still trying to explain it to his own satisfaction. His abiding theme is historical change, and it's evident that structure of feeling is at the heart of his thinking about it.[2] And yet despite (or perhaps because of) all this relitigation, the idea never seems fully to resolve itself. Williams himself is aware of the problem; by the late 1970s he sounds almost apologetic: 'To this day I find that I keep coming back to this notion from the actual experience of literary analysis rather than from any theoretical satisfaction with the concept itself.'[3] His followers haven't been satisfied either. And so while no British critic on the Left is more admired, since Williams's death in 1988 the idea of structure of feeling has enjoyed a curious half-life. As David Simpson comments, it has never proved 'exportable':[4] subsequent critics have not refined or developed it, or by and large even employed it in other than a glancing, ad hoc fashion. A signature invention of a major intellectual figure, it endures as a kind of phantom device.

Allowing, then, for its chequered past, and taking due note of its opacities, what does the concept now leave us to work with? First, the seeming paradox that *feeling has shape and regularity*: 'as firm and delicate as "structure" suggests, yet [. . .] operat[ing] in the most delicate and least tangible parts of our activity.'[5] We may think of feeling as amorphous and ungovernable, a medium of unbridled subjectivity. But feeling doesn't simply pour out of us: feeling is antecedent, it surrounds and informs us, a structure in the sense of being a framework that we are always negotiating. In the epoch of 'theory', anti-expressive assumptions of this kind will become routine. Even so, 'structure of feeling' has not lost its counter-commonsensical shine. And it still has its own distinct promise when it comes to reading cultural change. Crucially, that is, and secondly, *feelings are historically contingent.* With a new generation comes a new subjective regime; the structure of feeling is repeatedly transformed, so that each generation 'feel[s] its whole life in certain ways differently'.[6] This holds implications, thirdly, for the way that Williams thinks about historical context, setting him at odds with the Marxian tradition that is his home base. Structure of feeling is a historical determinant that slips through the mesh of a materialist analysis. We can reconstruct 'the material life, the general social organisation, and, to a large extent, the dominant ideas', but when it comes to the shaping of a cultural form (in this case drama) there still 'remains some element for which there is no external counterpart.'[7] This elusive element is structure of feeling: not as a superstructural effect (epiphenomenon of some deeper cause), but as *a historical determinant in its own right*. The way that each generation 'feels its life' is an active ingredient of cultural change.

All of which, needless to say, begs a great many questions. It's not a surprise that Williams's followers on the Left have parked it to one side as a subjectivist aberration. But nor is it hard to see why Williams himself remained so attached to the idea, and why later readers, too, without knowing quite what to do with it, have nonetheless kept circling back. It touches on so much in literary (not to mention 'lived') experience that we know we need to talk about more effectively than we do. Not least, the problem of *feeling* itself. Feeling belongs, as Williams puts it, among the most 'delicate' parts of our activity, the writing and reading of texts being a case in point. The practice of reading is saturated in feeling. And yet we tend to bracket it off as subjective or even private; it's hard to find the language to bring it confidently into literary discussion. Embarrassingly obvious, infinitely subtle, this vein of cultural experience is somehow everywhere and nowhere. It's also quite evident, as Williams insists, that the language of feeling is historically variable. A quick illustration, a 'usual suspect': the sentimental streak in Victorianism. Modern readers hold out against it; it turns us off; it creates a barrier. And yet the original readers of Dickens or Meredith had no such problems. Between their time and ours something has been lost, an emotional context that the writing in question unthinkingly assumes, in which its affective vocabulary felt right, but which presents itself now as a sense of foreignness or opacity. The same goes, too, in more subtle degrees, for writers who may only be a couple of decades older, or indeed younger. As Williams puts it, 'no generation speaks quite the same language as its predecessors.'[8] We don't speak theirs, and they don't speak ours. They write according to their structure of feeling, and we read them through the prism of our own. The point once again is somehow almost too obvious. But if we want to read historically we need to keep thinking about it.

Structure of feeling, as I have come to see it, is an intuition on Williams's part that never quite becomes a theory. It offers no set procedure, no *method* of reading. And yet it points to what, for me, are among the most insistent problems in our literary history. As a critical hunch, it can't be 'applied'; it won't stand guarantor of anything. But it can be explored, and permitted in this process to underscore specific analytical priorities. Thus, to rethink the history of New Zealand writing by way of structure of feeling to me implies three things. First of all, a constant alertness to where I am reading and writing from—in every sense possible, but not least a generational sense. Second, a curiosity about the repertoire of feeling that impinges on each generational moment, about the way this compels and constrains what gets written, and about the ways in which writing can help us to reconstruct this affective context. And third, a mapping of literary-historical development onto a generational grid marked by changes in the climate of feeling: a genealogy of feelings; or, better, a *seismology* of feelings.

This last point demands clarification. A 'generational grid' is hardly a novel proposition; we know there's a well-established convention that sees the history of New Zealand writing as a generational procession: the *Phoenix* generation, the Baxter generation, the *Freed* generation. Structure of feeling, as Williams makes clear, favours the same demographic rhythm: 'The way in which I have tended to apply the term in analysis is to the generation that is doing the new cultural work, which normally means a group that would have a median age of around thirty, when it is beginning to articulate its structure of feeling.'[9] But note that Williams's model is not primarily agonistic; it doesn't default immediately to a narrative of struggle, of sons trying to murder their fathers. Not that sons *don't* murder their fathers (of course they do!), but this is only one story. An oedipal account tends to personalise matters, focussing on the players and the rituals of literary contest in a way that can deflect us from the scale of cultural transition. Without it—without that historical scale—there is no way to speak accurately of the writer as agent.

This, in my view, leaves an unresolved problem in our understanding of events between the wars and of the impact (whether for good or ill) of Curnow, Brasch and the other young men around them. What makes Williams instructive here is the firmness, but also the subtlety, of his historical determinism. In trying to outline a structure of feeling we are reading for the pattern of a subjective regime, whose 'characteristic elements of impulse [and] restraint' at once enable, and put limits upon, literary expression.[10] We are warned away, in other words, from naïve ceremonies of blame or veneration addressed to individual authors. But not to the point where the author is elided: while writers are not 'free' agents, they are agents nonetheless. Authors help to write the affective codes that they are constrained by; or as Williams puts it, 'The new work will not only make explicit the changes in feeling, but will itself promote and affect them.'[11] The key to understanding what literary nationalism achieved is to keep hold of both implications of this process. We need to be able to recognise not just the limited resources that writers had to work with—what I called earlier the cards they were dealt—but also the skill with which they shaped this given menu to their own (sometimes further self-inhibiting) ends. It is entirely too easy to reduce nationalist writing to those attitudes and assumptions that we no longer find sympathetic, and then to sheet home those values to individual authors as if this somehow exempted us from reading these writers thoughtfully.[12] This misconstrual of agency is not so much unfair as short-sighted. It closes down texts in which a more tolerant form of reading might seek to discern the larger cultural patterns that these writers are articulating.

Nationalism and modernism

It has long been understood that New Zealand's literary nationalism adopts certain features of Anglophone modernism. But in taking this modernist dimension as read we have paid less attention than we might have to a rather startling anomaly. Like 'the 60s', like television, like coffee and wine-drinking, cultural nationalism is one of those things that comes late to New Zealand. One might think almost prohibitively late. The assertion of national cultural sovereignty is, after all, a quintessentially Romantic impulse. And yet, emerging in New Zealand only at the beginning of the 1930s, it demands to be articulated in terms of a new, and in many ways antithetical, cultural dominant. To forge a literary nationalism at the height of international modernism: the task, if not literally impossible, is at the very least paradoxical. And the outcome here is a unique local variant whose oddness—whose no. 8 wire singularity—I believe we have not yet made enough fuss about.

Born of the Age of Revolution (the abolition of slavery, the revolutions of France and America) Romanticism's kaupapa is radical, salvific change. It is always looking for the blissful dawn, and one of the places it finds it is in the New World, most obviously America. The writers of the New England Renaissance were second and third-generation Romantics: Emerson (b. 1803) was eight years younger than Keats; Thoreau and Whitman were fifteen years younger than Emerson. And it was Romantic ambition, impatience and optimism that blossomed on the American frontier. The autonomy of the Romantic 'self' offered a model of an autonomous culture; and just as the transcendental subject could apprehend in Nature its own spiritual likeness, so in the plenitude of the frontier America needed to recognise the contours of its emergent identity. 'New lands, new men, new thoughts', demanded Emerson.[13] The New World *was* the break with the past that Romanticism dreamed of effecting, and it was the task of the American artist to deliver the fresh start that this implied.

The demand made of the writer by this millennial opportunity was the same one that Curnow would make a century later: to 'deal direct with life'.[14] Whitman describes himself as writing 'like a man unaware there was ever [. . .] such a production as a book'.[15] His vision, he insists, is entirely unmediated; the one book that matters is the American scene in front of him. The stakes here, of course, are political as much as intellectual or spiritual. Books mean Europe; they mean the risk of importing not just the cultural manners of the Old World but the morbid political thought embedded in them: 'monarchies' and 'priestly conventions', 'notions [. . .] founded on the idea of caste.' Of himself, on the other hand, Whitman announces: 'Along his words spread the broad impartialities of the United States.'[16]

There would always be something implicitly egalitarian in the claim to be dealing directly with New World experience. By the time we reach Australia in the years leading up to Federation in 1901, the Romantic impulse has inevitably become somewhat etiolated. But in the nationalism fostered by A.G. Stephens and the *Bulletin* Red Page, the belief that a new land can produce a new political consciousness is as powerful as ever. In the *Bulletin*, Lawson, Paterson and others establish the durable narrative of the nation's bush psychogenesis. The formative encounter with the New World environment has by this stage been largely desacralised. The bush is not Emerson's realm of 'spirit', but the scene of an accumulated history of adaptation and struggle. Even so, it still serves admirably in settler identity formation. Forged in the battle with this challenging foe, the subject who emerges—presumptively male—is tough, independent and resilient. The bush has shorn him of his Britishness and of any inherited class pretensions. He has learned optimism and mateship. Above all he has learned a trenchant egalitarianism. The demands of making do in the bush have rewritten the rules of political and social engagement.

Challenges to this Romantic narrative were not long in coming. By the early 1920s, as David Carter explains, the Red Page was fretting about 'the manifestations of modernity all around it—Cubism, Futurism, Freud, Joyce, Pound, jazz, free verse and free women'.[17] And this to a large extent prefigures the shape of the conversation through the 20th century: on the one hand, the myth of the nation's bush origins (the narrative that second-generation nationalist Vance Palmer will call 'the legend of the Nineties'); on the other, a succession of flank attacks from one or other form of modernism, arguing the inadequacy of the bush legend in the name of sophistication, urbanity and cosmopolitanism. While Palmer, his wife Nettie, and P.R. Stephenson will stick to the bush, and in particular accent the legend's socialism, the so-called 'Cold War intellectuals'—Vincent Buckley, A.D. Hope, James McAuley—will try to wrest the nationalist high ground away from them, arguing a cautious modernism that draws strongly on T.S. Eliot and the Southern agrarians, but without abandoning Matthew Arnold and F.R. Leavis. Similarly, the primitivist nationalism of the Jindyworobaks will be targeted by the avant-garde modernism of Max Harris and the Angry Penguins—the latter anathema equally to the Palmers and to the Cold Warriors (who, in the persons of McAuley and Harold Stewart, will sink the Angry Penguins in the Ern Malley hoax).[18] It's a history with complex cross currents. But the basic outline is legible enough: a Romantic, bush-bound nationalism on the defensive against varieties of urbanity and modernisation.

To cross the ditch, then, and approach our local version of this history is not just to cross the four decades from the *Bulletin* writers to the 1930s. It is to leap the gaping chasm of World War I, and to enter the labyrinth of modernism. When we think of it like this—that is, of just how much history separates us from the nearest available models of a kindred literature—the emergence of our own belated variant almost defies logic. How was the angst-ridden turmoil of modernism to be reconciled with nationalist self-invention? Modernism, after all, was not just international and cosmopolitan, but urbane, mandarin and formalist. Literary nationalism, by contrast (on the models of America and Australia, and also for Curnow the Ireland of the Celtic Twilight), was localist, populist and representational. Equating identity with physical locality, nationalism favoured the pastoral, and authenticated itself from Nature; although modernism sometimes showed primitivist leanings, it was the child of the City, and of a typically deracinated realm of culture. Where modernism was analytic and experimental, nationalism tended to the oratorical and the coercive. And where modernism cued off the disaster of the war, nationalism spoke of continuity, opportunity, plenitude. This list could be even longer, but the problem is stark enough. How could a settler literary identity possibly be constructed under the aegis of modernism?

And yet, remarkably, it was. Somehow these antithetical imperatives were wrangled, manipulated, teased into dialogue. Courtesy largely of Allen Curnow, they were even made to yield a coherent cultural programme. Too much so, we have since learned to argue; thus, the blindnesses and the alleged prescriptivism of the nationalist intervention have come to occupy us to the exclusion of almost all else. But have we really said enough about the movement's sheer finesse? Have we even conceded what an odd thing it is, that striking accommodation that Alex Calder, in the best account of this problem that I'm aware of, labels *critical* nationalism?[19] Yes, one can think of (distant) parallels: in the Harlem Renaissance, or in the second-generation localism of William Faulkner and William Carlos Williams. But the singularity of this transaction—this grounding of the modern in the 'local and special'—demands a deeper appreciation. And it's this which, for all my own reservations, and for the many and varied ways in which I find fault with our nationalist writers, is most apt to make me want to write like a cheerleader. In the paradox of a modernist nationalism, there remains a cunning, a sophistication—dare I say it, even a Kiwi ingenuity—that our critical discourse has never quite caught up with.

Modern sexuality

As a 1930s phenomenon, nationalist writing travels in the slipstream not only of literary modernism but of what Christine Stansell has dubbed *sexual* modernism.[20] The sexual revolution of the 1920s is easily overlooked in the shadow of its 1960s counterpart. But this was a period in which gender relations, and more specifically sexual relations, were reimagined dramatically and with far-reaching consequences. On the gender front, the decade brought an atmosphere of masculine *ressentiment* and defensive self-assertion. Threatened, it would seem, by suffrage feminism, and unmanned too by the carnage of the war, an embattled masculinity bulked itself up and evolved new norms of gendered behaviour. At the same time, more disruptively still, the thriving new science of sexology applied itself to physical sex, and specifically to the sexuality of women. Women were reinvented as sexually responsive subjects; contraception was modernised; marriage was eroticised. In many respects of course these developments were liberating; it is here in the 20s that we see the emergence of a sexual regime that seems recognisably modern. And yet for women between the wars—the women who lived through and processed these changes—the repercussions would be distinctly ambivalent.

How these developments ramify in literature has not been precisely articulated, even in the Northern Hemisphere. But it's clear when we think about the structure of feeling which comes with the nationalist 1930s that changes in the climate of sexual consciousness need to be explored. Here I am happy to take my cue from groundbreaking work of the 1990s by Michele Leggott and Kai Jensen. Between them, in their different ways, Leggott and Jensen have detailed the masculinisation of New Zealand writing in the nationalist era: a transformation evident in equal measure in the language of male writers, in the dominance of male writers, and in the virtual disappearance of literary writing by women. Thus Jensen is able to propose in *Whole Men* that the excitement of the 1930s is about masculinity as much as about national identity. Leggott, with her emphasis on Robin Hyde, has addressed the way that the entrenchment of literary nationalism not only disabled women at the time, but now makes it all but impossible to engage with a literary aesthetic that pre-dates it.

Revisionist work on gender, then, has already changed the way we think about nationalism. Where I would like to steer the conversation now is in a more international direction, and towards a thicker social context. Where does all this literary manliness come from? And how does an apparent shift in literary subjectivity intersect with those gendered identities that are being remade between the wars? The literature of the hard frost coheres, we understand, around geography and place—a mythology constructed on the frozen ground of what its authors like to paint as a prohibitively hostile landscape. But nationalist writing is also built on the assertion of a rigidly masculine sexuality, and if we wish to understand why it proves so effective we need to explore the sexual dynamics that accompany it.

'Literary history'

While structures of feeling appear to track with the generations, the correlation is not watertight. Nor are the generations in question precisely those of routine demography. The phenomenon known as the Baby Boom, for instance, is conventionally identified with the birthdates 1946–65. But as anyone around my age will recognise, this period in fact encompasses two distinct cohort experiences. Structures of feeling, I am tempted to say, are a bit like astrological charts—except that it's not so much a question of the stars under which a generation is born, as of the constellations under which it is formed and educated, and then enters the ambitious terrain of its early adulthood. For Baby Boom I, as I'll call it, this meant the late 1960s: Woodstock and Vietnam, sexual liberation, the golden age of rock music, psychedelia, Paris 68. This familiar litany describes the generational experience that shaped the way this cohort felt its politics, its sexuality, its cultural ambitions. For 'us', by which I mean Baby Boom II (born 1955–65, give or take), the heavens were configured quite differently. AIDS, feminism, soft masculinity, the 1981

Springbok tour, Rogernomics, the Mervyn Thompson affair: these factors helped to shape a cultural style far removed from the long-haired ebullience of our elder siblings. Our music was punk and new wave. We took drugs, not to transform our consciousness but simply to get wasted. And our activism, as it sporadically emerged, retained little of our elders' Romantic self-confidence; our sense of fun may have been nihilistic, but our politics were sober, chastened and self-critical.

These dispositions that I'm outlining hastily remain to be explored in the distant future (they belong to the twilight of what I've called a 'long' literary nationalism). They need to be brought to the table, however, if I wish to explain where I'm writing from. At the bar of History, every cohort can expect to be held accountable for its own particular vices. My generation of literary scholars, trained in the graduate schools of the 1980s, has its failings lucidly catalogued by Rita Felski in *The Limits of Critique*. Critique in this sense is a blanket term for those habits of sceptical or 'symptomatic' reading that prospered as the language of European cultural theory took hold in the Anglo-American humanities. Deconstruction and psychoanalysis, Michel Foucault and Fredric Jameson, new historicism and queer theory, would teach us in a dozen different ways that the text was always harbouring a (guilty) secret, and that our mandate as sophisticated scholars was to ferret it out. This was the vein of excitement that greeted us as academically minded young adults. Those chastening experiences of the early 80s had primed us for something stricter than the Romanticism of our immediate elders, and we found it in what Felski, after Paul Ricoeur, calls a 'hermeneutics of suspicion'.[21]

In New Zealand's universities the effect was less systematic, less codified and I think less rigorous than in the Northern Hemisphere, or in Australia. But we felt it nonetheless, and our literary discourse was transformed accordingly. 'And so we bring disaster to the tired New Zealand literature that we know,' wrote Leigh Davis in the first issue of *And* in 1983,[22] and he was right. Finally, it seemed, there was a way to get past Curnow, and a way around the *Freed* generation into the bargain. The nationalist tradition was transformed overnight from a procession of historical landmarks into a heinous texture of oversights and exclusions. Again I'm speaking in shorthand here about events that await more patient exploration. But for now it's enough to register two outcomes. In the first place, the atmosphere was unquestionably invigorated. The vocabularies of French feminism, postcolonialism and postmodernism complexified local critical writing beyond recognition. However, as the impulse waned a collateral effect was also apparent. Whatever we might have believed we were doing inside our high-minded specialist enclaves, from the outside the impact was massively off-putting. Critique was 'political correctness' with a PhD: the language was so specialised, the prose so impenetrable, the voice of default so grim and censorious, that critical reading acquired an image problem it still hasn't recovered from. Nor was it just that it put people off, exaggerating the divide between the academy and the general educated reader. It also had a cost inside the specialised discourse that it over-ran. I'm reminded of Roger Horrocks's remarks, in an essay to which I've alluded already, reflecting on his sense that younger readers have come to know only a 'cartoon version' of cultural nationalism.[23] For all its vaunted complexity, critique was too fond of contextual shortcuts, too quick to reduce the text to its hidden determinants, and too well rehearsed in the way it thought about what those determinants might be. When I think about Horrocks's comment, and about my own experience as a New Zealandist in a university English department, it occurs to me to wonder if we didn't unwittingly teach a generation of students *not* to read.

So where does all this leave me today, still trying to write about New Zealand literature, but now against the backdrop of a literary culture whose disposition seems as much 'post-critical' as it does 'post-national'? Should we simply toss out the last 30 years, the questions we've asked and the language in which we've asked them? When I put it like that, of course the answer must be no. I'm too much the stern-minded child of the 80s to accept that settler monoculturalism is suddenly a dead issue, or that the questions that proliferate around sex and gender have ceased to be productive and rewarding. These are not contexts I am ready to dispense with: I am still a 'suspicious' and 'symptomatic' reader; in Felski's terms, I am still *digging down*, searching for the non-obvious meaning beneath the obvious one.[24] It remains for me a fundamental presumption that texts know more than their authors know, and that teasing out this incipient knowledge is among the irreplaceable functions that critical reading can perform.

Let me explain this another way, as sometimes I have had occasion to. When someone asks me 'What do you write?' I have a simple answer: *literary history*. It's a good, plain, protestant phrase; no one could fault its modesty. At the same time, it leaves me enough to be getting on with. The expression as I use it covers two ambitions. The first aim is textual, or, as I prefer to say, curatorial: to write the history of what has been written, to frame it, to try to keep it visible and useable. The second, inevitably, is broader in scope: its object is not the history *of* literature, but history *by way of* literature. It implies using texts to try to read and write other histories, searching out dimensions of historical experience that literature can potentially make legible. But are these two ideals compatible? The first, after all, is a mode of appreciation, addressed to literary texts as what Horrocks calls 'high-energy works of art'.[25] Meanwhile, the second—the *contextual* procedure—has a habit of producing just the opposite effect, reducing the text to a sketchy illustration ('cartoon') of a pre-digested politics. Is this the inevitable outcome of a contextually focussed criticism? I don't believe so. Contextualism can bring historical texts to life, not just politically, but in a literary sense as well. But this demands fresh lines of inquiry. And it also requires us (again I'm persuaded by Felski on this point) to relinquish the ideal of critical detachment.[26] We need to accept our own involvement, as feeling subjects, in the narratives we construct.

Like other views of history from the last half-century—pre-eminently those that descend from Foucault—structure of feeling appears to frame the past as a sequence of stand-alone silos (cf. epistemes, paradigms).[27] We are reminded of what in the past—even the near past—is 'other', no longer fully recuperable. But this doesn't leave the reader safely detached; historical distance is not neutrality. While inevitably there is much that escapes in the space between our feelings and theirs, we remain enmeshed in affective relations. To return to a figure I introduced in my preface, I think of this project as a 'family' history, and any claim to critical objectivity is pre-empted in that metaphor. It's the history of a literature that I've grown up inside; I'm not a big player, but I'm 'in' the conversation. And I'm tangled up, too, in what Derek Attridge would call my 'idioculture':[28] as a reader I travel in a cloud of language, everything that has ever rubbed off on me, a personal past preserved in ways of which I am largely unconscious. The Freudian term for this entanglement is *transference*, and there's no space outside it from which to read or to write. An undertow of confusion and drift will always be an undeclared element of serious reading. I am writing, then, out of a transferential engagement in the intimate conversation that is New Zealand literature. In various ways I try to make this explicit. But it's bound to show also in more subtle colourings passing through the weave of the text, traces of the intricate complex of feelings that comprise the affective palette of 'family' life. I'm not *trying* to write in an indulgent manner—I try to be as clear and precise as I can—but I don't bother covering up my attachments. Sometimes I can't help writing bad-temperedly, even of writers I deeply admire. I don't refrain, either, from value judgements. Not that I expect my protestations that such-and-such a text is 'the best' or 'the strongest' or 'the most interesting' to be taken at face value. I *hope* the reader might agree. But I also trust them to understand that these must be strictly imaginary judgements. Far from affirming my own authority, I suspect they do the opposite: they declare things I 'have a weakness for'.

If I'm still reading symptomatically, then, I can't pretend to do so from a place of clinical safety; whatever I retain of the ambitions of critique I am pursuing from a position of engagement, not 'procedural objectivity'.[29] To this first proviso, I need to add a second: this is about the kinds of contextual questions that, for me, are still worth asking. I've said that I take it as axiomatic that texts know more than their authors know. But texts know more than their readers know, too. If they don't, then reading contextually is no help in appreciating them. There's a style of politically inflected critique that likes to pose questions to which it already knows the answers. The text is employed to prove the critic's suspicions; it helps to affirm a context whose implications are firmly established. The question whose answer is 'patriarchy' or 'containment' or 'the colonial gaze' positions the text as already redundant: the thesis needs so little from it that the text remains inert. The contextual question that can bring the text to life is one to which the answer is unknown.

I have already signalled two questions that fit this description: unresolved historical problems that leave the text room to inform and surprise us. One is about the relationship between modernism and New Zealand literary nationalism (we know that there is one; we don't know how it works). The second concerns writing by women in the 1930s (we know roughly what happens, but we don't know why). With each of these questions, there is no established context, no historical meta-narrative, ready-made to answer it. If we wish to establish a context, we need to seek it through the text, among those unknown patterns of feeling that writing can help us to reconstruct. This, I believe, is where reading contextually can turn up the wattage of the literary text. The context necessarily is broader than the text, as well as antecedent to it (it's not a hermeneutic circle, or certainly not a closed one); but the text is our best guide in seeking its shape, and in doing so—in coming to the text with these questions—we are obliged to put the text through its paces (we give it a chance to resonate). Context, as an open question, throws us back onto the intelligence of the text. My hope, then, is that in reading for the history of feeling we can find a point of synergy between the contextual and the curatorial, remembering the history of New Zealand writing in the process of trying to remember with it.

Chapter 1

'Nothing can ever be the same'

Mansfield's new worlds

A 'lost' writer

When R.A.K. Mason became editor of *Phoenix* in July 1932, printer Bob Lowry hailed him as 'a crack-brained socialist'.[1] It's an image that in one form or other would stay with him: the staunch and self-sacrificing servant of the Left, the remarkable poet who allowed politics to displace his muse. As James K. Baxter would later observe, 'Among the uncommitted he earned the special respect due to the committed man'.[2] Mason, then, seems an unlikely advocate for the inwardness of modernist fiction. And yet earlier that year he addressed a Hamilton meeting of the WEA, where his theme, as Rachel Barrowman records, was 'Modernism in literature':

> The great characteristic of the modern age was the realisation of change, and the greatest poet of change, [Mason]

> argued—the greatest of those who 'turn all their power to finding out more and more about the stream' [of continual change], among them Lawrence, Yeats and Housman—was Joyce. And of the social forces that had influenced the literature of the modern age [. . .] the most important was the development of the science of psychology. The insights of the psychologists into the subconscious had produced 'a wise, deep, fine interpretation of the human mind such as only the great Greeks ever dreamt of in the past', which in turn had deepened and introduced an 'almost mythical' dimension to literature, in the work, for example, of Joyce, Virginia Woolf and Dorothy Richardson.[3]

This excitement about the inner world of modernist fiction—that 'fantastic twilit jungle' where Joyce and company 'prance hand-in-hand to the sweet pipings of Professor Freud', as he sketches it elsewhere[4]—sounds a curious note, but not only in Mason; in fact it goes against the grain of the entire literary movement which the first appearance of *Phoenix* two months earlier has been understood to signal. The New Zealand writing that is shortly to emerge will be indifferent to this inward, subjective impulse. In one respect, however, Mason does sound like a writer of the 30s. As the new literary nationalism begins to take hold, it will be as if nobody has bothered to read Mansfield.

The version of Katherine Mansfield who is the subject of this chapter is that writer whom the nationalists might have read, but didn't—a writer whom it seems they were obliged to forget in order to invent a literature that began with themselves. Ironically, they fashion their distinctive modernist nationalism by ignoring our most accomplished and original modernist author. But Mansfield is not so easily dispensed with. She haunts the texts of mid-century nationalism—and haunts the pages of my own account—as the thing that goes missing in the selective way that nationalism takes up the modernist challenge. In turning their backs on Mansfield, the *Phoenix* generation close off the very possibilities that Mason is extolling. It's a move with its own historical necessity. It will prove enabling in numerous ways. But it leaves a kind of scar tissue embedded in nationalist writing, something dull and insensate where Mansfield's intelligence has been excised.

No one makes this quite so clear as Frank Sargeson in 1948. For the most part the nationalists preferred to represent the inherited state of writing in New Zealand in terms of poetry. Their strongest spokesman, Curnow, was a poet; and it was easier to assimilate Mason and Ursula Bethell than to join issue directly with a precursor as formidable as Mansfield. When Sargeson eventually fronts up to the topic, he is forced into moves that seem wilfully naïve:

> 'Prelude'. It is mainly about children, and it begins with a horse and cart journey which rather resembles the beginning of the chaise and pair journey in Chekhov's excellent story, 'The Steppe'. Next, 'At the Bay': the same children and adults appear, and among other things the story is notable for the wonderful evocation of the New Zealand seaside [. . .][5]

Predictably, in trying to cut Mansfield down to size, Sargeson fastens on her expatriatism—the problem of having 'spent much of her life in a state of suspension between two hemispheres.'[6] Conventionally travel broadens the horizons; yet Mansfield's decision to return to Europe (she left New Zealand permanently in 1908) has in Sargeson's view a narrowing effect. It produces a kind of solipsism, a detachment from some implicitly more substantial social context: 'You have to depend on yourself too much—and what you find *in* yourself. Suspension (or to use another word, freedom) always has its dangers, and it is particularly dangerous for a writer to be virtually free from any sense of social tradition.'[7] From a nationalist point of view it's a knock-down argument. However, what this ignores is that exile and deracination formed the matrix that gave birth to Anglophone modernism. Joyce, Eliot (*early* Eliot), Ezra Pound, Gertrude Stein, Samuel Beckett, Jean Rhys, even the internal émigré D.H. Lawrence: modernism was the language, not so much of a 'social tradition' as of an emergent *anti-social* tradition, a convergence of New World restiveness and Old World alienation. A drifting constellation of bohemian outsiders would form what Mansfield's first biographer Antony Alpers calls her 'Wandering Tribe'.[8] This is not to say that she found solidarity among the modernist avant-garde; her relations with some of the bigger—and lesser—names were on occasion poisonous. But exile was the condition of the moment, and it situated Mansfield, not in the provincial writer's airy daydream of the metropolis, but at ground zero in her century's literature.

If World War II belongs to Sargeson and company—who will make of it a measure of 'reality' and 'experience'[9]—New Zealand's definitive writer of the Great War is Mansfield. As Vincent O'Sullivan puts it, she is 'among that group of writers who understood early on how the First World War was a *permanent* fragmentation of what living in Europe implied.'[10] O'Sullivan quotes her uncensored opinion (she also wrote a critical but more diplomatic review) of Virginia Woolf's novel *Night and Day* (1919):

> My private opinion is that it is a lie in the soul. The war never has been, that is what its message is [. . .] I feel in the *profoundest* sense that nothing can ever be the same, that, as artists, we are traitors if we feel otherwise.[11]

As directly as anyone, Mansfield articulates the sense of historical rupture that drives the modernist revolution, a seismic upheaval that will demand a re-examination of the fundamental tenets of intellectual and creative endeavour. Where everything is shattered, everything must be remade, not least the means by which narrative seeks a hold on this shattered world. Mansfield's response will be the one that Mason applauds: her fiction turns inwards, always still 'realist', always intent on representation, but as Sydney Janet Kaplan puts it, on 'representation enlarged to include interiority, which itself becomes a prime subject for fictional treatment'.[12]

This is an altogether different version of Mansfield driven back on 'what you find in yourself'. That her fiction takes an inward turn is no more than we might say of Joyce or Woolf or Marcel Proust. But Sargeson, unable to envisage her in this context, is deaf to Mansfield's modernism. He appreciates neither her technical innovations nor the psychological acuity that today seems so apparent in them. New Zealand writers of Sargeson's generation will proceed as if none of this ground has been broken. A refusal of interiority—a kind of 'anti-psychology'—will become a characteristic feature of their own 'anti-myth'.[13] They will write as if Mansfield never existed, and the cost to New Zealand fiction will take decades to remedy.

Unseen realities

For novice printers Leonard and Virginia Woolf the prospect of hand-setting the 17,000 words of Mansfield's 'Prelude' must have been alarming. As Alpers reports, after presenting the first page to Mansfield for inspection they enlisted the services of an acolyte.[14] Bloomsbury by now was enough of an institution to act as a magnet for culturally ambitious young women; today they might be known as groupies—Virginia Woolf called them 'crop-heads' or 'Bloomsbury Bunnies'.[15] Alix Sargant-Florence, a bright young graduate just down from Newnham, was one of their number. She would prove, though, a less-than-willing camp follower. Swiftly concluding that typesetting was not the kind of literary apprenticeship she had in mind, she quit (to the Woolfs' astonishment) after only a couple of hours.[16] Her next appearance in the Hogarth Press story is in an altogether different capacity. Married to James Strachey, younger brother of Lytton, she would gain her place in literary history as the co-translator of the *Complete Psychological Works of Sigmund Freud*.

In the story that the future Alix Strachey almost typeset, she could have read—had she picked her way through it letter by letter—a prelude to all that is most Freudian in 20th-century fiction. But somehow it seems more fitting that she refused. Despite the importance of the Strachey translation to the Hogarth Press catalogue, between Bloomsbury and psychoanalysis there was always a certain failure of recognition. Freud's work first became available in English through the translations of the American A.A. Brill shortly before World War I, and Leonard Woolf wrote a thoughtful review of *The Psychopathology of Everyday Life* in 1914. Virginia's younger brother, Adrian, would become a psychoanalyst. Freud himself admired Lytton Strachey's work. However, as Douglass Orr demonstrates in his survey of the topic, what little was known about psychoanalysis never worked deeply on the Bloomsbury sensibility.[17] Alix Strachey recalls that when she and her husband returned from studying with Freud in Vienna their immersion in psychoanalysis earned them no credit: on the contrary, it made people nervous and even 'a little contemptuous'.[18] Virginia Woolf proof-read the first Hogarth edition of the case histories, but enjoyed making fun of them;

her knowledge of Freud's work, concludes Orr, was never more than casual.[19]

Mansfield appears to have known even less. According to Claire Tomalin in *Katherine Mansfield: A Secret Life*, she could be 'caustic about the Freudians'—that is, Lawrence and his analyst friend David Eder.[20] It was Lawrence who Mansfield had in mind when she told Beatrice Campbell, 'I *shall never* see sex in trees, sex in running brooks, sex in stones and sex in everything.' She also reports advising Lawrence that he ought to christen his cottage 'The Phallus'.[21] Frieda Lawrence had been romantically involved with the maverick psychoanalyst Otto Gross, and exposure to Frieda and her husband has been cited as an opportunity for Mansfield to have discovered Freudian theory.[22] But Mansfield and the Lawrences were ambivalent company, and Lawrence's cranky metaphysics of sex wouldn't have made him an ideal interpreter. In Mansfield's letters and journals there seems to be no direct reference to Freud whatsoever. The literary roots of Mansfield's psychologism lie not in psychoanalysis but in the literary impulse known as Symbolism.

At the origins of English modernism there are few works more important than Arthur Symons's *The Symbolist Movement in Literature* (1899; reissued 1908). Symons's enthusiasm for the French poets of the 19th century influenced Yeats, Pound, Joyce and, most importantly, Eliot; it was reading Symons in 1908 that Eliot first discovered Arthur Rimbaud and Jules Laforgue.[23] In New Zealand we have always lacked a Symbolist tradition: unlike the Australians we don't have a Christopher Brennan or an early Kenneth Slessor; Charles Spear, our one Symbolist poet in this fin de siècle vein, would not publish his slim volume *Twopence Coloured* until 1951. But while still a teenager at Queen's College in London, Mansfield was lucky enough to have a German teacher, Walter Rippmann, who introduced her not just to Oscar Wilde, on whom she developed a formative crush, but to Walter Pater, and to Symons and the French poets he championed. Mansfield and Eliot were exact contemporaries, born within a couple of weeks of each other, and oddly enough it was the colonial teenager who encountered Symons four or five years earlier than Eliot himself.[24] Whether she read *The Symbolist Movement in Literature* is not clear, but according to Clare Hanson and Andrew Gurr she knew at least two of Symons's critical works, in addition to his poetry, and was well acquainted with the boiled-down version of Symbolist aesthetics that Symons was advancing.[25]

Symbolism exaggerated both the inwardness of the Romantic tradition and its impatience with rationalism. The French poets promoted to English readers by Symons rejected the realism of Honoré de Balzac and Émile Zola, and the rhetorical certainties of Victor Hugo. Instead they turned to a penumbral realm of intuitions and intimations, a world of phenomena obscured by material surfaces; this they referred to as the *au-delà*, and the symbol, as they conceived it, was the means to apprehend this 'other' dimension. In the Symbolist orientation, key modernist elements are already in evidence. Pound's advocacy of the concrete image and his hostility to abstraction and rhetoric, Eliot's 'objective correlative', the Joycean epiphany, all proceed more or less directly from the Symbolist impulse. However what the doctrine lacked in its 19th-century incarnation was a metapsychology. Symons had a ready string of metaphors to name the experience that Symbolism targeted: 'the luminous darkness of the universe', 'the irresistible empire of the unseen'.[26] But so long as it was grounded only in hieratic phrase-making, its pursuit of the numinous always threatened to devolve into fin de siècle occultism—the iconic instance being Yeats, initiate of the Hermetic Order of the Golden Dawn. What modernism required was that this 'unseen reality', as Symons called it,[27] be situated more robustly and objectively. Following Bergson and William James, and then above all, and increasingly, Freud, this for the 20th century would mean *in the mind*.

The Freudian formulation of the unconscious, which named this dimension for a new era, would shape the environment in which modernist literature developed and in which its subjectivism achieved default status. Modernism would be the literature of the Freudian century. But not until the generation of W.H. Auden and Robert Lowell would literary writers be ready to embrace Freud explicitly. Pound invokes 'the newer psychologists' when it suits him,[28] but first-generation modernists were more apt to view the formalised language of psychoanalysis as a threat to their own creative processes. The great psychologists-in-fiction of the period are 'Freudian', therefore, in spite of themselves. If Proust or Joyce or Woolf 'sound like' Freud, it is because they are breathing the same atmosphere, confronting the same problems—problems which to them, of course, are *literary* problems, but which now produce an inwardness psychologised, a theatre of the mind. In this psychological turn, which sets the course of modernist fiction, no one will be quicker on the uptake than Mansfield.

Ciphers and symbols

Symbolism as a historical movement is one thing; symbolism as a literary technique presents a different order of complexity. Habitually celebrated as the means by which literature generates those meanings that are most dense and recondite, within literary studies the symbol has been the object both of high ceremony and of deep obfuscation. It is probably no less difficult to write plainly about literary symbolism than to explain efficiently the symbolic functions of language itself. But it can't be avoided, and so in the paragraphs that follow I am going to try to separate three different orders of symbolism. If this involves shortcuts and simplifications, I ask the reader to bear in mind that it may be the lesser of two evils.

The ever-dependable M.H. Abrams begins with the kind of symbol that he calls 'conventional' or 'public'.[29] The Cross, the heart, the silver fern: these signs bear meanings which are potent but relatively stable (or, as Abrams puts it, 'determinate within a particular culture'). If writers inevitably use symbols of this order, it's because their meanings have been naturalised within our culture to the point where we scarcely notice ourselves employing them. In a literary context, it seems to me, this notion of 'determinate' reference can usefully be extended. In my usage, then, it also covers a vocabulary of low-density symbolism whose interpretation demands little conscious effort. When Laura heads down the gully at the end of 'The Garden Party', we take in the tweed caps that represent class difference and the basket of party food that represents *noblesse oblige* with the ease that one takes in the scenery from a passing vehicle. When Stanley's walking stick goes missing in a comic episode in 'At the Bay', we know that what's at issue is his patriarchal authority. The stick as office power-dressing, the stick that a father might beat someone with, the stick that he might thump on the floor like the Late Colonel, and yes, inevitably, the stick as phallus, concur in representing that authority without difficulty or ambiguity. This conventional symbolic vocabulary is not much more than a convenient shorthand. These are literary devices, and they are not used idly, but nor are they points of any great semantic complexity.

Where symbolism makes greater demands is where it becomes, as Abrams puts it, 'private' and 'personal'[30]—still often drawing on conventional associations, but overlain and overloaded with meanings that will be in varying degrees subjective, enigmatic and ambiguous. As generations of English tutors and their students have been able to agree, the eponymous fly in Mansfield's famous late story immediately invites us to think of Lear: 'As flies to wanton boys are we to the gods. They kill us for their sport.' As the banker ('the Boss') drowns the hapless creature in a pool of ink, we recognise the workings of a kind of cosmic conspiracy, an allegory which, given the status of Shakespeare in our culture, rests on a symbolism that is more or less 'determinate'. But of course what has fascinated the same generations of readers is the 'over' determination (the *surplus* of meaning) that supplements and complicates this reading. The context of the Great War, in which the Boss has lost his son, reminds us of the trenches and of the young men who sometimes quite literally drowned in them. And this historical contingency, in turn, opens into a thicket of more personal conjunctions: the death of Mansfield's brother in France; the ubiquity in her fiction of these Harold Beauchamp-like 'Pa men' (as she calls them); her likening of herself in her own struggles to a fly fallen in a jug of milk;[31] her private association of the war with her illness (describing her lungs as 'that old battlefield');[32] the reader's grisly knowledge that the author of this very late story is inexorably drowning in her own blood. It's this mode of symbolism—dense and auratic—that has traditionally been such an object of fascination to literary criticism. 'The Fly' is one of a number of Mansfield's best stories (think of 'The Doll's House', or Bertha Young's pear tree in 'Bliss') to revolve around this kind of enigmatic, grand-manner symbolism. It is one reason, no doubt, why these classic texts have cast such a spell over critics and classroom instructors.

But while these figures are indispensable to Mansfield's work, they don't represent her most original mode of symbolic writing, or her most historically significant. At first approach the breakthrough fiction 'Prelude' would appear to belong in the catalogue above. At its heart looms the aloe, perhaps the most iconic of all Mansfield's symbolic inventions, and certainly from her own point of view the most heavily freighted. In the manner of the classic, high-literary symbol, it is situated at a conjunction of public and private discourses. Mansfield probably came across it first in Walter Pater: 'A certain strangeness, something of the blossoming of the aloe, is indeed an element in all true works of art.'[33] For Pater it is an emblem of creative mystery, a generative opacity at the heart of Symbolist aesthetics. Mansfield will incorporate this imagery into her own fantasy of a mysterious, creative fruition; she imagines, somewhat against her better judgement, 'a self which is continuous and permanent; which [. . .] thrusts a sealed bud through years of darkness until, one day, the light discovers it and shakes the flower free and—we are alive—we are flowering for our moment upon the earth.'[34] The aloe, then, operates as a hinge between the two kinds of 'prelude' implicit in the title: between the narrative of Linda Burnell's pregnancy, fictional prelude to the birth of Mansfield's brother and muse; and the meta-narrative of her own creative emergence. As has often been remarked, though, the significance of the aloe in 'Prelude' depends on who's looking at it. To Linda, for whom marriage to Stanley is a fearful cycle of sex and parturition, the aloe is alarmingly, implacably phallic: 'Linda looked up at the fat swelling plant with its cruel leaves and fleshy stem [. . .] the blind stem cut into the air as if no wind could ever shake it.'[35] But to her sexually innocent daughter Kezia it is simply an unknown: 'Whatever could it be? She had never seen anything like it before.'[36] Even for Linda, the aloe's symbolism depends on the inter-subjective context in which she encounters it. In the company of her mother, Mrs Fairfield, her own position becomes childlike; now she imagines the aloe as a ship bearing her safely out of reach of Stanley and his attentions.

This protean, perspectival quality locates the aloe between two poles. At one extreme we meet the servant girl Alice, working in the kitchen with a book propped open in front of her, reading:

> 'To dream of black-beetles drawing a hearse is bad. Signifies death of one you hold near or dear, either father, husband, brother, son, or intended. If beetles crawl backwards as you watch them it means death from fire or from great height such as flight of stairs, scaffolding, etc.
>
> 'Spiders. To dream of spiders creeping over you is good. Signifies large sum of money in near future. Should party be in family way an easy confinement may be expected. But care should be taken in sixth month to avoid eating of probable present of shell fish [. . .]'[37]

Alice's text is like a caricature of what, after Abrams, I've called determinate symbolism: a 'dirty, greasy little book, half unstitched, with curled edges',[38] its system of rigid correspondences is demonstrably worn out. Its appearance here underlines a sense in which 'Prelude' is a story preoccupied with symbolism itself. Amplified by Mansfield's not untypical class-coding (a hermeneutic for the serving class), the cipher book counterpoints the leisurely, listless and explicitly modernist internal life of Linda Burnell:

> 'How loud the birds are,' said Linda in her dream. She was walking with her father through a green paddock sprinkled with daisies. Suddenly he bent down and parted the grasses and showed her a tiny ball of fluff just at her feet. 'Oh, Papa, the darling.' She made a cup of her hands and caught the

> tiny bird and stroked its head with her finger. It was quite tame. But a funny thing happened. As she stroked it began to swell, it ruffled and pouched, it grew bigger and bigger and its round eyes seemed to smile knowingly at her. Now her arms were hardly wide enough to hold it and she dropped it into her apron. It had become a baby with a big naked head and a gaping bird-mouth, opening and shutting. Her father broke into a loud clattering laugh and she woke to see Burnell by the windows rattling the Venetian blind up to the very top.[39]

Linda is the most intricately drawn character in Mansfield's fiction. She is also, in a manner of speaking, the most 'Freudian'. Not because she 'sees sex in everything'—though indeed she does—but rather because the quotidian patterns of her thought are so insistently and *self-referentially* symbolic. The wager that opens up the Freudian unconscious is not, after all, that symbols can be interpreted; nor is it merely that the mind thinks in symbols, that symbols shape the subjective worlds we live in, nor even that these symbols are the bearers of meanings which remain opaque to us even as we are subject to them. None of these ideas is foreign to Symbolist poetics. But the difference in Freud is in the specific metapsychological way that he locates an 'other scene' of meaning which the symbol intimates. In short, the Freudian unconscious is *personal*. It can't be decoded with a cipher book (we can say that an image is 'phallic', but this doesn't tell us what it *means* in any given context); nor is it a storehouse of archetypes, as in Jung's 'collective' unconscious. The symbols that emerge in Freudian analysis can be interpreted only by referring them back to the subjective structure in which they are embedded: their meanings arise in the subject's own interior world, or as Lacan will later insist, in the subject's language. As O'Sullivan points out, then, what's so plausible about Linda's dream is how closely it tracks her waking life.[40]

In fact sometimes the difference is hard to discern. When Linda, a little later, after Stanley's departure, is tracing patterns on the floral wallpaper—'She could feel the sticky, silky petals, the stem hairy like a gooseberry skin, the rough leaf and the tight glazed bud'[41]—it's not entirely clear if she's awake or asleep. But what Freud would call the 'dream-work' carries on regardless: the continual transformation of external objects into patterns of private symbolic significance. This is the radical aspect of the symbolic language in 'Prelude'—an assimilation of the symbolising function into the self-delineation of character.

Arguably, this depth in characterisation may best be described, not as psychological, but as narratological. Free indirect style—sometimes known as 'narrated monologue'—is described by Dorit Cohn as 'the technique for rendering a character's thought in his own idiom while maintaining third-person reference and the basic tense of narration.'[42] First used consistently by Jane Austen, and then widely by French novelists of the 19th century, most famously Gustave Flaubert, free indirect style has traditionally been seen as a compromise between external and internal narration. For the modernists, the style fits seamlessly with their psychological and subjectivist ambitions. It mimics the new fiction's default line of sight, delineating not the objects of an external world but objects as perceived by and affecting an internal consciousness.

No modernist writer is more skilled at the technique than Mansfield. Here is Linda watching her husband return from his bath:

> Back came Stanley girt with a towel, glowing and slapping his thighs. He pitched the wet towel on top of her hat and cape, and standing firm in the exact centre of a square of sunlight he began to do his exercises. Deep breathing, bending and squatting like a frog and shooting out his legs. He was so

> delighted with his firm, obedient body that he hit himself on the chest and gave out a loud 'Ah.' But this amazing vigour seemed to set him worlds away from Linda. She lay on the white tumbled bed and watched him as if from the clouds.
>
> 'Oh, damn! Oh, blast!' said Stanley, who had butted into a crisp white shirt only to find that some idiot had fastened the neck-band and he was caught. He stalked over to Linda waving his arms.[43]

For this performance Linda is definitely awake (albeit watching 'as if from the clouds'), but once again it shows us her metamorphic process of consciousness. The diegetic markers are subtle; only the directional statement 'Back came', and the possessive pronoun 'her', source these observations explicitly to Linda. And yet the insight into Linda's perceptions is alarmingly visceral. Her husband's clumsy physical ebullience—straining at the fastened collar, threatening to tear his way through it—speaks, yet again, to Linda's compound fear: of his sexual impositions ('There were times when he was frightening—really frightening'), and of the 'great lumps of children' he is so determined to father on her.[44] Not that Linda consciously interprets these images. The point is a more fearful one: that her mind habitually works this way.

The most obvious innovation in Mansfield's free indirect narration is in the quick-fire interplay—often likened to filmic montage, by which she may well have been influenced—between the points of view of a range of characters. Stanley, of course, is not a man given to introspection; arguably, his characterisation is more an effect of the external narrative voice than is the case with Linda. But in places he, too, is presented in free indirect mode, and the reader's understanding of Stanley is as much an outcome of his unspoken reflections as of his narrated actions. In Stanley's thought patterns, just as in Linda's, we meet those half-formed perceptions of self and other that underwrite the failures of connection in their relationship.

In 'Prelude' the problems of the marriage bed are signalled by Linda's absence of appetite; she is no more excited by mutton chops than by Stanley's 'amazing vigour' in physical relations. Her husband's best effort to sweeten her up is the armload of treats he brings home from the city. The cherries and the (conventionally aphrodisiac) oysters come fully furnished with their erotic associations; as outlined above, their symbolic meanings are 'determinate'. It's the third gift, the pineapple—'in the pink of condition', as Stanley proudly tells himself[45]—that resonates more deeply in this contingent, personal context. With its prickly rind and its green spiny crown, the pineapple is a little aloe. But not only that, it is also a little Stanley Burnell. Like the 'tip-top' mutton and 'tip-top' cows, its optimum condition is a projection of his narcissism. Stanley, too, 'glowing' from his bath, would like to believe he's in the pink of condition: 'I haven't a square inch of fat on me. Feel that.'[46] It's a fragile construct that needs constantly to be humoured. And yet for Linda there is nothing fragile about Stanley's physicality. Thus, in all its guileless desire to please, the gift can only re-inscribe the impasse of their relationship—Stanley's physical self-delight being precisely the last thing his appetite-less wife wants thrust upon her.

As C.K. Stead once put it, 'Prelude' and 'At the Bay' together 'make up a portrait of a marriage as subtle and complete as you are likely to find in fiction.'[47] Mansfield never wavers in her realism; the mimetic capacities of language are not under challenge, as they are in, say, Stein. But the realist narrator is no longer satisfied to serve as what Henry James once called his heroine's 'biographer'.[48] The new Mansfield narrator is also a psychological impersonator, unfolding the symbolic patterns of consciousness as if from inside her characters' own language.

We come to know the Burnell marriage so deeply because we see it, not just from both points of view, but from 'inside' and 'out', continually alerted to the transactions between behaviour and interior consciousness. We discover how the couple relate in both conscious and unconscious registers: not because Mansfield is a student of Freud, but simply because her mapping of that interior world is so nuanced that a Freudian unconscious can be—one might almost say *demands to be*—mapped onto it. She arrives, in other words, by way of her passage through Symbolism, at a realism perfectly attuned to her modernist moment.

Second selves

Just occasionally Mansfield's stories are more explicit in the way they address psychological issues. The story 'Psychology' signals as much in its title—I'll return to it shortly. More enigmatic is the unfinished late fiction 'A Married Man's Story'. Though written at the same time as 'At the Bay',[49] this work feels wholly at odds with the New World lyricism of the Burnell fictions. It is one of only two Mansfield stories (the other being 'Je Ne Parle Pas Français') to be narrated by a male protagonist; and by contrast with the plotless verisimilitude of the great New Zealand fictions, 'A Married Man's Story' feels plot-driven, melodramatic, gothic. Its first-person narrator is a chilly piece of work, whose indifference towards his wife and infant child appears both cruel and calculated. It hasn't always been like this. Initially, he tells us, they were happy. But since 'last autumn' something has gone wrong—they exist in a state of undeclared hostility—prompting the narrator to reflect on the mystery of what keeps couples together:

> You see—you've reckoned without the unknown quantity—which is their secret relation to each other—and that they can't disclose even if they want to. Thus far you may tell and no further. Oh, don't misunderstand me! It need not necessarily have anything to do with their sleeping together . . . But this brings me to a thought I've often half-entertained. Which is that human beings, as we know them, don't choose each other at all. It is the owner, the second self inhabiting them, who makes the choice for his own particular purposes, and—this may sound absurdly far-fetched—it's the second self in the other which responds.[50]

To understand what has gone wrong in the marriage we need to take account of this 'secret relation', and the role of the narrator's 'second self' whose promptings point back to the gloom of his childhood: 'But really to explain what happened [last autumn] I should have to go back and back—I should have to dwindle until my two hands clutched the banisters, the stair-rail was higher than my head, and I peered through to watch my father padding softly up and down.'[51]

And so the married man's 'story' becomes a psychological case history. The ambience is that of a vaporous high Symbolism: powders and potions, nocturnal transformations, intrusions of a sinister demi-monde. We learn about his father—'old D.P.' (for 'Deadly Poison')—a pharmacist, who sells his 'famous fivepenny pick-me-up' to 'gaudy' young women, and who appears, in this dreamlike recollection, to have poisoned the narrator's mother. The child has studied his father intently: 'His manner was discreet, sly, faintly amused and tinged with impudence. Long before I could appreciate it I knew the mixture . . . I even used to copy him in my corner, bending forward, with a small reproduction of his faint sneer'.[52] This 'mixture', of course, refers both to the father's dubious potions and to the toxic behaviours that the narrator has learned from him. The story breaks off shortly into its eighth numbered section. Since Mansfield's long stories default to 12 sections—as in 'Prelude' and 'The Daughters of the Late Colonel' ('At the Bay' adds a vestigial 13th)—we can guess that the existing story is roughly two-thirds complete. But already, as Stead observes, it seems fairly clear what the past is going to tell us about the present.[53] The thing that went fatally wrong 'last autumn' can only have been the birth of the couple's child. The narrator, as a father, has become *his own* father, and has begun psychologically to 'poison' his wife.

That we're able to deduce this from the incomplete story is perhaps a weakness more than a strength. As a teasing out of the substructure of a relationship it's all a bit mechanical, which may explain why in the end the work remained unfinished. But if the story is an outlier in Mansfield's oeuvre, this attention to the way in which intimate relationships are swayed by the dialogue of these occulted 'second selves' is equally crucial to other stories whose status is more central and whose ambiguities are more intractable. In 'At the Bay' there is the puzzling triangle of Beryl Fairfield and Mr and Mrs Harry Kember, where it's Beryl's seduction by the 'fast' and threatening wife that appears to have morphed by the story's end into an ambivalent desire for her husband. 'Why in God's name did you come?' demands Kember, to which Beryl can't reply because consciously she doesn't know.[54] There's also 'Je Ne Parle Pas Français' and the murky trio of Raoul Duquette, Mouse and Dick Harmon. Here again, no desire is quite what it seems: Duquette's protestations of a grand passion for Mouse are not enough to dampen his infatuation with Dick, any more than Dick's pretend marriage to Mouse is able to surmount his obsession with his mother.

The supreme instance, however, is that snapshot of erotic

indeterminacy, 'Bliss'. The story gets straight to the business of the title: the 30-year-old protagonist Bertha is awash with 'a feeling of bliss—absolute bliss!', a diffuse state of emotional arousal, 'as though you'd suddenly swallowed a bright piece of that late afternoon sun and it burned in your bosom, sending out a little shower of sparks into every particle, into every finger and toe'.[55] The external action consists of Bertha and her husband hosting a mildly bohemian dinner party—duly satirised—while the internal drama follows Bertha's inquiry into the cause of this excitement that she can't put her finger on. The most obvious explanation lies with her new 'find', Pearl Fulton, with whom 'Bertha had fallen in love [. . .] as she always did fall in love with beautiful women who had something strange about them.'[56] The elastic nature of homosocial bonding allows the erotic implications of this crush to remain ambiguous. So, does her state of excitation come from the discovery of same-sex desire? 'What was there in the touch of that cool arm that could fan—fan—start blazing—blazing—the fire of bliss that Bertha did not know what to do with?'[57] Initially, it seems we're being steered in this direction. But in a sequence punctuated by abrupt filmic cuts her focus slides from object to object. First to her husband, as Bertha discovers 'for the first time in her life' that she desires him—'ardently! ardently! The word ached in her ardent body! Was this what that feeling of bliss had been leading up to?'[58] And then to her husband and Pearl together, discovered *en tableau* as they plot a sexual assignation.

What makes Mansfield's depiction of relationships so knowing and so irreducibly 'modern' is this sense of the *otherness* of sexual desire, of desire as the language of those occulted 'second selves' and their 'secret relation[s] [. . .] that they can't disclose even if they want to'. Bertha, it seems, is confused and turned on by a knowledge she doesn't know she possesses, a secret known only to her second self. It speaks to her between the lines of her husband's overstated indifference: 'Oh, Harry, don't dislike her. You are quite wrong about her.'[59] And it's there in her inchoate but resolute conviction that she and Pearl share a secret understanding; perhaps, Beryl thinks, 'she will "give a sign" but 'what she meant by that she did not know, and what would happen after that she could not imagine.'[60] And no wonder, since Beryl doesn't know what she knows. The desire that suffuses her is not her own, but her unwitting apprehension of the hidden desire of Harry and Pearl. Or, as I'm struggling not to say, her *unconscious* apprehension—one refrains with difficulty, just as it's an effort not to translate 'bliss' as *jouissance*, or Bertha's diffuse excitement into Lacan's 'desire of the Other'. It's important, however, to resist this urge, if we wish to see Mansfield clearly and above all historically. Yes, her terms readily translate into Freud's: for 'second self' read 'unconscious'; for the dialogue of second selves, read 'transference'; and while we're about it, for Bertha read 'case study in hysteria'. But what Freudian theory brings to these stories is just another language for what they supply of their own accord. They don't (as I ventured earlier) *demand* that language. We don't need psychoanalysis to decipher them. The requisite framework—the metapsychology—is furnished already by the fiction itself.

Modernist renewal

'Psychology' (from 1919, a year after 'Bliss') is about a couple, or rather a couple manqué, who collude in using the discussion of books to keep each other at arm's length;[61] like Eliot's Prufrock, they can't find the nerve to 'force the moment to its crisis'.[62] This is the spirit in which the unnamed 'he' ventures his thoughts about the direction of contemporary fiction:

> 'I have been wondering very much lately whether the novel of the future will be a psychological novel or not. How sure are you that psychology *qua* psychology has got anything to do with literature at all?'
>
> 'Do you mean you feel [. . .] the young writers [. . .] are trying simply to jump the psychoanalyst's claim?'
>
> 'Yes, I do. [. . .]'[63]

Despite the way her work reads today, it's not clear how Mansfield herself would have answered this question—what she would have understood as a 'psychological' novel, and to what extent she was aware of the ground she shared with psychoanalysis. To Mason, however, in 1932, the answer was obvious: the best and most innovative fiction to have emerged in the preceding two decades had been determinedly psychological. Today, with the benefit of a longer hindsight, we can add to this two equally emphatic statements. First, that alongside James, Proust, Richardson, Joyce, Woolf and Faulkner—the 'A-list' from Leon Edel's admirable mid-century monograph *The Psychological Novel* (1955)—we have to acknowledge Mansfield herself; that within the compass of her brief career and comparatively slender output, her 'interpretation of the human mind' (Mason) is as 'wise, deep [and] fine' as any. Second, however, on a less sanguine note, that back home in New Zealand, where Mansfield's subtleties would prove unreadable, this channel would run dry and a nationalist literature evolve as if in ignorance of modernist interiority.

To the writers of Sargeson's and Mason's generation, Mansfield's work presents problems that they are unable to see beyond. Each of these obstacles to engaging with Mansfield demands, at least initially, to be outlined in its own terms. There is first of all the problem of her critical fame, or more precisely her critical mythology. A much broader issue is one of this book's recurrent themes: a general eclipse of writing by women, in the context of a wholesale re-gendering of literary culture. In this light the failure to read Mansfield appears indicative rather than exceptional. A third problem though is more specific to her own work. There is something in Mansfield's project—in the specific manifestations of her modernism—that goes a long way towards explaining why that modernism finds no audience among the mid-century nationalists.

Before I investigate this, however, a word about the critical mythology. As any of today's Mansfield scholars will tell you, her critical reception has been muddled and frequently unedifying. In the last few years of her life she achieved a good measure of fame and at least some acknowledgement of the aspects of her work that were genuinely modern. But her death in 1923, and her husband's entrepreneurialism, changed all that. John Middleton Murry set about publishing every scrap that Mansfield had written—'boiling Katherine's bones to make soup', as one of their circle unkindly put it.[64] And this, combined with Murry's partisanship ('the most wonderful writer and the most beautiful spirit of our time'),[65] and with his insistence on what he saw as Mansfield's spiritual journey as opposed to her craft and intellect, granted his wife a kind of mawkish celebrity but obscured her role as modernist innovator. Occasionally a critic—for example the American short story writer Katherine Anne Porter[66]—would put a finger on the kind of 'grown up' Mansfield we recognise today. Woolf, of course, had acknowledged Mansfield as the only writer she was ever jealous of, and Eliot in 1934 cited 'Bliss' as an exemplary experimental fiction.[67] But by and large Mansfield was left stranded in Murry's cultish cul-de-sac, while the discourse on modernism in fiction evolved a canon that ignored her.

In fairness to the literary nationalists, then, they would need to have been reading Mansfield more acutely than just about anyone else in order to be able to access the kind of writer I have been describing in this chapter. And after all, why should they? The Mansfield of the Murry cult was already a figurehead for exactly the kind of thing they despised: a cosy, genteel, book-loving culture that stood between them and the hard-minded *critical* discourse that, in their view, the settler situation demanded. Worse, this local book culture was not just complacent, but naïvely *nationalist*. Mansfield the famous New Zealand author stood for precisely the idea of New Zealand writing that they were determined to displace.

In Mansfield, in typically modernist fashion, a sense of social disintegration contends with and motivates the pursuit of a residual coherence. 'These fragments I have shored against my ruins,'[68] writes Eliot in a phrase that has become a shorthand for this dynamic: the artist, among the ruins of a shattered post-war culture, searching for the traces of a lost ideal order (Pound's Confucianism, Eliot's unified sensibility, Lawrence's arcadian vitalism). For Mansfield, this 'useable past' is in New Zealand, in those memories that have been galvanised by the disaster of her brother's death in the war:

> Now—now I want to write my recollections of my own country. Yes I want to write about my country till I simply exhaust my store—not only because it is a 'sacred debt' that I pay to my country because my brother & I were born there, but also because in my thoughts I range with him over all the remembered places. I am never far away from them. I long to renew them in my writing.
>
> And the people, the people we loved there. Of them too I want to write—another 'debt of love'. Oh, I want for one moment to make our undiscovered country leap into the eyes of the old world. It must be mysterious, as though floating—it must take the breath. It must be 'one of those islands . . .' I shall

> tell everything, even of how the laundry-basket squeaked at '75'—but all must be told with a sense of mystery, a radiance, an afterglow, because you, my little sun of it, are set. You have dropped over the dazzling brim of the world. Now I must play my part.[69]

At the threshold of her major work—it's 1915 and she's writing 'The Aloe', the first iteration of 'Prelude'—Mansfield alights on her 'undiscovered country'. Here, compacted into the form of her own family, is the bedrock that will hold together her fractured 'subjective epic'.[70]

I am drawing here on Lydia Wevers, who describes Mansfield's work of reconstruction as follows: 'The voice which speaks [. . .] a loss specifically identified with European modernism [. . .] can answer its loss with discovery and renewal [. . .] As Europe scatters itself, and Mansfield's life is broken into its different and often opposing parts, so in her work does New Zealand gather together, becoming itself, a country, a people, a family'.[71] This requires some careful discriminations, for at a glance Mansfield's representation of family life might appear prevailingly negative. There's so much loneliness and isolation; her characters so often are cut off from one another by those operations of consciousness that her fiction depicts so keenly. However, Wevers makes the case that this strictly dystopian view of familial and other intimate relationships is concentrated in the European stories.[72] New Zealand, the object of that 'sacred debt', is by contrast a site of mysterious renewal: 'It is so strange to bring the dead back to life again. There's my Grandmother back in her chair with her pink knitting, there stalks my uncle over the grass'.[73] Here, and most specifically in the Burnell stories—though in ways that may not be immediately obvious—family is the site of regeneration and repair.

The key is the portrait of Stanley Burnell. In a certain light Stanley is of course a minor domestic tyrant. But he's childish more than monstrous. He's not the Late Colonel, or the brooding 'Married Man'. He expects the household to revolve around him—'Look sharp! The stick's got to be found!'[74]—which it does; but so practised are the women in managing him that his comings and goings become a kind of tidal rhythm, a pulsation more comic than anxiogenic. In Linda's situation we hear an acute protest against patriarchal sexual relations. And yet, frightening though Stanley can appear to Linda, and cruelly though she sometimes thinks of him, her protest is silent, her proto-feminist resistance strictly internal. Sometimes she keeps her thoughts to herself; she imagines handing Stanley her feelings like so many wrapped packages ('this hatred, just as real as the rest [. . .] She could see his eyes as he opened that'),[75] but of course this never actually happens. At other times she is unable even to recognise her thoughts, unconscious of her own resentment as she voices it, silently, to herself. Similarly Beryl, 'buried' in Karori, sees plainly how her dependence on Stanley has brought her to this spinsterly impasse: he has been 'threatening to take a place in the country' ever since she has lived with them.[76] But the closest Beryl comes to expressing her resentment is in an unfinished letter, or in leaving the sugar out of Stanley's tea. It may produce confused, symptomatic behaviours, but nothing approaching open revolt.

In the same way that the gender threat to Stanley's regime is neutralised, so is the pressure of class relations that might otherwise undermine its bourgeois complacency. As Wevers demonstrates, class inequality is preserved, and yet at the same time contained, located precisely 'on the edges *but inside* the large house of white middle-class New Zealand.'[77] Thus Alice, the maid, may be busy at the kitchen sink, but she still gets to share with the other women in the collective relief at Stanley's departure. Class stratification has had its edges softened—it becomes the kind of inequality that needn't make the middle class feel bad about itself. Stanley, in characteristic fashion, congratulates himself on his 'new man' Pat: 'There was nothing servile about him—and if there was one thing he hated more than another it was servility.'[78] When it comes to the subtleties of liberal patriarchy, Stanley is a natural adept; he 'wouldn't mind' giving Pat a handful of cherries, '—but no, better not. Better wait until he had been with him a bit longer.'[79]

A disconnection emerges between the modernist insistence that 'nothing can be the same' and the mysterious, sacred duty of 'bringing the dead back to life'. As Mansfield reveals her undiscovered country to the admiring gaze of her European audience, what the Old World discovers is an image of itself refreshed and renovated in the New. Drenched in the afterglow of nostalgia, the bourgeois order of Mansfield's New Zealand is an image of the old European order—'the same'—only stronger for being more inclusive, more yielding. It is, by design, a *consoling* fiction, a putting-back-together of the world that has been ruined by the death of her brother. In the process, at an ideological level, this New World repairs the social order of the Old, discovering to the eyes of the bombed-out centre a view of regeneration at the imperial fringe.

Something different

'Katherine Mansfield's *At the Bay* is one of the minor masterpieces of our language,' wrote V.S. Pritchett in the *New Statesman* in 1946. To this, however, he attached the caveat to which these questions of continuity and consolation inexorably lead: '—but who are these people, who are their neighbours, what is the world that they belong to? We can scarcely guess. Too self-sufficiently, they drop out of the sky and fill the little canvas.'[80] As Alpers does, one can fend this off as an Old World failure to grasp a New World scenario. But for New Zealand writers, too—the Curnow–Sargeson cohort—this will be the problem with the kind of country that Mansfield discovers. This complaint will emerge as one of the key motifs of the nationalist mid century: that New Zealand writing has been habitually unreal in its refusal to account for *how we got here*. What has been applauded in the name of an emerging literature has been a cultural prosperity without history. In 'Prelude' the Burnells, making their initial night-time journey from Thorndon to Karori, re-enact this colonial magic. When the family wake in the morning it is to a lifestyle-block arcadia already in full production: orchard and flower garden, rhubarb and blackberries, 'three tip-top cows and enough fowls and ducks to keep them in poultry'.[81] This pastoral abundance has dropped from the heavens with no more explanation than that Stanley has picked it up 'dirt cheap'. Of the long chain of cause and effect—the history—that has set the family down in this replete environment, there is no account. 'History,' as Wevers judiciously puts it, 'has not yet invaded the modernist present.'[82]

Sargeson, writing in 1948, may well have read Pritchett's comments published two years earlier, and his own remarks about a lack of 'social tradition' in Mansfield's fiction conceivably reflect this. Yet Sargeson hardly needs prompting. The primary imperative behind his cohort's cultural critique is to make this 'invasion'—this belated historical reckoning—finally occur. 'Now all the history that did not happen / Begins, and stings like an unfrozen wound,' writes Curnow in his sonnet 'To M.H. Holcroft'.[83] Like Mansfield, reeling from the carnage of the war, the nationalists begin with a modernist sense of rupture. But where, for Mansfield, New Zealand is a site of repair, for the *Phoenix*–Caxton writers it is the site of a foundational trauma. This critical diagnosis will supply the rhetorical energy with which to rewrite the rules of literary engagement in the 30s and 40s.

Standing in their way—requiring to be displaced—was a literary culture that appeared to have acclimatised itself as nonchalantly and as painlessly as the Burnells. Just as Karori seems to spring fully formed from the sentimental bullishness of Stanley's imagination, the Dominion boasted a tip-top literature with no account of where it stood or how it had been arrived at. It was a literature which, by the mid 1930s, was deemed fit to be celebrated in the country's first ever national Authors' Week, an event designed 'to impress upon the people of New Zealand the wonderful volume and the high standard of work in the world of letters achieved by their fellow countrymen'. The encomium is from the organiser and official cheerleader O.N. Gillespie

General committee at the inauguration of New Zealand Authors' Week, 1935. Standing far right, Pat Lawlor; sitting far right, O.N. Gillespie; centre Sir Harold Beauchamp.

(who imagines that 'our lovely land' is about to become to the modern world what Greece was to the ancient one).[84] The event was the initiative of PEN NZ founder and Mansfield enthusiast Pat Lawlor, and invited to chair the organising committee was none other the Pa-Man himself, Sir Harold Beauchamp.[85] Posed at the centre of an admiring group, his face lit up with avuncular modesty, it is for all the world as if Stanley Burnell has climbed up off the page to be installed as patron of New Zealand literature.[86] Nor in the end should this greatly surprise us. Notwithstanding its gender protest, its worldliness, its acerbity, its pain, Mansfield's fiction still leaves itself open to co-option by a cosy, back-slapping nationalism. There is nothing in the world of Stanley Burnell to unsettle the amnesia of a national literature that doesn't know how it got here.

From a 30s point of view, then, Mansfield has to be sacrificed. Their argument with history leaves the nationalists no choice. The ground must be cleared for their more ruthless version of what Curnow calls the 'discovery of self in country and country in self'. Mansfield's demotion, of course, will be temporary; today her place seems increasingly secure as a major figure, not just in New Zealand terms, but in the still-evolving history of Anglophone modernism. Even so, the swerve to avoid her comes with a cost. Well beyond the horizon of this book—in the 50s, the 60s, and later still—our writers will struggle to re-legitimise a language of thought and feeling of equivalent sophistication. In contriving to forget Mansfield, the nationalist generation deny themselves access to another new world, the 'twilit jungle' of modernist interiority with all that it offers in terms of complexity and psychological intelligence. Declining to read our most original writer will inhibit New Zealand fiction for decades to come.

Chapter 2

Predecessors

Baughan, Bethell, Mason

In 1971, on the death of R.A.K. Mason, Charles Brasch wrote a tribute in *Landfall*: 'It is indeed with Mason's work, and that of another poet writing at the same time, the much older Ursula Bethell [. . .] that New Zealand literature as a continuous body of work begins.'[1] Since Mansfield had been so determinedly sidelined—and since the nationalists in any case liked to use poetry as a shorthand for New Zealand writing as a whole—this assessment would not have surprised *Landfall*'s readers. Bethell and Mason are surely the most convincing poets of the 1920s, the first to find an idiom that feels at home in the 20th century. These are the writers whom Brasch's generation are most inclined to acknowledge as elders. Their later publications grace the catalogue of the Caxton Press, and they seem to belong there.

But the reference to 'continuity' is not entirely helpful.

It's at odds first of all with the isolation of both writers, and their strangely shaped, discontinuous careers. It is also out of tune with the way that the writing of the 30s and 40s characteristically situates itself. The discourse of New Zealand literary nationalism is only secondarily a language of continuity. The preferred theme is rupture, or *dis*continuity: the difference that separates the New World from the Old, and the break that this distinctively 'critical' nationalism wants to insert between itself and earlier versions of local writing. Standing in the way of a real 'New Zealand literature' (so the argument runs) is an amateurism that has lacked the tough-mindedness to see, to face up to, and to articulate the settler condition. Curnow's New Zealand—and it is Allen Curnow with whom increasingly we need to grapple as we enter the force-field of nationalism proper—will emerge in the opening introduced by a vehement interruption of that moribund tradition.

Not that Curnow doesn't make exceptions. In his first severe pruning, in the 1945 Caxton anthology, he spares Bethell and Mason as well as (to the confoundment of nearly everyone) D'Arcy Cresswell. In the 1960 *Penguin Book of New Zealand Verse* he rediscovers Blanche Baughan. Beyond doubt Curnow owes a debt to these writers—if not so much in his practice as a poet, then certainly in the formulation of his critical thesis, where crucial perceptions are extracted from Cresswell and Mason in particular. And if Curnow owes them a debt, then the nationalist movement as a whole is indebted in turn. The task of this chapter is to itemise that debt. Here, more than anywhere else in this book, I'm canvassing a period and battening on its highlights. I'm not trying to unpick a governing impulse; the chapter is framed as three discrete profiles rather than a single-minded argument. Nonetheless I didn't choose these highlights at will. While I won't indulge Curnow's indulgence of Cresswell (the latter will have his say in due course), it is Curnow's version of the period that guides me, and with it the question of exactly what survives as the hard frost sets in.

To group these three poets as predecessors, then, is to read them, as I have been reading Mansfield, through the lens of literary nationalism. Whatever they offer in their own right, my first concern is what they mean to the 30s and 40s. It's hard to find a satisfactory metaphor, but 'predecessor' appeals for its neutrality. From the Latin *prae* (beforehand) and *decessor* (retiring officer, from *decedere* = depart), a predecessor simply 'goes before'. We are not talking, then, about a 'parent', a 'model' or a 'teacher'; a predecessor may be any of these things, but none is implied directly. The question of affiliation remains an open one, and it's in that space that the discussion needs to unfold. But what is *almost* implied—to the ear, at least, and bearing in mind that *decedere* means not just 'to depart' but also 'to die'—is the fate or status of a *pre-deceaser*. Again we come up against loss and forgetting. To read for continuity between the 20s and the nationalist mid century is to be struck once again by how much is left behind, or is passed over, or 'passes away'. The three writers under discussion in this chapter, each of whom is survived by at least a small quantity of distinguished verse, show us idioms and options available to poets in the decades leading up to the arrival of literary nationalism. But none will write well beyond the early 1930s. A modest number of poems will survive, but the places from which they were written will no longer be habitable.

Baughan: New World Romanticism

The little that is known about the life of Blanche Baughan (1870–1958)—and sadly, the trail now being so cold, there may never be a full biography—is enough to make her one of the most appealing figures in early New Zealand writing. Baughan has (in spades) the kind of girls-can-do-anything glamour that attaches to the independent woman of the suffragist era. The fullest account available comes from the PhD research of Nancy Harris.[2] Baughan grew up in Putney in southwest London, in material comfort, but haunted by alarming events in her family. In the early 1870s her mother's father was committed to Broadmoor for an act of insane homicide. In 1880, when Baughan was ten, her mother murdered Baughan's father. Her father's death left her with a modest private income; it also convinced her not to have children, in light of what she feared was a congenital mental illness. True to her word, Baughan never married, though a (possibly apocryphal) story has her running away from a finishing school in Switzerland with a bear trainer from a travelling circus. In 1887 she entered the Royal Holloway College of the University of London, graduating four years later with prizes in Latin and Greek and with a First Class Honours degree in Classics (the first awarded to a member of the College). She was then involved in settlement work in the East London slums, and was active in the suffragist movement; at the same time she was obliged to nurse her mentally ill mother who had been in the family's care since the death of Baughan's father. On a world trip in 1893 she appears to have visited New Zealand briefly, and in 1900, on her mother's death, she emigrated.

Her most notable period as a writer coincided with her 30s, spent chiefly at a remote settlement called Chorlton on the northern side of Banks Peninsula. Here she produced her two most substantial literary works, *Shingle-Short and Other Verses* (1908) and the short fiction of *Brown Bread from a Colonial Oven* (1912), as well as the first of the travel pieces later collected as *Studies in New Zealand Scenery* (1916).

But this burst of inspiration proved mysteriously short-lived; her active career as a writer would not survive World War I. Two related projects absorbed the remaining years of her life. One was the study and practice of Vedanta, then enjoying a vogue in the West, involving trips to California and to India during the war, and extensive correspondence with spiritual teachers on both continents.[3] The other, galvanised by the first, was the agitation for penal reform in which she remained active deep into old age. She helped to establish the New Zealand branch of the Howard League in 1924, and wrote the small book *People in Prison* (1936).

'A Bush Section', from *Shingle-Short*, was saluted by Curnow as 'the best New Zealand poem before Mason'.[4] But even this unconditional verdict doesn't quite do justice to its singularity: it's the best before Mason by a country mile—the poem seems to come from a different universe of discourse; more prosaically, it comes from a different continent. The model is Whitman, whose long free-verse line, freedom from end rhyme, and rolling compound sentences give Baughan the scope to reconstruct a ravaged frontier landscape (based on a period spent as a housekeeper at Ormondville in Hawke's Bay) whose realism feels strikingly modern:

> Logs, at the door, by the fence; logs, broadcast over the
> paddock;
> Sprawling in motionless thousands away down the green of
> the gully,
> Logs, grey-black. And the opposite rampart of ridges
> Bristles against the sky, all the tawny, tumultuous landscape
> Is stuck, and prickled, and spiked with the standing black
> and grey splinters,
> Strewn, all over its hollows and hills, with the long, prone,
> grey-black logs.

[. . .]
At the little raw farm on the edge of the desolate hillside,
Perch'd on the brink, overlooking the desolate valley,
To-night, now the milking is finish'd, and all the calves fed,
The kindling all split, and the dishes all wash'd after supper:
Thorold von Reden, the last of a long line of nobles,
Little 'Thor Rayden', the twice-orphan'd son of a drunkard,
Dependent on strangers, the taciturn, grave ten-year-old,
Stands and looks from the garden of cabbage and larkspur,
  looks over
The one little stump-spotted rye-patch, so gratefully green,
Out on this desert of logs [. . .][5]

No wonder Curnow seized on this poem: still, today, the immediacy is palpable. To turn back from here even to something as successful as Edward Tregear's 'Te Whetu Plains' or Arthur Adams's 'The Dwellings of Our Dead'—let alone any of those windier Victorians (Bowen, Bracken, Domett and co)—is to notice how intensely Baughan *looks* at what's in front of her. Curnow said all this more eloquently: 'No earlier New Zealand poem exhibits such unabashed truth to its subject.'[6] His rhetoric has become so familiar that it's now perhaps an obstacle to admiring Baughan's veracity. But 'truth to its subject' here really does mean something. How many poems (before Bethell, and even beyond) find a way to detail what the evening chores consist of, what's growing in the garden, or that the first crop planted in the 'stump-spotted' clearing is 'rye'? We learn about the first native shrubs to regenerate (konini, wineberry). We learn not just what the ruined landscape looks like, but even how it smells: the 'spicy breath' of macrocarpa, the 'acrid, familiar aroma' of smouldering logs.[7]

The liberties of Whitman's prosody serve Baughan in a way that English Romantic and Victorian models entirely fail to serve her colonial colleagues. But this is only the formal aspect of Baughan's debt to North America; behind her engagement with Whitman's verse is a deeper relationship with New England Transcendentalism. Baughan was raised as an Anglican but records having lost her faith as a child 'with a consequent agony indescribable';[8] while her reading and education can be reconstructed only in glimpses, it's enough to suggest that the German Idealist tradition took on a corresponding significance. She read her German and British Romantics and their Victorian heirs (Thomas Carlyle, John Ruskin). According to one appealing anecdote, she knew enough Hegel to be able to carry on a mock-philosophical debate with a German-speaking parrot.[9] But it's from Emerson and Whitman that she gets what Harris, taking the phrase from Whitman's *Democratic Vistas*, calls her 'New Worldism'—her sense that where the frontier has burst the boundaries of Old World culture, the sovereign Romantic self is the natural agent of building anew. This is the germ of the cultural nationalism expressed so triumphantly in the American Renaissance. And it's the formula that, 60 or 70 years later, in the decade before World War I, Baughan rehearses here in her remarkable one-of-a-kind poem.

In later years Baughan would consider herself a mystic, recording, in prose accounts edited by others, two specific supra-rational experiences. The first of these, at Chorlton in 1905, also produced a piece of verse:

> Breathed through by the winds, and in league
> with the stones of the field,
> From the light of the stars and the sun
> Unexcluded, unsealed—
> Out of all elements formed, to all
> elements kin [. . .][10]

The rhetoric here sounds very much like Emerson: the state of illumination reveals the interpenetration of Nature and Self. As Emerson famously put it: 'I am nothing; I see all; the currents of the Universal Being circulate through me'.[11] In a 'universe [that] is nowhere dead matter, but everywhere alive and active, bright Spirit throughout'—as Baughan writes in one of her scenery studies[12]—the individual subject is alive with that same 'bright Spirit'. This orthodox transcendentalist view is implicit in everything that Baughan writes about landscape. Harris suggests that the Chorlton experience must actively have precipitated the writing of 'A Bush Section'. To me this seems arguable. Nonetheless it's plain that Baughan's accounts of mystical 'Oneness',[13] and the New World ebullience of 'A Bush Section', are cut from the same transcendentalist cloth.

'Little "Thor Rayden"', the poem's organising vehicle, is presented as having come down in the world. As 'the twice-orphan'd son of a drunkard', he appears to have lost his homeland as well as his parents. He has also, in this levelling frontier culture, lost his aristocratic name, reduced from European privilege to 'dependen[ce] on strangers' and to a 'narrow round of monotonous labours' (working, perhaps, alongside the poet in the farming household at Ormondville). And yet, however reduced, he is anything but *fallen*: this is a Romantic scenario, not a Christian one. In this burned-out, 'desolate' and apparently static scene, where 'there is no change, nothing stirs', where 'all is mute, monotonous, stark',[14] the child's untutored and thus unsullied view is the lens through which the poem discovers energy and motion. In sequence, Thor contemplates his 'comrade' the river, still 'bright as a needle' as it picks its way through the fallen logs; the 'wonderful Train' that bursts into the landscape, its smoke 'like the glorious hair of some else-invisible Angel'; and the nightly passage of the constellations: 'The sky is a wide black paddock, without any fences, / The Stars are its shining logs'.[15] Each attests to a dynamism that is ready to remake this shattered frontier. But the key exhibit in this catalogue of Spirit is the child himself, with his fund of Romantic capital: 'spark of Life!', 'begetter, of changes', 'Offspring of elements all [. . .] their captain and ruler'.[16]

Like the landscape itself, the child has been damaged, a correspondence Baughan takes trouble to emphasise. Here, for example, it's impossible to say if the third and fourth lines refer to the landscape or to the child settler:

> Here on Earth, from what region unguess'd at?
> Here, to this rough and raw prospect, these back-blocks of
> Being, assign'd—
> Lean, cumber'd with ruin, lonely, bristling with hardship,
> A birthright that fires have been through—[17]

Thor, as much as the deforested landscape, is 'lean' and 'lonely', 'cumber'd with ruin'; the hillsides bristle with burnt standing logs, while the 'taciturn' child bristles at his dependency; and so on. In the process of settlement the child has been reduced to his solitary, elemental self. At the same time, however, the trials he has suffered affirm his kinship with the natural world. And it's this vital sympathy of child and Nature—the 'bright Spirit' that circulates between them—which holds out the promise of new growth stirring in the ashes:

> A Mind that moves 'mid the motionless matter:
> 'Mid the logs, a developing Soul:
> From the battle-field bones of a ruin'd epoch,
> Life, the Unruin'd, freshly upspringing,
> Life, Re-creator of life![18]

Implicit once more is the example of Whitman. Despite its ebullience, 'Song of Myself' doesn't shy away from contradiction and violence: in the midst of its jaunty, on-rushing catalogues, a slave is sold at auction, the crowd taunts a prostitute, 'malform'd limbs' drop 'horribly' in the surgeon's pail, and yet none of it dampens Whitman's mood.[19] 'A Bush Section' taps the same vein of enthusiasm. It can't be said that Baughan's world is unrealistic, or that she fails to take account of the destructiveness of settlement. But for every reminder that the landscape is 'silent', 'disconsolate', 'Ruin'd', 'forlorn' and 'blank', there's a 'Mind!', a 'Soul!', an 'outflowing Heart!' apostrophised in Baughan's rollicking lines. Even though the future is posed as a question, the exclamatory tone is already its own answer:

> O pioneer Soul! against Ruin here hardily pitted,
> What life wilt thou make of existence?
> Life! What more Life wilt thou make?
>
> Ah, little Thor!
> Here in the night, face to face
> With the Burnt Bush within and without thee,
> Standing, small and alone:
> Bright Promise on Poverty's threshold!
> What art thou? Where hast though come from?
> How far, how far! wilt thou go?[20]

The child embodies both the frontier's harshness and its vigour. Like Whitman's all-encompassing 'I', little Thor works a dialectical magic, absorbing the tumult and violence of settlement and playing it back as spiritual dynamism.

A short-lived burst of creativity that dissipates almost as swiftly as it arises: in this, Baughan displays the same pattern as Bethell and Mason. Baughan's case, however, is the most dramatic, and I'm tempted to say the most 'romantic'. In one or two of the stories, and in the self-conscious 'bush' accents of 'The Old Place' (a poem several times anthologised) there are hints of the kind of colonial realism that Mansfield tackles fleetingly around the same time. The 'scenery' studies sent home to *The Spectator* are of some interest as period pieces. For myself, though, I'm happy to go with Curnow's implicit judgement: Baughan's claim to be honoured as a writer is chiefly this one exceptional poem. That the poem exists at all is a mystery. *How on earth did she come to write it?* I don't mean to argue that the poem was a fluke, and certainly not that it hadn't been earned. Baughan was well educated. And she had worked at her craft for a decent period; a fat volume of routine Victorian verses was in print before she left Britain, and at Chorlton she produced a quantity of work that suggests a dedicated practice. 'A Bush Section', though, is *sui generis*. Nothing in our meagre colonial canon comes anywhere near its freedom or its realism. It's entirely without precedent. And with the partial exception of 'Maui's Fish', about which a little more in a moment, it's also unlike anything else in her own work. Nobody seems to have recognised its qualities, and it lay in obscurity until 1960. Nor is it clear that Baughan herself especially valued it. In a letter from the time of its first publication she writes: 'I set little store by *Shingle-Short* [in which 'A Bush Section' appears]—tho' I'm personally fond of the name piece and the song of the cabbage tree [from 'The Paddock'].'[21] It seems fair to say, then, that she barely knew what she was doing. Yet somehow, through her openness to Emerson and Whitman, and her openness to her own experience—with or without the prompting of a transcendental illumination—she managed to conjure this lone example of an inspiring colonial-Romantic poem.

Baughan is not a nationalist. Spirit, Nature, Life, Change: these Romantic proper nouns insist on their *universal* currency. Unlike Emerson and Whitman, American several generations over, Baughan doesn't argue that the life of the Spirit is to be enhanced in particular by 'this' soil, or 'this' Nature. The name 'New Zealand' barely figures—for Baughan it is not a potent signifier; nor do we encounter the kind of negative leveraging against Europe so characteristic of the Americans (in the one place that this occurs, in 'Maui's Fish', the rhetoric is 'New Worldist' rather than nationalist). Baughan remains an English migrant, for whom imagining new beginnings does not necessarily imply a critical distance from British culture. 'Maui's Fish' appropriates Māori tradition in the cheerful manner of the day, and uses this requisitioned narrative in extolling a New World of youthful possibilities. The perspective, that is, remains wholly colonial: you can make something new, according to Baughan's allegory, and not step outside of imperialist assumptions.

Curnow rescues the Baughan who matters: in canon-making terms it's an impeccable call. 'A Bush Section' failed to speak to Currie and Alexander, to Holcroft (who might have known better), to Chapman and Bennett, or to McCormick.[22] But the moment Curnow points them out the poem's qualities become self-evident, and no anthologist since has failed to include at least substantial parts of it. Baughan, though, is different from Mason and Bethell. With this pair Curnow will maintain dialogue: he keeps coming back to make subtle adjustments; getting them right is essential to the stability of his narrative. Baughan won't be part of this fine-tuning process. As in Bethell and Mason, there are aspects of her work that under the right historical circumstances might have proved amenable to nationalist uses. But while Curnow rightly values her, he views her across the abyss of World War I, and her High Romantic vision of the new is left parked to one side as an admired curiosity.

Curnow's challenge in the 30s and 40s is to formulate a nationalism answerable to modernism; this, we'll see in Chapter 4, demands a reading of the outcomes of settlement that is historical and critical. Baughan's response is mystical. From within the limitations of her colonial perspective, she records the destructiveness of settlement. But her vitalism overpowers historical time: the drama of destruction already manifests, for Baughan, the promise of growth and repair. Curnow—notwithstanding a certain Pākehā sleight of hand—will seek to reinstate a more historical temporality. The experience of trauma, disruption and shock is amplified, not just in force, but in duration, while regeneration (Baughan's 'green clearing') is postponed, reduced to a horizon or hypothesis. Where Baughan's poem accelerates settler experience, Curnow wants to slow it down, prolonging that moment of historical rupture in which his critical anti-myth will take root.

Bethell: 'Before the all-wintry years'

Ursula Bethell (1874–1945) is Baughan's junior by just four years. They were personal friends, and their respective career paths track one another in significant ways. Although Bethell was born in North Canterbury, her education followed the approved colonial pattern: secondary education at an exclusive girls' school in Oxford, finishing school in Geneva, and later painting and music studies in Geneva and Dresden. Like Baughan, she was involved in London in feminist-inspired social work. And similarly, too, her father's early death would leave her with sufficient private income to be able to remain unmarried. Her work as a writer, however, came later. In 1924, at the age of 50, she moved with her friend Effie Pollen to the property she called Rise Cottage, on the Cashmere Hills above Christchurch; here in the course of the next ten years she completed virtually all of her significant work. Her first book, *From a Garden in the Antipodes*, appeared in 1929, two decades after *Shingle-Short.*[23]

Bethell wrote her poems in a different world, on the other side of World War I. It was a moment in which poetry was scaling itself down, as modernists and others pursued tightness and discipline in their flight from the overblown ambitions of the Victorians. So where Baughan went 'big'—'A Bush Section' runs to eight pages in the *Penguin* anthology; other poems from *Single-Short* are longer again—Bethell in the 1920s goes 'small'. Where Baughan embraced the expansiveness of Romanticism, Bethell, in the garden poems especially, crafts restrained, iconic miniatures:

> My garage is a structure of excessive plainness,
> It springs from a dry bank in the back garden,
> It is made of corrugated iron,
> And painted all over with brick-red.
>
> But beside it I have planted a green Bay-tree,
> —A sweet Bay, an Olive, and a Turkey Fig,
> —A Fig, an Olive, and a Bay.[24]

While Bethell will never be a modernist, in a poem like 'Detail' (quoted here in full) she could easily be taken for one. The poem seems entirely of its moment: if we cross-check with William Carlos Williams, for instance, 'The Red Wheelbarrow' was first published in 1922, 'This Is Just to Say' in 1934; halfway between them, 'Detail' looks perfectly at home. A signature topos of modernist poetics involves the making of key poems by rigorous subtraction. The two lines of Pound's 'In a Station of the Metro' are said to be the pared-back remains of a poem 30 lines long.[25] The familiar version of *The Waste Land* is what survives when Pound does the same job for Eliot, reducing the poem's original length by almost half. In 'Detail', this editorial pruning is recorded in the internal drama of the text. A minimal kind of drama, to be sure, and yet at the poem's end something does 'happen': a statement of 'plainness' becomes even more plain as the final line strips out the qualifiers. Precisely what we're hearing in the parallel construction—a second voice answering the first, perhaps, or the preservation of alternative drafts?—the poet leaves ambiguous. But in this pointed reduction, this *excess* of plainness, 'Detail' reads explicitly as a minimalist manifesto.

Faced, then, with Bethell's minimalism there's an urge to inquire about her reading. Although in the 1940s she would sometimes refer to Eliot, it doesn't seem likely that she knew Pound or Williams, especially by 1929.[26] So how did she write, with such nerveless assurance, a poem that feels as if it's channelling them? A convention has arisen that she must have read Arthur Waley, whose translations from Chinese and Japanese traditions were much admired in the years just after the war. While I'm not aware of any concrete evidence,[27] this explanation seems inherently plausible; Waley's translations were more extensive, and more widely circulated than Pound's. But there's another way to think about Bethell's scaling down: not in terms of what she'd been reading, but in terms of who she was writing for. Holcroft, who knew the poet relatively well, records: 'The garden poems were spontaneous, sometimes artless, and written at first for sister and friends in England, an audience she knew would be responsive.'[28] It was only with the encouragement of this first, private audience that eventually the poems were submitted to a public one,[29] and their freshness, their lightness, their lack of will-to-literature, may all be explained in part by the context that first supported them. Likewise their sometimes elliptical quality: the lack of explanation, of stage directions, of meta-discourse. What can be *assumed* doesn't have to be *said*. It's a recipe for economy and, as we'll see shortly, for the staging of a specific kind of intimacy.

Given Curnow's predilection for poetry that's concrete, grounded and local, it's curious that the garden poems don't seem particularly to attract him. In 1945 he includes five poems from the first book (in a total representation of 19), and in the 1960 anthology, four (of 13). He doesn't ignore *From a Garden in the Antipodes*, but neither does he particularly embrace it. In 1945 he leaves out 'Response'; in 1960 he leaves out 'Pause'; and in neither anthology does he include 'Detail'. For later anthologists all three have been automatic choices, and partly, one can't help feeling, because they're so much the kind of thing that Curnow has taught us to value. But there's something odd about Curnow and Bethell; his response is unpredictable, as if swayed by unseen currents. Bethell herself even raises an eyebrow when in the last year of her life Curnow makes his selections for the Caxton anthology; to Holcroft she admits that she is 'surprised and pleased that he chose some of what I might call the more Christian pieces.'[30] The complaint so often heard about Curnow's anthology choices is that he favours poems that flatter his own critical realist thesis. But in this case, if anything he seems to do the opposite. Where Bethell's Christianity distances her from Curnow, a selection that underlines it serves to emphasise that difference.

That the garden poems began life as personal communications is inscribed in their internal structure of address. They assume, initially, a specific reader: their 'you' is the poet's friend Ruth.[31] But Ruth is not just any friend, she's a friend in Britain, in 'loved and lost London' ('Mail'),[32] so that intimacy, and geographical distance, are introduced in the same device. The plainest illustration is the opening poem 'Response':

> When you wrote your letter it was April ,
> And you were glad that it was spring weather,
> [. . .]
> I write in waning May and it is autumn,
> And I am glad my chrysanthemums
> Are tied up fast to strong posts [. . .][33]

However much the speaker insists she's 'glad' (she repeats the phrase three times), she knows that most of all she's talking courage to herself, and that hers will always be poems of exile: 'But oh, we have remembering hearts, / And we say "How green it was in such and such an April"'. We learn as much from the volume's title: 'the Antipodes'—literally 'the other side of the world'. She writes from New Zealand *as viewed from London*, and in light of the assumptions that come with that vantage point.

A more subtle poem on the same theme is 'Erica' (Erica being the botanical name for heath or heather, 'New Holland' a historical name for Australia):

> Sit down with me awhile beside the heath-corner.
>
> Here I have laboured hour on hour in winter
> Digging thick clay, breaking up clods, and draining,
> Carrying away cold mud, bringing up sandy loam,
> Bringing these rocks and setting them all in their places,
> To be shelter from winds, shade from too burning sun.

See, now, how sweetly all these plants are springing
Green, ever green, and flowering turn by turn.
Delicate heaths, and their fragrant Australian kinsmen,
Shedding as once unknown in New Holland, strange scents
 on the air
And purple and white daboecia—the Irish heather
Said in the nursery man's list to be so well suited
For small gardens, for rock gardens, and for graveyards.[34]

The speaker invites her distant friend to travel in her mind's eye: like Mansfield responding to the death of her brother, she wants to make the New World visible in the eyes of the Old. But not with Mansfield's sense of mission; while there's pride in the garden as a labour of settlement, there is no implication that the Old World needs repair. Instead we hear the exile's insistent grief. The final line is a plea to sympathise—appealing to those shared colonial assumptions—with one who will be buried on the far side of the world, who in the course of making a garden is also digging her own grave.

Reviewing the posthumous *Collected Poems* in *Landfall* in 1951, Lawrence Baigent celebrates Bethell in terms that Curnow could never countenance: 'Like the early settlers with whom she felt such a profound kinship, she endeavoured, in her poetry, to reconcile her immediate experience of New Zealand with all that she valued most in the English way of life.'[35] Where Bethell strives for colonial continuity, Curnow insists on settlement as an experience of separation. And though Curnow applauds Bethell for her 'visual authority' over her region (which also happens to be *his* region, Canterbury), again we can sense an impediment to his own project in the form of her religious faith. When Curnow first tries out the formulation that will come to be referred to as 'the South Island myth'—'the idea that we are confronted by a natural time, a natural order, to which our presence in these islands is accidental, irrelevant; that we are interlopers on an indifferent or hostile scene'[36]—it is Bethell who gives him his signature texts. As well as 'By Burke's Pass', he quotes 'Pause':

> In a very little while, it may be,
> When our impulsive limbs and our superior skulls
> Have to the soil restored several ounces of fertilizer,
>
> The Mother of all will take charge again,
> And soon wipe away with her elements
> Our small fond human enclosures.[37]

This is 1945. And yet by 1960 the poem is no longer part of his Bethell selection (again, that oddly unsteady view). It's as if in the interim he has looked back harder and been forced to acknowledge that Bethell's 'natural order' is not his own. Her 'Mother of all' may disguise the issue, but it's still too close to her Anglican God—whose act of destruction is its own consolation, His gift of 'tak[ing] charge again'. When Bethell lifts her eyes to the Canterbury hills, she discovers the eternal, the transcendental: 'Earth sleeps wrapped round / with the sure purpose of eternity' ('Looking Down on Mesopotamia').[38] But for Curnow that landscape is always the occasion of a failure of recognition that he insists is historical, and if nature is to play this role then it has to be desacralised.

The interval, then, between Baughan and Bethell makes less difference than one might have assumed. The formal behaviour of Bethell's poems—the restraint, the precision, the exaggerated plainness—anticipates better the manners of literary nationalism; in this respect Bethell feels later, more 'modern'. But from a nationalist point of view the same disabling features persist: the sightlines are unapologetically colonial; and the natural scene, which in nationalism will be there to provide 'a test of strength', is already subdued, indeed colonised, by the 'sure purpose' of spiritual belief. For Curnow, as I've suggested already, it may be that Bethell, being nearer, is more difficult to assimilate—nearer, that is, not just in the sense of being leaner and more exacting, but in the sense of being 'closer to home', where 'home' is Christchurch and Anglicanism. These are speculative thoughts; I won't delay to unravel them at length. But I can't help hearing, as a kind of background static, Curnow's flight from the same faith (his father having been a Canterbury vicar, and he himself having set out to train for the priesthood), and the afterimage, too, of his grandmother, Rose Gambling, memorialised in 'Tomb of an Ancestor' as the embodiment of colonial melancholia. This factor separates Bethell from Baughan: that where Baughan's colonialism is simply a given (her poems don't actively develop its moods), Bethell's is consciously experienced as grief. Pain will be a positive value in Curnow. But it has to be pain of the right kind, and Bethell's, implicitly, is not. Hence the arresting formula that he uses to explain why Mason 'stands on a plane above' her: that 'though he has recorded less of visible New Zealand, he has suffered more as a New Zealander.'[39]

'One of the surprises still in reading *From a Garden in the Antipodes* is to realise how little Bethell gives away in poems that seem so personal.'[40] I know what Vincent O'Sullivan means, writing here as editor of Bethell's *Collected Poems*. But equally we might turn this statement on its head: what makes these poems feel intimate is how little they explain. Their intimacy (or personalism) and their reticence are the same thing. Curnow catches something of this in 1945: 'As statements they remain somehow private, gestures which might be significant among a few where much else [is] taken for granted.'[41] And this, it seems to me, is the poems' big 'reveal': the fact of their self-containment, their refusal to explain, and the way this attests to the sufficiency of a self-contained world. The circuit of discourse that these poems presuppose is coherent, discrete and—even in the moment Curnow is observing it—already historical. If we wish to map the distance between the 20s and 30s, there is no more crucial story than the one these poems are (not) telling us.

The personalism of the garden poems is an effect of what I have called above their *structure of address*: the signals that tell us who is talking to whom, engaging or positioning the reader accordingly. The 'you' who 'wrote your letter [in] April' plainly isn't *me*, the unknown audience. We are reading someone else's mail, and the effect, as this metaphor suggests, is voyeuristic. Alternatively, though, we can think of it as dramatic: rather than speak directly to us, the speaker (as on stage) addresses a third party, offering the reader not a confidence but a spectacle, the act of addressing and relating to another. This axial shift, or redirection of the speech act, will be refined and popularised in the confessional poetry of the 60s: think of writers as different as Frank O'Hara and Sylvia Plath. It's a signal ingredient of the confessional drama. But it doesn't take relational *Sturm und Drang* or edgy sexuality to promote a sense of immediacy. The relationship in question may be quite mundane. The drama here is not in the intensity but in the structure.

The insistence of data that is left unexplained is often vital to the way such poems act on their public audience. In Bethell the most eloquent signal of this kind is the reliance on proper names: pet names, nicknames, personal designators whose bearers are never formally introduced to us. It's easy enough to work out who's who: that 'O metropolitan' and 'gracious urban' are forms of address for Ruth in London; that Michael is the cat; that Omi-Kin-Kan is a particularly cossetted orange tree; and that 'little Raven' and 'coadjutor' refer to Effie Pollen.[42] But this is not to say we can *interpret* these names. Nicknames persist as the vehicles of narratives: they commemorate the occasions that gave rise to them, or features of personality acknowledged within the friendship circles in which they have currency. Why is Effie the speaker's 'little Raven'—is it simply because her hair is black? Probably not, but we're never going to know, because the poem's internal audience knows already, which is Curnow's point. I don't mean to argue that the text contains secrets, as if the task of interpretation were to crack a private code. The secret of these poems is their indifference to a general audience; they don't care enough to bother hiding things from us. And yet in this indifference the text reveals something: the circulation of a body of signifiers which, to the very degree that they are opaque to the uninitiated, begin to trace the contours of a discrete social space. We infer such a space—we can *read* this space—precisely in those meanings which, to us, are indecipherable.

I believe it's fair to say, with O'Sullivan, that the garden poems 'in a sense are love poems expressing themselves as something else.'[43] They document a shared world—the life the poet shares with Effie—and they share it in turn with a trusted circle to whom their signs and assumptions are internally familiar. At times it can be tempting to translate this 'something else' into a different kind of love poem with which the modern reader is more familiar. Take the gorgeous lyric 'Elect':

> You have been my treasure, Rose Pilgrim,
> Because of your beautiful name.
> But because of your name I would not pamper you,
> And I chose you to be planted in a difficult place,
> In the pathway of the east wind
> [. . .]
> You have been my treasure, Pilgrim Rose.

And you are up near the frontier, near the gateway,
So that when I come home, tired, in the evening,
Home to my hill-garden, Rose Pilgrim,
You are the first flower I find there,
You are the very first flower, my Rose Pilgrim,
Pilgrim, my sweet rose.[44]

Plainly the given frame of reference is Protestant: Bunyanesque pilgrimage, Puritan election. Just in case we're tempted to doubt that Bethell is addressing a 'real' rose, we get the particularity of the wicked Christchurch easterly and (elided in my quotation) the poet with her 'thirty foot hose'. By editing out the bathos of that detail, no doubt I'm already starting to 'translate'. But it's hard not to read for an earthier, more intimate kind of 'election'. The more the poet delights in the name, rolls it around on her tongue, caresses it, the more romantic the poem feels and the less she sounds like someone talking simply to a rose bush. And after all, Effie is also her choice ('I *chose you* to be planted here'); also, too, a pioneer of sorts, a survivor in this 'difficult place', as well as the reassuring presence who alone makes the hill-garden 'home'. Personifying the rose bush so lovingly, the mode of address turns itself inside out, until behind the rose bush apostrophised as a person we may suspect we can hear a person represented as a rose.

Is it true to say, therefore, that the poem carries an erotic charge? For a reader in our own time the resonance may be difficult to avoid. But in reading this poem historically our own modern ears are of limited use. The more exacting question is: what would its original, domestic audience have heard in this text? And in putting it like this we are back with Curnow, aware of a conversation that we can't hear properly, in which the language may be familiar but the signs that the poem builds with it are oriented away from us. This is so, even when the couple's love story becomes explicit, as eventually it does, in the very last poems that Bethell writes. The terms of this late candour are not the sexualised terms of modernism. When Bethell becomes direct, it is within her own structure of feeling, in an idiom of sentiment, of grieving and of Anglican spirituality.

The great majority of Bethell's poems, and particularly those for which she remains best known, were written in the years at Rise Cottage with Effie. Her friend's death in 1934 left her devastated, and all but ended her poetic career: from the remaining decade of her life there survive two or three characteristic landscape poems and the 'Six Memorials', written to commemorate Effie's death each year from 1935 to 1940. The memorial poems remained unpublished in the poet's lifetime, and are, I think, the most untidy poems that Bethell left behind. They are documents, certainly, of great force, but a part of their eloquence inheres in this patchiness. They are pervaded, not just by grief, but by a sense of spiritual desperation provoked by that grief. As Holcroft records, Bethell always insisted on the literal truth of the Resurrection—not as a symbol, but as a physical reality: 'There must be a complete *reversal* of mortality'.[45] With Effie's death, this belief becomes so urgent (so explicit) that it overpowers the formal integrity of the poems. The 1938 memorial ends with a supplication in brackets, '(Creator, pitiful Redeemer, love-reviving Spirit, make it so!)',[46] as if the poet despaired of resolving her task poetically, and a *poetic* resolution were in any case beside the point.

To put the matter bluntly, Effie's death is recorded in the waning of Bethell's creative powers. The memorials are searing, but they're not great poems, or so at least readers have concurred. To borrow a phrase from Curnow (speaking of his own work), 'none [. . .] has been an anthologist's favourite.'[47] They are the poems, however, in which the relationship finds its fullest expression.

Spring 1940
(Christchurch, August)

This morning I saw suddenly a weeping willow green,
Beside the mechanic streets and grey, stone-heavy bridges
In solitude of grace above the sullen river
It stood, all green again.

Marvel! Apparition!—Before the all-wintry years
How often we had watched, in Spring, the purple-misted
Veils to a green haze dissolve about the willows,
Condense to a green rain.

Out to pastures, then, we went to seek our Spring.
Now, in the city pent, Spring sudden overtakes me—
As in time past my joy, hear my complaint now,
Spirit of Beauty, hear.

What shall be done with Spring? Until this grief
Meet vaster renaissance, now for immortal symbol
Here to sustain me, I may take your willow,
Your bright tree of tears.

Faith for the putting off of the vesture, and the fall,
Hope for the long nakedness, and last is charity—
The clothing of expectant boughs with amplitude
Of living green again.

Match Spring with vision, Spirit of Beauty, bring
With your persuasive love to the inward eye awakening,
Lest looking on this life to count what time has taken
I cannot bear the pain.[48]

This 1940 poem is I think the most effective. It's also the last, prompting the thought that, six years after her friend's death, Bethell at last achieves, in poetic terms at least, some kind of resolution. The verse is still patchy, rough-hewn, impatient. But it does find its way to a symbolic revelation that feels adequate to the task it sets itself. As the poet remembers the spring willow stems, as they were 'before the all-wintry years'—softening, dissolving, finally condensing into a 'green rain' of foliage—it seems to be a question of whether spring is now even conceivable. But the poem then discovers in stanza four the signifier that's been hiding inside the symbol. The willow reveals itself as a *tree*: not just an evidence of natural regeneration, but of the resurrection promised in the sacrifice of Christ. And the loveliness, and ache, of 'your bright tree of tears' is exacerbated surely by its local mundanity, weeping exactly where for Bethell it must, in the 'stone-heavy' heart of her Anglican city. It's a glorious image (however clumsily the stanza labours to unfold it); and yet the poet, it seems, is not satisfied by it, as if after all it were 'merely' a symbol. Finally, then, she reverts to what in context feels like a new kind of minimalism, as if, in the poem's last two lines, she were trying to reach beyond poetry itself in a statement of such *excessive* plainness that its qualities as verse barely signify. This is not the Bethell who gives so little away, but a poet driven in her desperation to an utterance of such devastating candour that, even 75 years later, the reader stands uncomfortably within the blast radius of its pain.

Like the garden poems before them, the memorials in their genesis are private events. Bethell herself didn't choose to publish them; they are deeply, even disconcertingly, intimate. But their resonance is also historical: they are the final chapter in a love story like no other in our literature. For all their reticence, Bethell's poems are among the most vivid testimony we have to the importance of these kinds of relationships:

the friendships and domestic alliances between women that underwrote so much creative, social and political work during (and for a short time after) the era of of first-wave feminism. I return to these homosocial partnerships in the next chapter, but we won't find their ambience evoked more tellingly than in Bethell's poems for Effie Pollen.

We glimpse this friendship, however, through a closing door. The conditions enabling Bethell to write are shattered by Effie Pollen's death. Writing to Eileen Duggan in 1937, she describes herself as 'a tree struck by lightning—dead—I can think of things, but not feel them—One must feel to write—All joy is lost.'[49] Her tragedy is her own, it's personal: the death of her friend is what undoes her (we can't blame 'history'). But what is *not* personal is what happens next: that after Bethell, Duggan and Baughan, among the generation to follow, there will not be a new crop of unmarried, independent women to assume their mantle. We glimpse in Bethell a homosocial culture on the threshold of its historical demise, a culture which in the next generation will collapse beneath the pressures of a new literary and sexual regime. The passing of the feminine world of Rise Cottage occurs against the backdrop of the eclipse of a structure of feeling, a climate change that will wipe women's writing from the map through the middle decades of the century. Behind Bethell—writing in 1940, one year after the suicide of Robin Hyde—looms this historical devastation, as writing by women enters its 'all-wintry' years.

Mason: Suffering like a New Zealander

As we know, Curnow nearly always backed winners. If they weren't winners already, with his Olympian endorsement they almost inevitably turned out that way. There was just one exception, one glaring lapse of judgement, when he discovered in assembling his 1945 anthology that a viable tradition in New Zealand verse began, not with Mason and Bethell (as Brasch so reasonably assumed), but with Mason and Cresswell:

> Two poets could hardly be less alike [. . .] Yet in the story of New Zealand verse these two poets cannot be kept far apart. About the same time—that is, in the years following the first World War—both seem to have discovered in verse an object worthy of a life's devotion. That might not have been so remarkable in this country, if they had not insisted that, as poets and *because* they were poets, they remained responsible adult New Zealanders: more responsible, because set apart for a special task. That was new; it was 'taking poetry seriously', and it marked the end of the undisputed reign of whimsy in New Zealand verse. The early work of both was of a new kind among New Zealanders because, in whatever else it fell short, it was not sentimental and committed the whole man to the poetry.[50]

Curnow affirms this valuation with the generosity of his Cresswell selections: 21 poems in the 1945 anthology, 15 of which he retains in 1960. It's the one important canonical judgement that subsequent anthologists will feel obliged to reverse.[51] However, in a more subtle way he is also wrong about Mason: not about his value, but about his sense of vocation. Curnow wants Cresswell and Mason to exemplify a level of commitment that will separate the nationalist 30s from the genteel amateurism he associates with the 20s. But Mason in the end will not 'commit the whole man'. Sadly, by the time Curnow brings down this judgement, Mason's career will have gone the same way as those of Bethell and Baughan. Of all of them, only the poetaster Cresswell will oblige by treating verse with an unswerving dedication.

So much for Mason and Cresswell; but what about Brasch's pairing, Mason with Bethell? Admittedly they are still an odd couple. The two are separated, not just by age, but by gender, class, politics and faith. They are also, at least during the active phase of their careers, seemingly oblivious of each other's work (an effect of geographical distance, and of the limitations of local publishing). And yet, for everything that divides them, there are also precise resemblances. 'About the same time' they somehow converge—the Cantabrian in her 50s and the Aucklander in his 20s—on the narrow ground of 1920s minimalism. Mason, like Bethell, will produce a body of poems which in context are immediately striking for their compaction. It's what Curnow calls, in Bethell, a 'proportioned' response,[52] although in Mason the effect will be, if anything, more frugal: short lines, an unsparing self-image, and a super-slim corpus, stark and acidic. They collaborate, then, in that post-war project of scaling down the modern poem. But they meet, in another sense, in an even more constrained space. The bulk of Mason's poems are composed between 1922 and 1930; his active career as a poet is over by 1936.[53] Bethell begins a couple of years later, moving to Rise Cottage in 1924; Effie Pollen dies in 1934, after which, as we've seen, Bethell too writes almost nothing. Their careers are not just historically synchronous (despite the disparity in their ages), but each is interrupted, at the same moment, in an equally abrupt manner. Neither is able to sustain a poetic practice in the altered climate of the 30s and 40s.

'Prelude' introduces what is effectively Mason's final volume, *End of Day* (1936). But it serves in many ways as a prelude to his complete oeuvre, a manifesto in four terse stanzas:

This short straight sword
 I got in Rome
 when Gaul's new lord
 came tramping home:

It did that grim
 old rake to a T—
 if it did him,
 well, it does me.

Leave the thing of pearls
 with silken tassels
 to priests and girls
 and currish vassals:

Here's no fine cluster
 on the hilt, this drab
 blade lacks lustre—
 but it can stab.[54]

As we saw in Bethell, the poem's decorum conjures aspects of early modernism. Not in its rhyme and formal regularity. And not, as in Bethell, in the visual 'hard edges' of imagism; Mason is not primarily an image-maker, and where he is the effect tends to be more oneiric ('Body of John', 'Be Swift O Sun'). In Mason instead we find 'hardness' recalibrated: a masculine (phallic) physicality, a stoical toughness, a hardness of attitude. Mason's compaction—for he is an unrelentingly economical poet—answers to several parallel impulses. Like his master, Housman, he is an accomplished Latinist, and here as elsewhere Latin models are plainly enabling. But the anti-aesthetic attitudes of this poem—the refusal of decoration, the monosyllabic dourness—are equally in tune, both with a prevailing secular puritanism, and with a vernacular masculinism. The poem is not an ornament, but an instrument, a weapon, with a combative (or critical) job to perform. It's a weapon, though, that Mason uses mostly against himself, and it's this self-mortification that, as much as anything, will resonate with his nationalist admirers.

So what does Curnow mean when he writes that, compared to Bethell, Mason 'has suffered more as a New Zealander'? Although Curnow doesn't say so, it must in part be a question of Mason's anti-colonialism. In this respect Mason presented a direct contrast to the other writers around him. He was alone among the well-known writers of the mid century in never having visited Britain (his two overseas trips were to Samoa, as a youth, and to China in 1957; of his fellow 20s poets, Bethell made the return voyage four times, and Cresswell the same, with a final one-way passage in 1950). For Englishness, Mason has a genuine anti-imperialist contempt. He expresses this jauntily in 'Latter-day Geography Lesson': 'here boys, ere disaster / overtook her, in splendour there lay / a city held empires in sway'.[55] In 'Judas Iscariot' the sentiment is more veiled. But this dark, oblique poem becomes less enigmatic if we accept, with Curnow, that Mason's Judas embodies a specifically English class sensibility.[56]

From the viewpoint of literary nationalism, this reads sympathetically; however, in Mason's agonistics Curnow is hearing something more subtle. In 1945, when Curnow 'nationalises' 'Sonnet of Brotherhood'—fastening on its imagery of isolation: 'this far-pitched perilous hostile place / this solitary hard-assaulted spot / fixed at the friendless outer edge of space'—Mason resists. The poem, he objects, was never intended as a national allegory.[57] But returning to it in 1960, and alluding to a dialogue that appears to have taken place in the meantime, an unrepentant Curnow reaffirms his first response:

> Mason has protested [against a 'New Zealand' reading] [. . .] He was thinking of the human race and the planet Earth. He is willing to suppose, nevertheless, that [. . .] both the choice of theme and the intensity of feeling point to an under-level of allegory implicating the poet as New Zealander [. . .] It may not be easy to find the man behind these various projections of the isolated, last-ditch, forlorn-hope situation, with its hero-victims who seem shocked into eloquence. It is not hard to find the New Zealander [. . .] I know that this area of New Zealand mind exists, and exerts its pressures on the more relaxed, good-natured, well-nourished surfaces of New Zealand living: we are uneasy underneath, and must respect a poetry which cuts so deeply to the sources of unease.[58]

This passage is vital if we wish to understand how Curnow judges the veracity of a New Zealand poem. It has much less to do than is often assumed with the naming of local places and things; it has far more to do, and in Mason's case *everything* to do, with a complex of feelings—loneliness, isolation, shock—that for Curnow are the hidden condition of the New Zealand psyche. By Curnow's calculations, to 'suffer as a New Zealander' is to find a language for those feelings that a national false consciousness conceals from itself.

In suffering *the right way* Mason is greatly advantaged by his agnosticism. The only consolation in his 'perilous' and 'friendless' universe is to look at the world with an undeceived realism. The untitled opening poem of *No New Thing* (1934)[59] is again a manifesto:

> If the drink that satisfied
>   the son of Mary when he died
>   has not the right smack for you
>   leave it for a kindlier brew.

For my bitter verses are
  sponges steeped in vinegar
  useless to the happy-eyed
  but handy for the crucified.[60]

Mason's is a poetry that neither accepts existential comfort nor offers it. In this sense, 'agnosticism' becomes too mild a term. His frequent repurposing of Christian imagery, particularly in this 1934 volume ('Footnote to John ii 4', 'Judas Iscariot', 'Ecce Homunculus', 'In Manus Tuas Domine'), has a sardonic, even gleeful quality, as if the poet were amusing himself with the thought that weaker minds than his ('the happy-eyed', or what Spender would call the 'non-recognizers')[61] might succumb to such trifling blandishments as those of Christianity. For the lapsed Anglican in Curnow this mock-biblical motif no doubt presses the appropriate buttons in the same way that Bethell's Christianity presses the wrong ones. More than this, however, an irreligious attitude opens the door to an uninhibited embrace of those concealed home truths. Mason's poems 'cut [. . .] to the sources of unease' because there are no false comforts to dull their edge. Where Bethell seeks desperately for proof of the resurrection, Mason finds what Eliot called 'the skull beneath the skin':

Oh I have grown so shrivelled and sere
    But the body of John enlarges,
    and I can scarely summon a tear
    but the body of John discharges

It's true my old roof is near ready to drop
    But John's boards have burst asunder
    and I am perishing cold here atop
    but his bones lie stark hereunder.[62]

Not just the skull, one might add, but the skeleton, and the process of decomposition which exposes it. 'John', as Barrowman informs us, is the name by which Mason was known in his own family.[63]

In this bleakly unredemptive vision Curnow will identify the way ahead for New Zealand poetry. It is an expression of our colonial dependence, he argues, that 'in New Zealand we lack capacity for the tragic emotions [. . .] We are stunted emotionally because we have not dealt direct with life'.[64] Mason is the first of our poets to have overcome this squeamishness. He knows 'that evil, pain and error can be final and absolute; that triumph and evil run parallel,' and the suffering that suffuses his work is a 'permanent rebuke' to those who believe otherwise.[65] Curnow quotes his English contemporary George Barker: 'every poet writes the nicest rather than the best poems he can: for the best poems leave him so much more short of blood'; Mason, he adds, is the New Zealand poet who 'has most consistently tried to write his best poems.'[66] It's an attitude, or implicit equation, essential to the truth claims of Curnow's nationalist anti-myth: the truth is more painful than everyone else assumes, and so the poem's negativity is the guarantee of its realism. Curnow, throughout his long career, will never leave this posture behind. But nowhere will it serve him better than in the inauguration of literary nationalism. In a characteristic flourish from 1951, looking back to the origins of the movement, he writes: 'We had to cut ourselves, taking up the edged tools of language, where it had been safe to play with those that were blunt or rusted.'[67] Nationalist poetry will be just this, a series of calculated acts of self-harm, and it's Mason, whose poetry 'cuts so deeply', who models what a tough-minded New Zealand poem should feel like.

And yet, for all that he offers to nationalist poetics—the right kind of sharp edge, the right kind of suffering—Mason will never be a writer of the 30s. He is not, it turns out, quite as tough as he pretends to be. While Curnow identifies with Mason's agonies, and even in some sense appropriates them, his own suffering heroism is grounded quite differently. Curnow has been fortified by the bracing lessons of modernism. But Mason's roots are in a milder literary culture, and to press-gang him into the struggles of the 30s is to wrest him out of an earlier context in which his work feels more at home.

Mason was poor at self-promotion, but in 1924 he made an unlikely gesture. He bundled up 50 copies of *The Beggar* and mailed them to publisher and bookseller Harold Monro.[68] Through his celebrated Poetry Bookshop in Bloomsbury, Monro would shift a surprising number. More to the point, he was so impressed that he immediately reprinted 'Latter-day Geography Lesson' and 'Body of John' in his occasional verse anthology, *Chapbook*. This was no ordinary coup: Mason was in the company of Edith and Osbert Sitwell, Richard Aldington and T.S. Eliot. In 1929 Monro published him a second time in the anthology *Twentieth Century Poetry*.[69] Of the 77 contributors, who included the giants of contemporary verse, four (including Eliot and Pound) were Americans; the rest were British and Irish; and then there was Mason. As far as it's possible to tell, these anthology publications were his first introduction to modernism in verse (it's clear from his comments on reading 'The Hollow Men' in 1929 that Eliot was still a novelty).[70] His poems, in their terseness, their compaction, their pessimism, already seem to show modernist affinities. And yet Mason discovered the modernist poets only when he appeared alongside them.

As in the case of Bethell's imagism, we're faced with a curious synchrony. With Mason, however, the lines of affiliation are more easily reconstructed. As C.K. Stead demonstrates, Mason sits comfortably (both in his economy and in his sombreness of vision) with the earlier phase of Georgian poetry, and with the Georgians' favourite precursors, Housman and Thomas Hardy.[71] For readers who learned their trade in the modernist era, 'Georgian' has become more or less a term of abuse. The poets associated with Edward Marsh's five anthologies of *Georgian Poetry* (1912–22) have been understood merely as a force of resistance—one which modernism, thankfully, drove from the field. But on first appearance, Stead explains,[72] the Georgians too were greeted as agitators, while (initially at least) there was mutual recognition between the group around Edward Marsh and Rupert Brooke, and the imagist group centred on Ezra Pound and T.E. Hulme. The anthologies of both were published and promoted by Monro; and both were equally averse to patriotic tub-thumpers like Rudyard Kipling and Sir Henry Newbolt. Only with the later Georgian anthologies, and the rising influence of J.C. Squire, did the now-familiar caricature of Georgian poetics (genteel, tweedy, escapist, effete) begin to obscure the common ground they had shared originally with the modernists. Consider the terms in which Monro praises Housman: he is sparing, Monro writes, in his use of 'poetical devices'; his poems 'contain [. . .] not a word too many,' showing 'complete resistance to the common temptation to add ornament'; and his totemic volume *A Shropshire Lad* (1896) is 'the antithesis of that bulky pomposity of late Victorianism.'[73] There is nothing in this verdict that wouldn't sit comfortably with Pound. And there's nothing either that could not be said equally of Housman's staunch admirer, Mason.[74]

But modernism and Georgianism could only travel together so far. They parted ways definitively around the question of form. Where the Georgians made the best of inherited models, modernism insisted that the received forms of verse would have to be broken down entirely. Nor was it just a question of technique or prosody (*vers libre*, speech rhythms, pulverised syntax), because with modernist experimentalism came a specific set of assumptions about audience, and about poetry in its social applications. The pursuit of formal complexity, and a conscious commitment to density and even opacity ('poets, in our civilisation, as it exists at present, must be *difficult*,' as Eliot maintained),[75] ruptured the contract with a general audience that had persisted, in however attenuated a form, since the time of the Romantics. Modernism priced itself out of that general market, concentrating its operations in the hands of a self-selecting elite. From this point of view, if the poet were to have any impact on the culture at large it could only be through a trickle-down effect, as if by refining a mandarin language—purifying the dialect of the tribe (Eliot)—the poem were priming the cultural economy and other folk further down the food chain would (mysteriously) benefit.

For Mason this aestheticism holds no message at all. He will never accept that the poet's responsibilities lie so heavily at the level of literary form. In 1933, as editor of *Phoenix*, he writes: 'This is no time to be studying the tonal value of the minor works of T.E. Brown. It is the greatest hour in history [. . .] the hour for realism is at hand.'[76] Curnow, by contrast, is a modernist native, and modernist assumptions about elite cultural practice saturate his nationalist programme. The writing of settlement demands more than a vigilant realism; it also demands complexity, difficulty and daring. For too long, says Curnow, the job has been left to the dabblers, the 'hobbyists and ungifted amateurs'.[77] The assignment, predictably, has proved too much for them; the settler world is *different*, and bringing it into language is a more exacting task than this insipid tradition has ever supposed. An adequate local writing will need to confront it on its own terms, 'taking up the edged tools of language', committing itself wholly to the challenge of the new. Once more, then, in this repurposed avant-gardism, a middle-brow contract has to be revoked to allow a professional minority to work at an appropriate level of complexity. Nationalist writing will retain strong vernacular sympathies. But these will be expressed in a system of aesthetic codings through which an educated minority communicates primarily with itself.

In 1937 Curnow published *Enemies*, the slim book in which, fleetingly, we can first glimpse the terms and the mood of the nationalism he would articulate, grounded at once in the history of settlement and in a language of disaffection cribbed from Eliot: 'London has spawned. Here are banks in the egg, / foetus Beaverbrooks, Edens and Baldwins'.[78] The same year, Mason was writing to Glover about his commitment to communism and the fact that he was no longer writing. He has 'no excuse', he tells Curnow's publisher, for 'stuff of the old defeatist kind'. Instead, he now 'want[s] to bring [his] artistic feelings into line with [his] intellectual knowledge', where by 'intellectual' knowledge plainly he means *political* knowledge: 'I fancy I have about got there & in the future hope to publish some reasonably decent proletarian stuff.'[79] By this date his 'literary' work was all but complete (after 1937, I count eight lyric poems).[80] This is not to say that Mason would write nothing else: still to come were 'This Dark Will Lighten', a poem 'for mass recitation' performed in 1939; a short history of the Cook Islands (1947); a radio play, 'Strait is the Gate', broadcast in 1968; and a handful of other polemical prose pieces and dramatic sketches ('simple plays for special purposes',[81] as Mason called them). But ahead, too, lay the blanket refusal of his literary admirers to take this work seriously. The Mason whom Curnow and Glover admired was the poet, and the poet had fallen silent. We see Curnow and Mason crossing on opposite tacks, Curnow with Eliot and Pound in his sails, and Mason disappearing into the Bermuda Triangle of agitprop and service to the Trade Union movement.

There is, then, a softness to Mason, a humanism, that leaves him out of tune with an emergent literary nationalism. As we have seen, he is unmoved by the formalism underlying Curnow's sense of vocation. Mason isn't ruthless enough to accept poetry in itself as 'worthy of a life's devotion'. And nor does he share the misogyny that will become so familiar as we venture deeper into the mid century. 'Prelude', admittedly, appears to suggest otherwise: the poem as a frankly phallic weapon, the denigration of ornament as feminine. But in this respect the poem is untypical. Elsewhere in his work, what Michele Leggott has called 'the scapegoating of feminine consciousness' (identifying it, accurately, as a characteristic reflex in nationalist poetics)[82] is not in evidence. Once again, Mason has not absorbed this modernist habit. In his attitude to women, as in his attitude to form, he turns out on closer inspection to be less 'hard' than he first appears.

Among the last of Mason's poems is a curious piece called 'Payment':

> Fool I've been wax to fashion
>   for hot winds to mould me
>   like a girl let passion
>   subdue and hold me:
>
> Now doom in his just season
>   seeks a bitter levy:
>   with fruit of unreason
>   my womb is heavy:

Now pangs of fruitless bearing
  all night long will rend me
  alone and no one sparing
  a hand to friend me.[83]

It's a poem that seems to work equally well whether we take its subject to be unrequited love, or a dark Romantic view of poetic inspiration. In either case it's a long way from the emotional decorum of nationalism. The feelings that infuse it, even while it notionally complains of them (malleability, passion, infatuation, unreason), occupy a register that in the years to follow no male poet except Fairburn is likely to entertain. Certainly no one will figure himself as a woman surrendering to passion, to pregnancy and to childbirth. 'Payment' was first published in 1934.[84] But it speaks from the 1920s side of a masculinisation of poetic values that from around this moment will effectively close down a wide range of expressive gestures. It will be a long time, then, before any male poet is going to be caught dabbling in cross-gender identification; and a long time too (again, the possible exception is Fairburn) before anyone will attempt something as sensuous as 'Flow at Full Moon' or as courtly as 'Be Swift O Sun'. The causality, and the cost, of this expressive shutting down is a theme that will recur throughout the rest of this book.

The story of how Mason dumped 200 unsold copies of *The Beggar* off the end of Queen's Wharf is one of the most indelible in New Zealand literary folklore. No wonder Rachel Barrowman begins with it; as Mason's biographer she could hardly do otherwise. The story may be apocryphal, as Barrowman acknowledges, but its truth is of a different order: 'It is a symbol of a time—the 1920s and 1930s—when a true, vital, native literature struggled to be written or heard in a provincial and puritanical country. Mason on Queen's Wharf is the archetype of the poet ignored by a society which he in turn despised.'[85] And so he is, it couldn't be plainer. First Fairburn, and then Curnow, tell the story to similar effect.[86] But Barrowman, I suspect, in setting out to write Mason's life, has further implications in mind. This is not an image of just *any* provincial poet, but of Mason himself, of his career, and of his demons. Of all the interrupted careers of this period, none presents a more melancholy spectacle: the most original talent, and the one whose failure to keep writing leaves behind the deepest sense of loss and puzzlement. The question is apt to be framed in terms of Mason's political activities (the same question sometimes asked of Baughan): 'Did the poet fail because of politics; or did politics fill the space when poetry failed?'[87] But Mason was a man beset with all kinds of obstacles. His father died when he was eight years old, probably by his own hand. The desperate possessiveness of his mother, and his own helpless response to it, emerge dismayingly. Late in life he was diagnosed with what we would now call bipolar disorder.[88] Meanwhile, Barrowman traces a pattern of self-defeating behaviour: he could have had a career as a Latinist (like Housman) if only he'd sat his exams; he could have made more of the opening with Harold Monro, but wouldn't answer his letters; and so on. Is the failure of his poetry, then, just one more expression of an entrenched psychopathology, the suicide he never succumbs to but stages symbolically at the end of Queen's Wharf and in that ultimate 'drowning of the books' which is his silence?

And yet while Mason's legend hinges on the loss of his creative gift, I'm not convinced that the most revealing answer is strictly biographical. The pattern we've been tracing in this chapter suggests another: not that he 'loses' his gift but rather that history destroys its habitat. As the 20s become the 30s, the ground shifts under his feet; the new decade takes the game away from him; a structure of feeling emerges in which Mason is left marooned. Comparing Mason to Baughan and Bethell we can see that he's lost their spiritualism. But Mason retains their humanism, and it grounds him irrevocably on the 20s side of an historical divide. As a left-wing humanist, Mason will insist that writing can only renew itself through the people: 'Once an art becomes divorced from contact with the masses, it becomes flabby and sterile.'[89] So while he 'takes poetry seriously', he doesn't take it *seriously enough*; he isn't prepared to 'commit the whole man' where this means committing to a self-sustaining middle-class vanguard. In this light, Mason's premature silence, grievous though it is, no longer appears exceptional. Instead his career joins the pile-up of those that litter the threshold of the 1930s. He falls at a barrier that no one gets over: not Baughan or Bethell, not Jessie Mackay or Eileen Duggan. So what *is* this barrier, how can we conceptualise it? What are its contours and its historical conditions? These tricky questions occupy the chapter to follow.

Chapter 3

'Stridently sex-conscious'

Writing and gender (and mountaineering) c. 1928

The Depression thesis

'Rightly or wrongly,' Raymond Williams tells the *New Left Review* in 1977, 'we [. . .] usually identify the point at which a cultural generation seems to form with what is often [. . .] just a decade of their activity'. We employ this shorthand, Williams explains, because if a new generation is going to shift the governing structure of feeling, this will be their moment: 'The way in which I have tended to apply the term [structure of feeling] in analysis is to the generation doing the new cultural work, which normally means a group which would have a median age of around thirty'.[1] The writers who inaugurate New Zealand's nationalist literature are a cohort of 'thirty-somethings' in exactly this sense. Between 1935 and 1939 the writers who will form the hard core of the nationalist movement emerge with their first significant works. Fairburn writes the long poem *Dominion* in 1935, when he is 31; Sargeson publishes *Conversation with My Uncle* in 1936 at 33; in 1939 comes Mulgan's *Man Alone* (age 28), Glover's *Thirteen Poems* (27), Curnow's *Not in Narrow Seas* (28) and Brasch's *The Land and the People* (30). Despite so much that will happen later, for Sargeson and Curnow especially, we are right to think of this as 'the generation of the 1930s', and of their nationalist renaissance as an event that dates from this specific moment. It is here, in the years leading up to the war, that the future of New Zealand writing is re-routed by the energy of a group of young writers in the first flush of self-assertiveness—or as Williams would say, by a new generation 'beginning to articulate its structure of feeling'.

It's small wonder that in the historiography of literary nationalism so much weight has been attached to the Depression. In a chapter titled 'The Awakening of Poetry', M.H. Holcroft puts it like this:

> It sometimes happens that a large experience, shared widely by the people, brings to a generation of poets the conditions for which they might have sought vainly as individuals. The economic depression of the early thirties is usually regarded as an evil thing [. . .] Nevertheless [. . .] it was a fortunate season for New Zealand literature which brought so many of its apprentices into a close association with the realities of the slump.[2]

The Depression hits at precisely the right moment; it accompanies this phase of creative 'apprentice[ship]'. As the Great War did for the first wave of Anglophone modernists—and as the Vietnam War and sexual liberation will later do for the young local writers of the 1970s—for the nationalist generation it's the Depression that furnishes the soundtrack to the formative years of their early and mid 20s. Or so it appears. It's a straightforward matter to read the influence of the slump in the emergence of a nationalist house style (its realism, vernacularism, dystopian pastoralism, and so on); from Robin Hyde to Robert Chapman, Alan Mulgan to Eric McCormick, writers of the mid century routinely cite the Depression as a catalyst.[3]

On occasion the argument is challenged or subtilised. Curnow, who objects to the sociological tone of McCormick, grumbles that the 'poets concerned are more than a social seismograph, recording bumps; [. . .] they had some potency of their own'.[4] Later critics on the Left will question how deeply the Caxton writers engaged with the crisis politically.[5] But in terms of the Depression's influence in shaping New Zealand literature, the conclusive point isn't how realistically the nationalists represent economic hardship, or how firmly their texts position themselves on the Left; what is crucial is the sense of rupture that they derive from it. As Chapman puts it, 'The overturn in social conditions broke up the crust of complacency, allowing artists to see into what lay beneath.'[6] Holcroft and Brasch draw the same conclusion—an illusion has been punctured, a 'cold blast of reality' has intruded on a comfortable slumber—articulating in capsule form the nationalist anti-myth that will be formalised by Curnow.[7] Hence Curnow in his 1960 introduction:

> The economic stresses of the thirties forced the New Zealanders to look to themselves, and when they looked outward on the world again, it was with altered vision [. . .] The offence was rank: it cut through and down to the nerves of collective self-esteem.[8]

In this dialectic of complacency and 'offence' is the kernel, not just of Curnow's historical thesis, but of his critical game plan: his nationalism will seek to do for New Zealand writing the very thing the Depression has already done for the Dominion's collective consciousness. It's a nationalism deliberately designed to *give offence*. For all his suspicion of McCormick's seismography, Curnow learns his history under the tutelage of the slump.

The economic hardships of the early 1930s, then, are not just a catalyst for literary nationalism, but are written into the structure of its historical argument. Nonetheless, as an explanatory context this 'Depression thesis' only goes so far. Most of all, it doesn't address the changes taking place between women and men. The rigours of the nationalist hard frost will not be experienced evenly: with the rise of literary nationalism, and setting in at exactly the same time, comes a wholesale re-gendering of literary culture that will shape the course of New Zealand writing for decades to come. As we see in the work of revisionist critics writing in the 1990s—and I'm indebted, in particular, to Michele Leggott and to Kai Jensen—we can map this re-gendering in two related ways. We can read it, first of all, in the texts of the nationalist canon: subject matter, settings, language, tone, all take a markedly masculine turn. So too (drawing on first-generation modernism) does the critical rhetoric with which Curnow and others promote their own cohort and denigrate their competitors and predecessors. Leggott in her work on Hyde and Duggan refers to a 'scapegoating of feminine consciousness',[9] and in Sargeson, Curnow, Fairburn and Glover we can hear precisely what she means. Secondly, in the same moment, the practice of writing is re-gendered: women themselves disappear from literary publication. In *Whole Men* Jensen draws a gender 'Manhattan' to chart what happens to women's stake in literary production.[10] In the first two decades

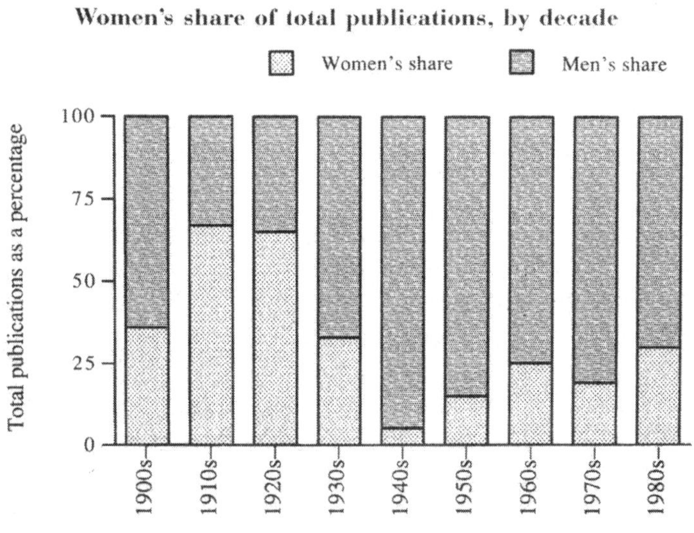

Kai Jensen, *Whole Men*, 101

of the 20th century, women publish *more* than men. But with the advent of nationalism their share falls catastrophically, and in the 1940s will be cut almost to zero.

Leggott observes this more specifically in the fractured tradition of women's poetry. As Baughan remains silent, as Mackay and Bethell reach the end of their careers, and as Eileen Duggan is sidelined in her tussle with Curnow,[11] younger poets fail to appear (as do younger writers of literary fiction, after Jane Mander). Speaking back to the new masculine hegemony will be the lone voice of Robin Hyde. After Hyde's suicide in 1939, silence.

This 'fortunate season' in which the nationalists gain their ascendancy is a more intricate event than economic conditions alone can account for. Exposure to the Depression in the early years of adulthood is a vital aspect of these writers' generational experience. However, it is only one element in the emergent structure of feeling. This is why I'm interested in 1928, why I've picked it out in my chapter title, and why I keep circling back to it. It's not that I systematically investigate this year. But it catches my attention because whenever we come across it we know we're dealing with a moment that (narrowly) pre-dates the Depression. These young men, as they are first finding their voices, are riding a wave of historical change, but they are not just riding the urgency of the slump. They are propelled, as we'll see in Chapter 4, by the imperatives of literary modernism, and by something else: another wave, a groundswell, lifting them up and driving them forward. 'No age,' writes Virginia Woolf some 12 months before the Wall Street Crash, 'can ever have been as stridently sex-conscious as our own.'[12] It's an observation that rings as true in New Zealand as it does in Britain. To appreciate the brute force of New Zealand's literary nationalism, we have to understand the sex-consciousness that informs it. We need to find a path through the history of gender, and through the history of sexuality, in the decade after World War I.

Masculinity at bay

Woolf's remark about her sex-minded era refers to the fiction of her male contemporaries. Reading them, she is struck by the emotional inhibition that results from a peculiarly masculine self-consciousness. The reasons for this, she concludes, are historical: men have had their cage rattled.

> The Suffrage campaign was no doubt to blame. It must have roused in men an extraordinary desire for self-assertion; it must have made them lay an emphasis on their own sex and its characteristics which they would not have troubled to think about had they not been challenged. And when one

> is challenged, even by a few women in black bonnets, one retaliates, if one has never been challenged before, rather excessively.[13]

According to Coleridge, as Woolf explains, a 'great mind' is androgynous. Two capacities, male and female, cooperate intellectually and spiritually; such a mind is 'resonant and porous; [. . .] it transmits emotion without impediment.'[14] But on the defensive, the masculine mind becomes 'crude and immature' (she cites Rudyard Kipling and John Galsworthy): 'virility has [. . .] become self-conscious—men [. . .] are now writing only with the male side of their brains.'[15]

The text that would eventually become *A Room of One's Own* was conceived for an audience of bright young women. In October 1928 Woolf travelled to Cambridge to speak at Newnham College. A week later she repeated the journey, this time to address the second of the two women's colleges, Girton.[16] Again, I emphasise the date to remind us that we haven't yet reached the Depression. And I emphasise the audience because it was these young women, born in the decade before World War I, who had the most to fear and the most to lose from the climate of masculine feeling that Woolf is describing.

On the face of it, the outlook should have been so much brighter. After all, Woolf's generation of women writers had done extraordinary things. As Sydney Janet Kaplan has argued, first-wave feminism needs to be read not simply as a correlative of the modernist revolution but as one of the energies informing it.[17] The first, heroic modernist moment may still have been the 'era' of Pound, Eliot and Joyce. But it doesn't take more than a cursory rollcall to remind us how extensively women writers also prospered. Call them the generation of the 1880s: Dorothy Richardson (b. 1873), Willa Cather (b. 1873), Gertrude Stein

(b. 1874), Virginia Woolf (b. 1882), Mina Loy (b. 1882), H. D. [Hilda Doolittle] (b. 1886), Marianne Moore (b. 1887), Edith Sitwell (b. 1887), Katherine Mansfield (b. 1888), Jean Rhys (b. 1890), Zora Neale Hurston (b. 1891), Djuna Barnes (b. 1892). For women a generation younger, following in the wake of this massively accomplished and influential cohort, the door to elite literary practice ought to have stood wide open.

As it proved, nothing could be further from the case. Who are the women writers of the mid century? Who, that is, in the second modernist cohort, carries forward the achievements of the women writers of the first? An answer isn't easy to summon; in fact this is a generation in which literary writing by women undergoes a dramatic eclipse. Laura Riding (b. 1901), Christina Stead (b. 1902), Lorine Niedecker (b. 1903), Elizabeth Bishop (b. 1911), Gwendolyn Brooks (b. 1917): all, of course, significant writers, but collectively a thin muster by comparison with their immediate predecessors. On the men's side, as well, the second generation is less illustrious than the first; but Auden, Spender, Bunting, Lowell, Olson, Zukofsky, Langston Hughes, Dylan Thomas (among the poets), and Beckett, Lowry, Orwell, Isherwood, Golding, Patrick White, Flann O'Brien, Richard Wright, Ralph Ellison, Nathanael West (among fiction writers) build on the work of the previous generation in a way that their female contemporaries appear not to. Of the women I've listed, we might add that there is only one fiction writer, and that none of them is British. The most accomplished British women writers of this vintage are probably Rebecca West and Daphne Du Maurier. Across the Atlantic, a more inclusive discussion might take in Carson McCullers, Anaïs Nin, Elizabeth Smart, and playwright Lillian Hellman; however, there's no American woman who reads like a plausible inheritor of Mansfield and Woolf.

None of which need greatly surprise the student of New

Zealand literary nationalism. The most influential writing of the hard frost era will be hard in exactly that muscle-bound sense that Woolf is protesting. It will be a literature stricken with masculine self-consciousness: defensive, inhibited, at times outrightly belligerent. And in the repercussions for New Zealand women writers—women the same age as Woolf's student audience—here too we fall in with the melancholy pattern of the Northern Hemisphere. Like their Old World counterparts, women writers born in the first years of the century will fail to inherit from the generation of Ursula Bethell, Blanche Baughan and Jane Mander. In a hyper-virile structure of feeling, writing by women will find no purchase, a situation only confirmed by the isolation of Robin Hyde. The tragedy of Hyde's career has of course been extensively explored. But, to the best of my knowledge, she is yet to be situated adequately in this international context. Hyde is not just an isolated figure on the local stage, but an unusual figure on *any* stage. The fate that overtakes her generation in the Northern Hemisphere makes her struggle more comprehensible, and her testimony even more eloquent.

A short history of South Island climbing

And now an excursion: a different kind of context. We are looking at a photograph of Blanche Baughan. It appears above the caption 'Climbing an Ice Face' in her *Studies in New Zealand Scenery* (1916). Baughan began sending these descriptive essays to the *Spectator* in London shortly before the war; 'Snow Kings of the Southern Alps' first appeared in 1910, and she must have made her trip to Mt Cook not too long beforehand. Because it's an image that has always intrigued me I have often referred to it in public presentations. But I've noticed that it draws an

'Climbing an Ice Face'

uncertain response. With her bonnet, jacket and matching reticule, her ramrod-straight back and her purposeful stride, Baughan appears somehow parodically Edwardian. Always this seems to bring a ripple of amusement—yet briefly, even sheepishly, since not far behind comes the intimation that in some sense we're laughing at the climber's sex. The initial reaction corrects itself. At a second take we respond to the chutzpah, the aura of suffragist derring-do, and admire in appropriately tutored terms the figure of a pioneer feminist pushing the boundaries. All the same, it's an image that wrong-foots us. The woman climber seems out of place—we have difficulty placing her.

Baughan, as I suggested in the previous chapter, is one of the most romantic figures in our literature, and among her many appealing qualities is her self-possession in the Great Outdoors. In 'The Finest Walk in the World' she guides us breezily over the Milford Track ('three and thirty miles in length—traversable, therefore, by the practised walker in one day').[18] In 'Forest and Ice' she climbs the Copland Pass, pausing on top of the Main Divide: 'You can sit on the rock-ridge and dangle one foot in Canterbury, the other in Westland.'[19] But we start to go wrong if we fetishise Baughan as a woman doing something unduly heroic. By her own account, her experience of Mt Cook could be that of any other athletically minded visitor. Think of the modern travel writer who takes a bungy jump or goes whitewater rafting: this is the sense in which Baughan 'does' Mt Cook. She walks on the glaciers, she hikes to admired viewing points, she engages a guide from the Hermitage to take her on a climb. She catches us out, then, posed on her ice face, not because she happens to be a remarkable woman, but instead because we no longer recognise the context that would make what she's doing here feel routine. Supporting her (represented here by the guide who steadies her ascent with an ice axe) are the practices, language and infrastructure of what I am going to call 'premodern' climbing. It is these that now appear so 'other'. For ever since this premodern culture was superseded—a process that begins once again in the 1920s—its modern successor has supplied the only imagery of alpine recreation that makes sense to us.

What did climbing feel like before it was modernised? Let me begin with a convenient visual census, an image precisely contemporary with the first. From Sally Irwin, biographer of

Freda Du Faur (1882–1935), we know that the shot was taken on Christmas Day, 1910. Several days of bad weather had left three separate parties stranded at the Malte Brun Hut; but on 25 December the weather broke long enough for the group to throw snowballs and pose for photographs.[20] Just three weeks earlier, the Australian-born Du Faur (rear, second from left) had become the first woman to climb Mt Cook. Her guides on that occasion, Peter and Alex Graham, are shown here, rear right and third from right, respectively. It is more than likely one of the Grahams in the ice-climbing photograph with Baughan.

The first incarnation of the lodge known as the Hermitage was built in 1884. In 1895 it was purchased by the Liberal government, and in 1901 brought under the control of the newly established Department of Tourist and Health Resorts. The Ball Hut dated from 1891, the Malte Brun Hut from 1898. As we can see, these outlying structures were not palatial (Baughan

Malte Brun Hut, Christmas Day, 1910

describes the Malte Brun's 'hardy comforts'),[21] but they offered a platform, a staging-post from which to tackle the high summits. Premodern climbing is all about this infrastructure: on the one hand, the Hermitage and the huts; on the other, the role of professional guides. The guides did the leading, the heavy packing, and the step-cutting essential to negotiating ice. Nobody climbed high without their help, and the best-known among them—like Jack Clarke (rear left) and Peter Graham—were the most influential personalities in the sport.

Reliant on accommodation and guiding, climbing in this era was narrowly confined; only within reach of Mt Cook were these amenities available. The same factors helped determine who could participate. Travel was costly and time-consuming, and Mt Cook was difficult to get to; there was the price of accommodation; there were guiding fees. Anyone mounting a serious campaign could easily spend 100 pounds over six weeks or so.[22] As a leisure activity, then, climbing was strictly class-stratified. The guides (including the Grahams and Clarke) typically came from working-class backgrounds. But these were the hired hands, the professionals. Their clients were either well-heeled tourists, like Du Faur, or members of the colonial upper middle class.

In gender terms, however, the culture of guided climbing was notably inclusive. Among the group at the Malte Brun Hut are four (male) guides and seven clients; the clients (readily distinguished by appearance) are four women and three men. This distribution was not out of the ordinary. The name best remembered is undoubtedly that of Du Faur, not just the leading woman climber of her day, but the best-known amateur climber, male or female.[23] She made the second ascent of Mt Tasman (the most challenging peak in the area), the first of Mt Dampier, and the first traverse of Mt Sefton. Most notably of all, in 1913, with Peter Graham and Darby

Thompson, she made the first 'grand traverse' (all three peaks in a single climb) of Mt Cook.[24] While Du Faur was the most celebrated and probably the most able, she was by no means the only distinguished woman climber of the period. By the end of the war, six women had climbed Mt Cook, including Jane Thompson, who in 1916 repeated the grand traverse at the age of 59. Muriel Graham, the first New Zealand-born woman to climb Mt Cook, Annie Lindon, Kate Gardiner and Ada Julius (front centre, looking away from the camera) are all names familiar to those who know this early alpine history.

But the face of climbing was about to change. In the summer of 1926–27 an Englishman, Ned Porter, and his Swiss friend Marcel Kurz spent a season climbing in the Southern Alps.[25] They climbed two-on-a-rope, without guides, who traditionally climbed in three-person parties. Porter and Kurz, however, employed crampons. These had been around for a while—they were first produced commercially in 1910—but until now no one in New Zealand had seen what they could do. Crampons transformed climbing on ice. Taking out most of the traditional step-cutting, they meant that ascents could be made faster and by more difficult routes. In 1928 a spike was added at the toe-end. This led in turn to the technique known as front pointing, making ice climbing faster again and the routes still more direct. Porter and Kurtz made climbing practices at the Hermitage look tame and old-fashioned, and before long young New Zealanders were taking up where the visitors had left off. In Philip Temple's stirring account, the apostle of modern New Zealand climbing is a young North Island schoolteacher, Dan Bryant.[26] In 1930 Bryant took a job at Waitaki Boys' High School in Oamaru and teamed up with Rod Syme and W.G. Mace. Like Porter and Kurz they climbed without guides but with modern equipment—most importantly, crampons. It was they and other young men like them who ushered in a new heroic chapter, the one that would culminate in 1953 with Edmund Hillary on the summit of Everest. (Bryant, not coincidentally, was the first New Zealander to climb in the Himalayas.)

The 1930s, then, saw the focus of New Zealand climbing transformed. Guiding didn't vanish entirely, but the Hermitage paradigm had been overtaken; the new approach was independent and expeditionary. Turning their backs on the Hermitage infrastructure (with hut accommodation giving way to tents, bivouacs and ice-caves) a new generation of tough young climbers was soon fanning out along the length of the Southern Alps. Decades of concentration on the climbing at Mt Cook had left literally hundreds of peaks untouched, but with improving transport (including the railway through Arthur's Pass), and with the willingness of the new breed of amateur to pack heavy loads into remote locations, all this changed. A plenitude of what climbing idiom called 'virgins' were suddenly crying out for conquest, and these confident young men were only too pleased to oblige.

By the onset of World War II virtually everything had been climbed. As noted above, though, the conquest of the Southern Alps was not yet the climax of this phase of heroic endeavour. With the end of the war, a small number of New Zealand climbers began to eye up larger targets abroad. As it happened, the game plan that had emerged in the South Island—hardcore expeditionary climbing with an emphasis on ice-craft rather than rock—was exactly what was required in the Himalayas. It was no accident that, following Dan Bryant, other New Zealand climbers performed so well there.[27] George Lowe, Norman Hardie, Edmund Hillary and a number of others had honed their skills and endurance on the high peaks of the Southern Alps. Hillary's triumph in 1953 was the summit of a climbing revolution with its beginnings in the late 20s.

Canterbury Mountaineering Club party, near Arthur's Pass, 1930

Not surprisingly, this modernisation transformed mountaineering's demographic profile. As the sport became less costly it became more egalitarian. Taking out the guides and the expensive accommodation and shortening the travel times (particularly from Christchurch) remade climbing as a DIY activity; money mattered less now than physical strength and resourcefulness, and the peaks came to be dominated not by tourists but by young New Zealanders climbing in their spare time. While most were probably students or urban professionals, the field was also open now to a broader class constituency.[28] Hillary, famously, was a beekeeper like his father. Hardie, who reached the summit of the world's third-highest peak, Kangchenjunga, with the first successful party in 1955, came from a large working-class family in Timaru. These were the kind of people who, before World War I, would only have climbed as guides (that is, hired labour).

But while in class terms the sport had become more

inclusive, when it came to the role of women the outcome could hardly have been more prohibitive. With the onset of the new expeditionary paradigm, women disappeared from the forefront of high climbing. There were no more Freda Du Faurs. In fact according to Graham Langton's research there were barely any women on the summits at all. At the end of World War I women's participation had reached almost 50 percent. In the 1932–33 season Langton puts it at below 5 percent.[29] Women still took part in alpine recreation, principally through the growth of tramping clubs. And there were isolated examples of high climbing by all-women parties. Greta Stevenson inspired a small group of women climbers in Otago for a couple of seasons in the mid 30s, and Betsy Blunden, the first woman guide at the Hermitage (1928–31) led an all-woman party up Mt Sefton in 1934.[30] But not until after World War II would the numbers of women climbers begin slowly to increase.[31] The North Island clubs, in particular the Tararua Tramping Club, maintained a better record of encouraging women into the outdoors. At the opposite extreme was the Canterbury Mountaineering Club. Formed in 1925, in 1927 the CMC officially excluded women from membership, a ban that would not be reversed until 1977.[32] With such a propitious hinterland at their doorstep, and with their young,

Canterbury Mountaineering Club members and their cars, 1930

ambitious and exceptionally active membership, the CMC were the dominant exponents of the new hardcore style.[33] But in their gender extremism, too, the CMC were paradigmatic. Expeditionary mountaineering emerged as a proving ground, not just for Kiwi independence and egalitarianism, but for an ascendant masculine homosociality.

Climbing and writing

By now it will be apparent that I am talking about climbing as if I were really talking about mid-century literature. But in truth I've scarcely deviated from the narrative mapped out by Temple and Langton. The *as if* effect is not poetic licence. It's simply that the moment one reads these accounts—reading as a student of New Zealand writing—the pattern of resemblance becomes irresistible. The history of climbing is a story we already know.

As the 20s passes into the 30s, the discourse of New Zealand literature is modernised and masculinised. An emergent cohort speeds up the game, installing a new scale of literary values. With the coming of what we now know as literary nationalism, New Zealand writing becomes more agonistic, more edgy, more critical, more strenuous, more difficult. Both in the content of the new writing, and in the collective behaviour that accompanies it, we can see the workings of a proactive homosociality. The effect on women writers will be swift and decisive. In the first place, women will cease to participate, at least in the register of 'literature'. Equally, this re-gendered regime will eclipse (make invisible) an earlier system of aesthetic priorities and values. Leggott puts it perfectly: the new literary nationalism is 'inimical to previous competences'.[34] There has always been more than one kind of writing—and more than one way of being a writer—but with the nationalist intervention its 'others' are taxonomically displaced. In a language that nationalism shares with first-wave modernism, the 'feminine' is aesthetically re-coded, so that creative priorities at odds with those of nationalism (beauty, for example, or spirituality or sentiment) must now contend, in unequal struggle, with the force of a militant masculinity. The effect is to rewrite literary history, until the exponents of those newly displaced aesthetic values (Duggan, parts of Bethell, the greater part of Hyde) begin to seem as distant and illegible as the Edwardian 'lady climber'.

The 'same' history, therefore, accounts for two quite different practices. But what does this homology mean? One way to manage this difficult question would be to argue that they're not really different at all: that in fact they're the same discourse, that the heroic age of New Zealand mountaineering is just settler nationalism in another register. Mary Louise Pratt supplies the necessary tools in analysing what she calls 'the anticonquest'.[35] By this she refers to those apparently benign practices (travel writing, natural science, cartography) through which European discourse takes command of other places and naturalises their occupation; not for nothing does the climber 'conquer' mountains. In these terms, one can readily argue that the naming of a locality (writing) and the physical mastery of a locality (climbing) are performing the same ideological work. Mountaineering fascinated the Caxton writers (as, in the figure of Hillary, it undoubtedly galvanised popular nationalism). The two cultures meet in ad hominem ways. Glover and Brasch both dabbled in climbing; climber and climbing historian John Pascoe was a friend of Glover's (and the source of the story of Arawata Bill);[36] Brasch's literary and romantic friendship with Harry Scott is memorialised in 'The Estate'. There is also an immediate connection through the South Island landscape. From this point of view, it may not be such a hike from the Canterbury Mountaineering Club across campus to the Caxton Press Club.

And yet however far we push this, the synchrony between these two sub-cultural histories confronts us with a question we are no closer to answering. *Why gender?* Why, at the hinge-point between these practices, do we find the same upheaval in relations between the sexes? Their masculine impetus can't be explained by whatever degree of investment they may share in cultural nationalism. We just need to think back once more to Woolf, in the year of the front-point crampon, 1928. The masculinism that Woolf describes, and which feels so familiar from our own local reading, is pressing on her *where she is*, in Britain and in contemporary British writing. So when the same manly energy manifests here in the writing or climbing of the 1930s, we can trust that it doesn't emanate from the South Island landscape (or from any other regional given: pioneering, pastoralism, puritanism). We are not looking here at something 'local and special' that materialises out of the conditions of settler nationalism. In their sudden and vehement turn to the masculine, these local modernist practices express a trans-hemispheric impulse.

Sighting across discourses, sighting across hemispheres, we begin to discern a new structure of feeling. At the turn of the 30s writing and climbing are reading from the same script. We hear Woolf addressing an audience of young women at Cambridge, warning them of exactly the conditions faced by women in New Zealand. Be it Newnham College or Christchurch, on the summits or at the printing press, everything seems to converge on gender. Yet still we can't say how, or why. We know that men have the wind in their sails—that collective momentum that Holcroft describes. We can sense how pervasive an effect it is, and we know already the cost to women. But we can't yet account for its potency, or explain how the tide of the 30s should sweep men and women before it in such contrasting ways. What are the historical energies animating this new climate of manliness? This question leads us finally to the role of sexuality, and the impact of its modernisation.

The science of sex

'The Suffrage campaign was no doubt to blame. It must have roused in men an extraordinary desire for self-assertion; it must have made them lay an emphasis on their own sex.' Woolf's explanation for an exaggerated gender-consciousness (or as she would say, sex-consciousness) is helpful as far as it goes. But a masculine reaction against first-wave feminism is just one part of the puzzle. Historians have placed equal weight on the after-effects of World War I. With its legacy of maimed and shell-shocked servicemen, 'feminised' by their physical and even more by their psychological injuries, the war was an affront to the collective self-image of masculinity.[37] Compounding this was the reluctance of women to give up their wartime advances in the workplace. In Britain, as Susan Kent explains, this traumatised manhood expressed itself, not just in anti-feminine *ressentiment*, but in an upsurge of physical and sexual violence.[38] In *Nor the Years Condemn* Robin Hyde details the same mood of antagonism in New Zealand.

And yet, vivid as they are, these repressive effects are still only half the picture. To understand the shift in relations between the genders, we need to come to grips with a *coercive* effect. At the same time that women were being vilified and physically assaulted, they were also on the focal end of a new science. With the 20s comes the golden era of sexology. In short, it is the decade in which women are hetero-sexualised.

The origins of the new sexual science can be traced to the

late 19th century. In 1886 Richard von Krafft-Ebing published *Psychopathia Sexualis*; Freud and Josef Breuer's *Studies on Hysteria* dates from 1895, and Havelock Ellis's *Sexual Inversion* from 1897 (to be followed by the remaining six volumes of his master-work *Studies in the Psychology of Sex*). But it was after the war that the science of sexuality burgeoned as an international movement. The original stronghold was Weimar Germany, where in 1919 Magnus Hirschfeld established his Institute for Sexual Research (visitors and sometime residents included Auden and Christopher Isherwood, André Gide, Ernst Bloch, Walter Benjamin and Sergei Eisenstein). It was Hirschfeld, too, who organised the first international congress in 1921, leading in 1928 to the establishment of the World League for Sexual Reform, which held annual conferences over the next few years in Copenhagen, London, Vienna and Brno (Czechoslovakia).[39]

The impetus of the movement was not just scientific, it was also emancipatory; sexology supplied the intellectual weight behind an international movement for the reform and modernisation of sexual relations. At the core of this revolution were the closely related issues of contraception and female sexual response. In America, Margaret Sanger, who popularised the term 'birth control', established the first clinic for the purpose in 1916.[40] In Britain, Marie Stopes, Dora Russell and Norman Craig were not far behind. Meanwhile, in the work of sexologists like Hirschfeld and Theodoor van de Velde, women emerged in a new light as active subjects of sexual pleasure. How closely the two issues track together is exemplified in the career of Ernst Gräfenberg, best remembered for his research into female arousal (hence 'the G-spot'); in 1931 he also developed the first IUD. When Gräfenberg was imprisoned by the Nazis (like Hirschfeld, he was both Jewish and gay), reportedly it was Sanger who negotiated his release and passage to the United

States.[41] And it was the right destination. If Germany was the cradle of the new sexual science, its ultimate fate was to be determined in America.

In *American Moderns*, her study of bohemian New York either side of World War I, Christine Stansell designates the attitudes emerging around sex with the useful label 'sexual modernism'.[42] As a modernism, the new sexual consciousness belongs with those experimental energies that inaugurate the new century, and without doubt the liberalisation of the 20s feels like the beginning of our own sexual modernity. To recognise women as active erotic subjects, and to unshackle sex from reproduction, reads from today's perspective as an unambiguous leap forward. But for the women around whom these changes occurred, the new climate offered a more ambivalent experience. There were costs as well as gains: in fact the dawn of this incipient modernity was marked by a virtual collapse of the feminist movement. Sex had long been a subject of contention, in the pages of the British pre-war journal *The Freewoman*, for example, and in its nearest American equivalent *The Masses*. While a number of prominent feminists were active in the sex reform movement, to others it was far from clear that sexual liberalisation was consistent with women's political and economic advancement. A division emerged between 'pro-sex' and 'anti-sex' feminisms. When the movement lost the galvanising focus of suffrage—the vote being won in Britain in 1918 (although women under the age of 30 would have to wait another 10 years), and in the United States in 1920—sex helped to drain its collective political will.[43] For women of the 20s, heterosexual liberalism orchestrated new ways of relating to men. But for 'anti-sex' feminists, who were often but not invariably older, it was easy to conclude that their own hard-won gains were already being traded for a new sexualised domesticity. As Stansell puts it, 'the structures of sexual modernism proved highly flexible in their ability to accommodate elements of the old sexual hierarchies'.[44]

Unlike its better-known descendant of the 1960s and 70s, the sexual revolution of the 20s was harnessed resolutely to the institution of marriage. The advances of sexual science were channelled not into free love but into a renovated, reinforced matrimony. A sequence of manuals from both sides of the Atlantic—Stopes's *Married Love* (1918), *The Companionate Marriage* by Wainwright Evans and Judge Ben Lindsay (1927), and most influentially of all van de Velde's *Ideal Marriage* (1926)—propounded a new erotic gospel: marriage was a romantic partnership that rested not on patriarchal authority, but on mutual sexual pleasure.[45] Sex for women undoubtedly improved. From Kinsey we know that American women of the 20s were having more sex before marriage and were more likely to experience orgasm, both before marriage and within it. Against a background of gradually increasing freedom, the sharpest division was between women born in the 1890s and the generation born in the first decade of the 20th century. Of women born before 1900, 14 percent admitted to having premarital sex before the age of 25; among women born in the decade following, the figure was 36 percent.[46] At the same time, contrary to the fears of conservatives, greater sexual freedom was not putting women off marriage. Marriage rates rose, while the median age at first marriage fell—all of this, confoundingly, just as the universities, the professions and the workplace seemed to be opening up. Indeed the trend towards earlier marriage was at its most pronounced among the increasing proportion of women with a university education.[47]

Liberalised heterosexuality helped to expand the empire of marriage. Women of an earlier generation had faced a choice: they could have a political and/or creative life, a career; or they could have marriage and children. Doing both appeared not to be an option. If they lived a public life it was from a place outside marriage. But now this enabling space was contracting. Sweetened by sex and consumer capitalism, the renovated marriage of the 20s was more coercive, more difficult to opt out of. Instead women found themselves facing a new dilemma: how to reconcile a career with heterosexual love, domesticity and children. It didn't help that the social sciences were redefining motherhood as an ever more demanding occupation.[48] And it can't have helped either that it was all so new, not just the juggling act, but each of its competing elements. The eroticised companionate marriage was new, and so, in some measure, were the expanding possibilities in education and employment. Women in the 20s were dealing with both, as well as with the now familiar problem of how they could be co-managed. The trials of women's writing in the century's middle decades are one indicative chapter of this enduring modern struggle.

'The last home of original Puritanism'

As gender historians themselves have lamented, the sexual and gender dynamics of the 20s and 30s remain under-explored.[49] By comparison with the so-called first and second waves (and the Cold War years that preface the second), the era of what Elaine Showalter calls 'the feminist crash' has received little attention.[50] Reverting to New Zealand we find the record is even thinner. As Caroline Daley observes, our knowledge of the pleasure-seeking elements in mid-century culture lags far behind our consciousness of a more familiar puritanism.[51] Needless to say, we have no Alfred Kinsey, no census; when it comes to sexual practices between the wars we seem to have no data at all. In trying to gauge what the sexual liberalisation of the 1920s might have meant in New Zealand, we are reduced to drawing connections among a sparse set of coordinates.

We do have at least, in Ettie Rout (1877–1936), our own home-grown heroine of the sex reform movement, once described in the House of Lords (by a bishop, no less) as 'the wickedest woman in Britain'.[52] Actually, Rout isn't strictly home-grown; she was born in Tasmania, but educated in New Zealand, her family moving here when she was eight. Though she never attended secondary school, in Christchurch around the turn of century she fell under the influence of the brilliant and free-thinking professor of chemistry Alexander Bickerton. Best remembered as the mentor of Ernest Rutherford, Bickerton was also responsible for a large-scale experiment in 'federative' (or collective) living in Wainoni on Christchurch's eastern fringes.[53] For the young Rout he was both a direct source of progressive ideas about sex and gender, and a conduit of relevant reading: Havelock Ellis, H.G. Wells (who would later become Rout's personal friend), G.B. Shaw and Edward Carpenter.[54] Most important of all was the Swedish feminist Ellen Key, whose *Love and Marriage* she would describe in 1913 as 'the best modern book written on the subject of marriage whether looked at from the viewpoint of the lover, the Socialist or the evolutionist'[55] (as the last phrase implies, Rout was a keen eugenicist). Rout's heroic work to combat venereal disease among soldiers was therefore no accident. She had done her homework in the era's progressive literature. And when she reached London in the years after the war she was speaking the same language as other women in the sex reform movement. Rout was forthright and not strong on tact, and she quarrelled with both Marie Stopes and Margaret Sanger.[56] But the colonial isolation of her New Zealand education didn't stop her joining the fray as their legitimate equal. The conversation about sex and gender, in other words, was already trans-hemispheric.

This is not to say that sex reform was part of official discourse in New Zealand. When Rout produced her own sex manual, *Safe Marriage* (1922), the book was promptly banned in her home country. In the same year, the *New Zealand Medical Journal* denounced birth control in marriage as a form of 'selfishness in its most revolting form'; women were principally to blame, and the practice contravened 'everything that is sacred in the name of nature, morality, science and common sense'.[57] So much for sexual liberalism. One can understand why Rout (in one of the book's several British editions) would refer to New Zealand as 'the last home of original Puritanism'. There wouldn't be a Family Planning Association here until 1936.

But however much official discourse resisted, to stem the tide of modern sexuality was impossible; it could only be a question of how swiftly the battle would be lost. As I've said already, it was in America that sexual modernism would find its true destiny. The sexualised 'new woman' of the Jazz Age was the first modelling of femininity to come packaged in a recognisably American form, and it wouldn't be long before New Zealand's cartoonists and leader writers were inveighing against the depravities of the 'flapper'.[58] With the 20s dawned the golden age of Hollywood, and Hollywood broadcast on a global frequency; New Zealanders, just like anyone else, could watch Greta Garbo in *Flesh and the Devil* and Clara Bow in *Mantrap*. The year of these two films, 1926, brought another new spectacle—the crowning of the first Miss New Zealand. As Barbara Brookes records, the winner, Thelma McMillan, was offered a Hollywood screen test which her mother forbade her from pursuing. Instead she went back to her job at Arthur Barnett's in Dunedin where she was 'mortified' by the hordes of customers who came by to 'gawk' at her.[59] Young women didn't have to go to Hollywood: Hollywood was coming to them, bringing them new ways of being looked at in a culture that was inevitably to become saturated with heterosexual eroticism.

Among all its other 'modernisms' (and to the horror of those Modernists proper who would see it only as evidence of language decay) the 1920s brought global mass media advertising, including for the first time the dominance of pictorial images. This again was an American-led development, and another potent conduit for an Americanised repurposing of feminine sexuality. It was also targeted directly at women. The role of advertising technology in co-opting women's aspirations for independence and diverting them into domesticity and consumerism is a topic too complex to be dealt with here.[60] What we do know, however, is that its language was increasingly ubiquitous. Robin Hyde, in *The Godwits Fly*, has Eliza Hannay working on a newspaper, 'razoring from foreign exchanges anything that might be taken as a hot tip for women' and absorbing 'the sex blackmail of a thousand advertisements'.[61] We may know very little about the real sexual experiences of New Zealand women in the 20s. But we can reconstruct what they were subject to as they tried to find their place in a modernising world: a new sexuality, and new technologies to impress on them how much they needed to be part of it.

Women with women: The fall of Rise Cottage

The earliest years of the 20th century saw a boom in what was then known as 'physical culture'. Ettie Rout's husband, the Irish-born Fred Hornibrook, was a pupil of the Victorian strongman Eugen Sandow. Arriving in Christchurch in 1900, Hornibrook established his own school and quickly became a local identity. As Rout's biographer Jane Tolerton puts it, 'while Professor Bickerton had the most wide-ranging and publicly displayed mind in Christchurch [. . .] Fred Hornibrook had its most powerful and most publicly displayed body'.[62] His Australian equivalent was former wool-classer George Zepherin Dupain, who opened his studio in downtown Sydney within a year or two of Hornibrook's. It was to the Dupain Institute, in the early months of 1910, that the 27-year-old Freda Du Faur came looking for help. In January her first attempt to climb Mt Cook had ended in failure. Bitterly disappointed, she was determined to get fitter and stronger.[63]

About physical culture for women, Dupain was ambivalent. But he had on his payroll two 'Lady Experts': one was his sister; the other, two years younger than Du Faur, was Muriel Minnie Cadogan. It was Cadogan who took Du Faur in hand. She had her own ideas about women and physical conditioning, and by the time her client returned to the Hermitage she would be, as Peter Graham discovered, 'trained to a hair'.[64] Cadogan, perhaps as much as the Graham brothers, helped Du Faur get to the top of Mt Cook. Their relationship would last 18 years. According to Sally Irwin, its sexual dimension blossomed when the couple reached Britain in 1914 (1912–13 would be Du Faur's last season as a climber). But from the end of World War I, Irwin's account makes distressing reading. With the 20s came a rising wave of homophobia targeted at women, a mood that Cadogan in particular appears to have internalised.[65] Suffering increasingly from depression and paranoia, she fell into the clutches of a medical establishment determined that the only way to treat her was to 'cure' her sexuality. Du Faur and Cadogan were separated, and each subjected to the treatment known euphemistically as a 'rest cure'—actually a drug-induced 'deep sleep' therapy, which in Cadogan's case may also have included electroconvulsive therapy.[66] Her condition continued to worsen until, with her debilitated partner powerless to intervene, she was dispatched on an economy-class passage back to Australia. She died on board, officially of a heart attack, in June 1928. Muriel Cadogan was 45. Du Faur would not get over it. In Sydney in 1935 she took her own life.[67]

I've observed already that the sexual liberalism of the 20s represented for women an ambiguous kind of progress. The female subject of the new sexual science was not only capable of sexual enjoyment, but desired it and was entitled to it. And increasingly there were the knowledge and means by which (other social factors permitting) women could control their fertility. Even a pathologising discourse about lesbianism may have had, for some women, a legitimating effect, allowing them to name their desires, lessening their sense of isolation or confusion.[68] These developments all prefigure the climate of the later 20th century. But in the meantime there were also distinctly adverse side effects. As we've seen, the institution of marriage was reinforced, while (then as now) women's sexuality could serve to deflect attention from other capacities and entitlements, most obviously in the workplace. A glamourised heterosexual norm pathologised not just homosexuality ('deviancy') but also indifference or abstention ('frigidity'). And the heightened visibility of female sexuality brought destructive pressures to bear on women's relationships with other women. As Nancy Cott explains, the Victorian insistence on 'women's moral influence and glorious maternity' had veiled female sexuality in a way that made the intimate friendships of women appear innocent. The Angel in the House, as Coventry Patmore notoriously called her, was someone who could safely be trusted outside the house. But not so the sexualised being of the 1920s: 'Since erotic drives were now admitted to be as important to women's nature as to men's—and valued apart from reproduction—women's relations with each other seemed to compete with heterosexual pairing and thus came to be suspected as threats to existing sexual and social order. This shift of concern was so emphatic as to constitute a backlash against the idea and practice of independent women.'[69]

One effect, then, was to open the door to the explicit homophobia that overtook Cadogan and Du Faur. In 1921, for the first time in British history, a bill was presented to the House of Commons that would outlaw 'any act of gross indecency between female persons'.[70] Queen Victoria, as legend has it, refused to believe that lesbianism existed. But now it was out there: one of the bill's sponsors, Sir Ernest Wild, could be heard in the House citing Ellis and Krafft-Ebing as he warned against this 'very prevalent practice'. In the end the measure failed, not for lack of moral outrage, but for fear that it might prove counterproductive (in other words, publicise the vice it was trying to eradicate). But the bill's existence underlined the ambivalent implications of a more visible sexuality. Seven years later—in that seemingly inescapable year, 1928—Radclyffe Hall's *The Well of Loneliness* was banned on the grounds of obscenity. The novel became the centre of a storm of publicity. In advance of the trial, one of those keen to testify in the novel's defence was Virginia Woolf. But others, including Woolf's husband and sister, counselled against it; their fear, as she explained to Quentin Bell, was that in doing so she might 'cast a shadow over Bloomsbury'.[71] A bohemian enclave like Bloomsbury was the sort of place where lesbian sexuality could pass quietly under the radar. But the new language of sexual enlightenment brought unlooked-for attention to what had formerly been safe spaces.

The knock-on effects would ramify across the entire spectrum of women's homosocial relations. Up until now, the presumption of female innocence had made it unexceptionable for women to set up house together. The advantages of this are particularly apparent in the careers of women born 1850–90, the modernist generation and the generation before them. Theirs was the heyday of the so-called 'Boston marriage', and it's evident at a glance how productive the arrangement could be. It was, in short, the most rewarding way of avoiding conventional marriage and child-rearing, and from Sarah Orne Jewett to Marianne Moore, from Jane Addams to Molly Dewson, writers and activists routinely built their careers on the platform of same-sex partnerships. In particular cases (Stein and Toklas, H.D. and Bryher) relations were evidently sexual; in others (for example, that of Marianne Moore, whose companion for most of her career was her mother) they plainly were not. More often, however, these partnerships inhabit that elastic, inscrutable ground in between. In creative terms, of course, such distinctions are beside the point: the importance of these relationships is the freedom they offered women to work.

But with the advent of sexual modernism—eroticising women, rescinding the presumption of their sexual innocence—that space closes down. Beyond the generation of the 1880s, then, these domestic partnerships disappear almost entirely, at least from the literary world. No doubt additional factors are at work. The decimation of the male population in World War I had skewed the demographics in the modernist generation as would not be the case for those who were born in the new century.[72] Inherited fortunes were eroded by the Depression, and with them the income on which these two-woman households often depended in an era when it was so much more difficult for women to find decently paid work. Historians have not yet analysed in detail this shift in the pattern of women's relationships. It is apparent, however, that from the 1930s these homosocial partnerships are not renewed.

In New Zealand as elsewhere during these generations, it

was space outside marriage that made creative work by women possible; in the late colonial period, the women who managed to write were those who by one means or other had eluded matrimony. Baughan, as we've seen, had a private income and the spectre of a history of family insanity that gave her a convincing reason not to marry.[73] Jane Mander (1877–1949) was another who remained wholly unattached, her biographer concluding that she never had a romantic relationship of any kind.[74] In her mid 30s Mander got as far as New York, studied journalism at Columbia, and wrote *The Story of a New Zealand River* (1919) in the heady atmosphere of Greenwich Village. But Mander lacked Baughan's private means, and although she completed six novels, a decade of hack-work in 1920s Britain took its toll on her writing. Had she been with a partner, perhaps her career would have unfolded differently. Instead she succumbed to the financial and emotional pressure to come home and care for her elderly father. Returning to New Zealand in 1932, she wrote nothing thereafter.

While Baughan and Mander remained single, others formed a variety of same-sex alliances. Jessie Mackay (1864–1938) set up house with her sister Georgina. Eileen Duggan (1894–1972) lived with her friend Julia McLeely, first in the Catholic hostel where they met, and then in the home of Duggan's widowed sister Mary. Ursula Bethell's life at Rise Cottage revolved around her friendship with Effie Pollen. If there's an exception to this pattern it might appear to be Katherine Mansfield. But Mansfield's marriage to John Middleton Murry was childless, and was conducted, like Woolf's, under the more elastic conditions of modernist bohemia. Crucially, too, Mansfield had not just a husband but also a 'wife', as she explicitly called her friend Ida Baker.[75] Baker's testimony in *The Memories of LM* returns constantly to her own inadequacies in the relationship, and to Mansfield's demands and cruelties. Nonetheless she also makes a very determined case to the effect that she was a better and more enabling partner than Murry.

By now it should be clear why, in Chapter 2, I placed so much emphasis on the relationship between Bethell and Pollen. Oblique though it is, the glimpse that we get in her poems is one of the clearest views we have into a lost creative space. Curnow detected, rightly, an air of privacy in Bethell's verse; the garden poems seem to be speaking to some other audience. But her work is by no means a purely private endeavour. The domestic worlds of these late-colonial women writers were a vantage from which they both looked out and spoke out, on causes that ranged from women's rights and temperance to Irish Home Rule and prison reform. As Leggott puts it, they were 'culture workers who believed also in a code of social service'.[76] Nor was it exclusively a homosocial world; although the friendships of women tended to form the domestic bedrock, the networks of these writers extended to the coterie that Chris Hilliard chronicles in *The Bookmen's Dominion*; even the publication of *From a Garden in the Antipodes* resulted from the enthusiasm of a male friend reading the poems in manuscript.[77] The point, then, is not that men were excluded, but that writers like Bethell, Duggan and Baughan were not yet constrained to *address themselves* to men. The world of Rise Cottage, like the world of Baughan's poems, and like the Catholic environment of the poems of Eileen Duggan, is a space which has yet to be invaded by the imperatives of sexual modernism.

Its demands, though, are only just below the horizon, and as that modernism dawns, the structure of feeling that supports these writing women will collapse. Again, we see this nowhere more clearly than in the circle of writers loosely gathered around Rise Cottage. As the *Landfall* tributes at her death make clear, Bethell was a dedicated mentor of younger writers and artists. Brasch, who was one of them, believed she saw herself as a kind of 'spiritual director'.[78] But the pupils we know about are exclusively men. Among them are names essential to the development of cultural nationalism: Rodney Kennedy, Paul Pascoe, Holcroft, Cresswell, Woollaston, Brasch; more distantly Bethell's encouragement extended to Glover and Curnow. But as for women, Rosemary Brewer concludes sombrely, 'the prevailing note—is silence'.[79] After Rise Cottage comes a break in transmission, a loss of filiation and continuity. The homosocial matrix that proved so generative for Bethell and her women contemporaries will have no inheritors.

The sex of nationalism

And so we arrive at the threshold of 'New Zealand Literature'. Around the corner, over the page, the Caxton generation are waiting to assume the earth. They are going to show us how to 'take poetry seriously', how to 'commit the whole man' to the task. And as they articulate their structure of feeling, displacing the literary culture of the 20s, writing by women will lose its footing—not just for a decade, but for the best part of half a century. In the 50s, the 60s, even into the 70s, the woman writer will remain an anomaly, as women in New Zealand (as in Britain and North America) struggle to find a way to speak either inside or outside the channels of heterosexual modernity.

As the writers of the 30s take control of the literary high ground, the language of sexuality will furnish an entire masculine ordnance; sex will serve variously as an instrument of knowledge, as a measure of aesthetic value, and as a vocabulary of diminishment and revulsion. And yet heterosexuality in the active sense—sexual intimacy between women and men—will go almost unrepresented in mid-century writing. For literary nationalism, heterosexuality is a setting, an assumption, a way of knowing the world. But it doesn't supply a language of connection, or even of romance. Instead we find a strictly homosocial economy, where intimacy and power are exchanged exclusively between men. The governing framework is always straight (male–male relations are policed by homophobia), and yet straight in the most impoverished sense. Sex as a mode of relationship, and the range of thought and feeling that sexual intimacy might generate, carry no weight in the nationalist imaginary. This is what Woolf warned her listeners about: men 'writing only with the male side of their brains'. Emotionally as well as erotically, hard frost heterosexualism will be frigid.

As I write I am aware of a familiar tone that comes with the language of gender critique. If this is the framework that best enables us to map the structure of feeling of the 30s, it also evokes those rituals of censure that, as I remarked in my introduction, are apt to close down our experience of nationalist writing.[80] The severity of the critical idiom threatens to mimic the effects that it's complaining of. Nonetheless, to read for structure of feeling offers a strategy for opening these texts up again—a way to make them available to a fresh and more susceptible response. It helps us to understand their force, the historical advantage that is the condition of their success. At the same time, it shows how these texts are constrained, the conceptual boundaries within which they are obliged to operate. Masculinism, for the nationalist writer, is enabling, but only on its own limited terms. It's not that an author, in relation to this structure, enjoys no agency whatsoever; as Williams puts it, 'The new work will not only make explicit the changes in feeling, but will itself promote and affect them.'[81] But no writer is free to devise the gender codes to which a given moment is subject. The Caxton writers don't *invent* the masculine impetus of the 30s, any more than do the young men of the Canterbury Mountaineering Club. They do, on the other hand, profit by it, and they invent something *with it*: a modernist literary nationalism.

Chapter 4

'All the history that did not happen'

Curnow's critical nationalism

Nation impossible

The months during which I have been working on this chapter have seen astonishing events on both sides of the Atlantic. Donald Trump has ambushed the White House, boasting that he's going to Make America Great Again and promising to build a wall between the United States and Mexico. In Britain (and beyond), 'progressive' opinion is still reeling from the Brexit referendum: Nigel Farage of UKIP declares that he has 'won his country back'; his opponents see only xenophobia and 'little Englandism'. And yet, mesmerising though these developments have been, in part they confirm what we already knew. Whatever our fears about globalisation, the answer can't be nationalism; owned as it is by the populist Right, the impulse seems irreconcilable with a generous-minded politics.

These feelings don't make this chapter any simpler to write.

Nationalism's degraded reputation is an obstacle that stands between ourselves, as contemporary readers, and a cohort of New Zealand writers who built their reputations on it. It's easy to forget, though, that even in the 1930s nationalism already came with baggage. We all know, or think we know, that Allen Curnow is a nationalist. And no doubt he is—but of the most reluctant, most ambivalent kind. He is a nationalist by force of historical accident, or of what he calls 'the problems set by his birth'.[1] As he'll re-state the matter many years later, nationalism was not 'an option but a circumstance'.[2]

To formulate a discourse of settler identity in the years leading into World War II: the proposition was far-fetched, as Curnow well knew. For a start there was the overwhelming force-field of modernism. While we lack a detailed picture of Curnow's reading in the 1930s, we know that he discovered Eliot and the imagists through Harold Monro's *Twentieth Century Poetry* (1929).[3] And from his biographer Terry Sturm we learn that around 1935 he 'began to read much more intensively in contemporary English poetry', both the first-generation modernists and the younger poets of the MacSpaunday group.[4] For someone of Curnow's age and ambition, the prestige of Anglophone modernism was irresistible. In his author's note to *Enemies* (1937) he coins a metaphor that Pound would have been pleased with: England, he writes, is 'the "technical research laboratory", where the finest and most advanced work is done with that subtle material, the English language'.[5] But how was metropolitan experimentalism to be reconciled with the Romantic assumptions of literary nationalism? The transcendentalist ebullience of the Americans, the poignant tones of the Irish Revival, the vernacularism of the *Bulletin* writers—all of these were an epoch away from the caustic, fractured, deracinated world that emerged so compellingly in Eliot and Pound.

Nor were the prohibitions merely aesthetic. If the timing was bad in relation to modernism, it read even worse as conventional history. Who could buy into the romance of nationality in the wake of one world war and leading into a second? In an epigraph from *Not in Narrow Seas* (1939) Curnow quotes J.C. Beaglehole writing three years earlier: 'it may be that in the 20th century the making of new nationalities is an anachronism, as it certainly is a danger.'[6] In *Island and Time* (1941) he witnesses grimly 'the old / Crime of nation tried again'.[7] Had nationalism ever shown an uglier face than in Europe under National Socialism? In 'Dialogue of Island and Time', it is the character identified as 'The Jew' who warns that 'Promise turns to poison [. . .] / When islanders seek a nation', and who is 'Pitifully [. . .] amazed' to hear New Zealanders 'claim / A destiny and a name'.[8] This, we might object, is the voice of a stereotype. But for Curnow it was also the voice of new friends who had been settling in Christchurch since the mid 1930s, families like the Binswangers, the Frankels and the Christellers, driven out of Europe by a psychopathic nationalism.[9] And still this wasn't the worst of it. More disabling even than Hitler—from the point of view of an incipient settler nationalism—was a modern awareness of 'crimes of nation' that settlement had visited on home soil. The two great wars were in part the unravelling of the system that had organised the globe under European hegemony. The Age of Empire was in the process of disembowelling itself. By the time Curnow published his first national anthology in 1945, the partition of India would be only two years away. In other words, it was far too late not to know better; and yet, even now, it was European imperialism that its settler inheritors had somehow to parlay into a discourse of legitimate occupancy.

The problem must have seemed insurmountable. But avoiding it was difficult, too: 'Everywhere nation is talked and taught; / In one-man schools, at public luncheons'.[10] As the 1940 Centennial approached, the 'old crime' was rampant, with a wartime Labour government leading the way: an extravagant exhibition covering 55 acres at Rongotai, Wellington; a literary competition with prizes in six categories, and so on.[11] Writing to Fairburn, Curnow is scathing; what's really needed, he says, is 'a festival of penitence and humiliation, for our having been here 100 years and added more human shit than human wisdom to this soil'.[12] A sentimental discourse of nation was particularly threatening to the arts. Curnow writes to Lilburn, again in 1940: 'For God's sake, never let them claim you as a "N.Z." composer. They are the great enemy, these publicists of "national" arts & letters. That road begins with the ignorant patronage of newspapers & ends at a Rotary Club dinner.'[13]

Curnow never relaxed his suspicions. To the end of his career he would resist the label 'nationalist', objecting as late as 1985 that 'the word travesties every idea I ever had about the subject'.[14] However, somewhere in the early 1940s, the question of local poetry begins to engage him in a new way. There's a hint of something different in his 1938 review of Fairburn's *Dominion*, where he states, characteristically, 'Neither Mr Fairburn nor any other honest man cares two straws about "New Zealand poetry" (leave it to the watery quarterly)'—meaning the magazine *Art in New Zealand*—yet adds: 'but if they will write so well, reference to it is unavoidable.'[15] The suggestion becomes stronger in his essay 'The Poetry of R.A.K. Mason' (1941), and more so again in 'Aspects of New Zealand Poetry', written for the Australian journal *Meanjin* in 1943.[16] There was something distinctive about Mason and Fairburn that had nothing to do with the conventional satisfactions of nationalism. *Something* was going to call itself New Zealand verse—this much was obvious—and perhaps after all it was too significant a matter to be left to the Rotarians (or to the genteel book-lovers who masterminded the 1936 Authors' Week).

And so, despite his profound misgivings, Curnow goes down the rabbit hole. By the end of the *Meanjin* essay he's admitting that 'New Zealand can hear the strange new speech of poetry coming to be her own'.[17] By the time he has edited the Caxton anthology, just two years later in 1945, he will have established himself as the arbiter and interpreter-in-chief of that 'strange new speech'. Many of his own misgivings will be confirmed. His project will be widely and sometimes wilfully misinterpreted, and for the rest of his career he will never be free entirely of the arguments that follow.[18] Yet what he achieves is remarkable. He initiates, almost single-handedly, a modern tradition in local criticism.[19] And he devises a framing of national identity that, in the settler world at least, appears to have no parallel. His critical thesis clears a space (a provisional space, and this will be crucial) in which New Zealand writing can articulate a 'self' without simply regressing to a naïve Romanticism. Not only that, but in this critical opening he discerns a way to speak, at least obliquely, to the dilemma of settlement as crime.

'Their present condition'

I have mentioned already Curnow's weakness for D'Arcy Cresswell. To bracket him with Mason is the most puzzling call that Curnow ever made. It's not just that Cresswell's poetry is feeble, but that it's riddled with precisely the received 'literary' qualities that Curnow loathed. How could he look past the archaisms, the poeticisms, the Romantic banalities, and persuade himself (but almost no one else) that Cresswell was a significant poet? Challenged by Fairburn, his defence is half-hearted: 'I don't repent giving him so much space. I was trying to make him, as kindly as I could, an interesting—

I wld say important—psychopathic disclosure of a common condition.'[20] While Curnow may not be the only Cresswell reader to question the author's sanity, he's out on his own if he truly believes that the question makes Cresswell an interesting poet. But does he? I think it's more likely, in fact, that Curnow is making allowances here, and that his backing of the verse is a displaced expression of his genuine debt to Cresswell's prose.[21]

Anything in Cresswell that's readable today can be found in the twin volumes of his autobiography, *The Poet's Progress* (1930) and *Present without Leave* (1939). The opening sequences of *Present without Leave* are without doubt his finest hour. Curnow would have noticed them in 1932, serialised in the Christchurch *Press* (if only because they were rumoured to have been part of the reason that the editor, Oliver Duff, lost his job).[22] But it's likely that he looked at this material more closely when the book itself appeared, since from 1941 he begins to reference, almost obsessively, one key paragraph in particular:

> The air of their islands is mainly fresh from the sea, and the rainfall abundant from the mountains whereon it condenses, from which, in some places, a violent sirocco results. Their present condition depends on the state of peoples a great distance off, and their communications with these. As yet they have no future of their own; and when at length one confronts them, they shall awake to find where they lie, and what realm it was they so rudely and rashly disturbed.[23]

Curnow quotes this passage, in part or in whole, on no less than seven occasions. It first appears (twice) in 1941, in the essay on Mason, and as an epigraph in *Island and Time*. It figures in 'Aspects of New Zealand Poetry', and in the introductions to both anthologies (1945, 1960). Peter Simpson uses Eliot's phrase: the passage has 'personal saturation value.'[24] To this

I would add that, with considerable precision, it anticipates the strategies that underwrite Curnow's nationalism. The paragraph serves as a kind of mnemonic—a reminder to himself, but also a shorthand that he continually presses on his readers. I don't mean that Cresswell literally *taught* Curnow how to think his way into nationalism. More likely, I imagine, is that Curnow discovered here, in Cresswell's eminently quotable prose, a capsule rendition of a position that he himself was already working from, or was working towards: that he recognised in Cresswell's rhetoric (his language, his argument, perhaps above all his tone) the combination of elements he needed in order to talk 'nation' in modernist terms.

The Cresswell passage underlines three key tropes around which Curnow's own strategy revolves. First, the premise of alienation, or distance. Cresswell's estranging pronoun 'they'—*their* islands, *their* communications, *their* future—is characteristic of the way he likes to place himself. This, after all, is the author of an essay memorably titled 'To Hell with the New Zealanders'. Even when he's not actively scolding his fellow citizens, Cresswell invariably speaks as an outsider; the voice which identifies 'their present condition' is in equal parts that of an anthropologist and a clinician. Curnow adopts a similar detachment. He observes from an analytical distance, exploring the case for 'New Zealandness' not as cheerleader but as critic. Just as importantly he shares Cresswell's time frame: 'As yet they have no future of their own; and when at length one confronts them [. . .]'. For both writers national self-discovery is a matter for the future, the 'as yet', the 'at length'. New Zealand is not an agreed reality; it is something we don't yet know about ourselves. This implies—thirdly—confrontation and shock as we address a situation that we have managed not to think about. As Curnow likes to tell us in a dozen different ways, we have failed to face facts, we have 'hid[den] from actuality'.[25] Ahead of us, before we can have 'a future of our own', is a reckoning with everything we have preferred to ignore. His signature move is to confront us, as readers, not just with the grubbiness and meagreness of settler history, but with our own disinclination to remember it.

Curnow's partisanship towards Cresswell is in contrast to his lukewarm engagement with M.H. Holcroft, whose meditations on landscape and local culture—*The Deepening Stream* (1940), *The Waiting Hills* (1943), *Encircling Seas* (1946)—are the most ambitious statement of 40s nationalism beside Curnow's own. They are also the nearest approach we have to a full-blown Romantic nationalism in the Emersonian mode. Holcroft is a transcendentalist. He believes in a 'mind' that is 'circumambient': 'mind surrounds the body [. . .] is in touch with other minds, or with a collective mind which may shade off into a region of pure spirit.'[26] He also believes that the land has a memory, that 'the country has lived a secret life of its own' and that this 'primeval' experience stays with us: 'nothing can be lost that has once been given its place in the general mind.'[27]

Initially, at least, Curnow treats Holcroft with respect. He quotes him approvingly the early 40s, and writes him a sonnet (from which this chapter takes its title) in *Sailing or Drowning* (1943). In the Caxton introduction he borrows an epigraph from *The Waiting Hills*:

> Their task is to acclimatize the muse, to open their minds and the minds of their readers to influences that can be found in this country and nowhere else; and in so doing to reach towards that primal force which lives like a pulse in the old themes of earth and sky and mutability.[28]

But Holcroft's Romanticism makes Curnow nervous, especially when his own critics begin to speak of them in the same breath.[29] When Curnow quotes this passage a second time, in a rather cruel review of Holcroft's *Dance of the Seasons* (1953), it's in order to distance himself from Holcroft's mysticism: 'the originality and value inheres not, of course, in his conception of a "primal force", but in his application of it [. . .] to an earnest study of poetic beginnings *in a society removed barely three generations from its colonial origins*' (emphasis mine).[30] Curnow wants nothing of 'shaping a soul', of 'the genius of the land', or of 'the discovery of an essential New Zealand'.[31] The Holcroft whom Curnow is willing to countenance is, like himself, a cultural historian. The object of his own inquiry is not an essential New Zealand spirit, but (in the preferred language of Cresswell) a historical New Zealand condition. Where 'spirit' and 'soul' derive from the intuitions of Romanticism, a national 'condition' speaks to the analytic temper of modernism. A condition can be diagnosed and critiqued. Potentially it can also be treated.

I have referred more than once to Alex Calder's label 'critical nationalism'. This describes a critical or disenchanted tone, and a critical procedure: 'New Zealandness' *by critique*. It's a term that, to put it another way, measures the distance from Holcroft to Cresswell. Colonial migration, as Calder explains, 'ought to have led to an identity crisis'. But the crisis was deferred: settler culture at mid century had still not confronted its 'inaugural dislocation'. By the 1940s, what was required was a bracing dose of revisionism—'tough-minded acts of looking and looking back'—to confront settler culture with its disavowed history. Calder describes this critical strategy as 'remedial': it made up for lost time; it was also potentially healing. But it was a treatment so aversive that it felt like something else. Such was the lesson of Cresswell and Mason, as exemplars of how to get real about New Zealand. The truth by definition was a painful truth. The remedy was always going to be difficult to swallow.

Cutting edge

Over the years I have talked about Curnow in university classrooms large and small. Almost invariably the experience has been frustrating. It doesn't seem to matter who makes up the audience—undergraduates, Honours students, even adult learners, typically so curious and biddable; much as I value Curnow's work of the 40s, and rewarding though it is to unravel and to write about, sharing that enthusiasm has always been a hard sell. The problem is partly of my own making: one might get more traction with the gentler poems of Curnow's old age.[32] Nor can I vouch, of course, for the approachability of my own teaching. But we're not talking here about 'approachable' poems:

> Small city your streets hold no particular legends,
> your brothels are as inconspicuous as your churches [. . .]
>
> London has spawned. Here are banks in the egg,
> foetus Beaverbrooks, Edens and Baldwins [. . .][33]

Or again:

> They arctic we antarctic;
> Colder the southern cap, emptier the seas;
> Horizon more emphatic
> Stamps out one by one our flickering days.
>
> Immature form, no nerves
> Twangling a meaningful music; stimulus
> Stops at a full gut; waves
> Cast up such creatures when the southerlies pass.[34]

I'm not sure I'll ever try to coax another class through 'New Zealand City' (from *Enemies*) or 'Polar Outlook' (from *Island and Time*), because I know already what my audience will tell me: *This stuff is horrible! Why are you making us read it?* Nor is it just a question of these characteristic but perhaps rather obvious examples; it's something that runs deeper, through the whole of Curnow's mid-century oeuvre, not least the prose. More than seven decades on—if my ad hoc ethnography is anything to go by—the abrasiveness of Curnow's tone has not lost its power to unsettle.

Curnow, I am guessing, would not be wholly displeased: that readers should find these poems 'confronting' implies that the text is (still) doing its job. For the modernist poet there was nothing to lose in alienating a non-specialist readership. To narrow and rarefy the audience, addressing without apology the trained and committed, was in step with a reconceived cultural economy in which modernism gave up sales and circulation for pure cultural capital (or what Pierre Bourdieu calls 'distinction'). There was more at play, though, than simple snobbism. When Eliot wrote in 1921 that 'poets in our civilisation, as it exists at present, must be *difficult*,'[35] he was drawing on the assumption that post-war modernity itself was difficult; poets needed to be pushing the boundaries—experiment and risk were the watchwords of the day—and only the kind of poem that was tough enough to repel the bourgeois reader was likely to be truthful. This idea translated readily into the context of critical nationalism. Here, as my students continue to discover, a modernist heroics of toughness, edginess and risk could be acclimatised with no more than subtle modifications. If the task was to face up to settler history, then the truthful poem couldn't be an easy experience. Conversely, where the reader felt threatened, the poet by implication must be touching a nerve.

Romantic nationalism exhorts its audience to wake up to its own good fortune: the abundance of opportunity at its doorstep (as in the American Renaissance); the depth of its native traditions (the Irish Revival). The message of critical nationalism is the opposite: not 'we don't know how lucky we are', as Fred Dagg used to tell us; but rather, 'our good fortune has been exaggerated'. Nothing arouses Curnow's scorn like the wish to pretend things are better than they are. In the Caxton introduction he makes a particular example of Eileen Duggan. At the height of her reputation in the 30s, Duggan was the country's best-known poet; but Curnow ceremonially strips her of rank: 'Prolific in the last twenty years, Miss Duggan has at least shown herself aware that life or land has posed her a problem; but the poem is most often a means of gentle evasion or confusing of the problem, as if she were trying to substitute for it something prettier, more easily borne'.[36] Evasion, substitution, confusion, prettification: it is with the help of this catalogue of soft-minded vices that 'we have so habitually upheld the pretended against the actual'.[37]

Of course, once this 'gentle' disposition has been lined up so invidiously with the forces of unreality, the corrective more or less writes itself. Where 'cheerfulness' has become a 'test of poetic merit',[38] nationalism simply reverses the terms: the other kind of poem—the truthful poem—will be measured by its harshness and despondency. These will be the salutary qualities of the nationalist reality check, the shock treatment that will jolt us out of the illusions that we have habitually permitted ourselves. The darker and more difficult the poem, the more this truth effect will cling to it. In this respect, inevitably, the key figure is Mason. With his poems like 'sponges steeped in vinegar',[39] Mason is the antithesis of Duggan and her gentle evasions. For Curnow, he embodies a 'mature knowledge that evil, pain, and error can be final and absolute'.[40] When he praises Mason's poems as 'sombre and vehement'[41] it becomes hard to imagine that grown-up writing could ever be anything else.

Mason's pain, as we saw in Chapter 2, is testament to his indigeneity: Curnow values his work over Bethell's because Mason 'has suffered more as a New Zealander'.[42] Suffering is a condition by which Curnow sets great store: 'our true poet is the suffering and demanding spirit of us all'; Douglas Stewart is guilty of 'a trick for evading the suffering a poem must entail'.[43] The figure of the poet in pain is an archetype we rightly associate with Romanticism. But where the Romantic poet's suffering implies subjective transcendence (unmediated access to a more than rational vision), the pains of critical nationalism are framed as a historical necessity. Curnow spells this out in his 'Note on the Second Edition' (of the Caxton anthology) in 1951. Rehearsing his familiar complaint about a 'long refusal to engage in poetry as a present adventure', he then describes how the poets of 30s broke through into a new kind of immediacy:

> The large and comfortable illusion gave way to the small and painful reality [. . .] 'New Zealandness' might follow; but was not what had been so much talked about. We had to cut ourselves, taking up the edged tools of the language, where it had been safe to play with those that were blunt or rusted.[44]

The complacency and timidity of the past leaves the poet of the nationalist present no choice. *Someone* has to suffer this 'painful reality'. I have mentioned Curnow's appeal to George Barker: 'Every man avoids his death as long as he can, and thus every poet writes the nicest rather than the best poems he can: for the best poems leave him so much more short of blood; but the nicest poems [. . .] do not bleed him so deeply'.[45]

It's an argument tailor-made for Mason, the New Zealander who 'has most consistently tried to write his best poems'.[46] But it resonates, too, whenever Curnow directs us to the painfulness of settler reality. In this context, only the poet who bleeds—who 'cut[s] [himself], taking up the edged tools of the language'—is taking poetry seriously enough to redeem it as a 'present adventure'.

In the history of settlement as told by critical nationalism, the sins-of-omission of the parents are visited on the children: 'The shock of so distant a migration, and the recoil of imagination from realities, were to be transmitted through two, three, even four generations'.[47] A problem of dislocation that the colonists couldn't face has been 'bequeathed unsolved'[48] to the generation of the 1930s; now comes the time, then, not just for remedial analysis, but for remedial hurt. The underlying metaphor is psychotherapeutic: the task of the nationalist poet is to lift our 'communal repression'[49] by confronting and making conscious that inaugural trauma. But the premise is also sacrificial. Where the poet pays the price for the illusions of earlier decades, the text becomes a strategic self-wounding; the hurt sustained in the writing of it is the proof of having risked an encounter for which others have lacked the fortitude. Every time that nationalism bleeds on the page, it confronts the reader with this stoic reproach. The pathos of the suffering poet signifies the urgency of this belated historical reckoning.

Anti-myth: Nation by negation

Curnow's reference to an 'anti-myth' has always been a critics' favourite. His own application of the term is oddly circumscribed. It first appears in an author's note in his *Collected Poems* of 1974, with reference to the 1939 volume *Not in Narrow Seas*: 'I suppose it could be called my contribution to the anti-myth about New Zealand which a few of us [. . .] were so busy making in those years.'[50] Immediately, though, he wants to put it behind him: 'Very soon after, I was writing the poems of *Island and Time* and *Sailing or Drowning*. I had to get past the severities, not to say rigidities of our New Zealand anti-myth'. We can sense here Curnow's habitual urge to make light of his engagement with nationalism; if he could, he would put 'those years' in a box and stow them as far away as possible. But scholars have seen it differently: the term has caught on because it captures so accurately not just the temper of *Not in Narrow Seas*, but of *Island and Time*, *Sailing or Drowning*, and the two definitive anthology introductions.[51] Nothing Curnow ever said goes more directly to the critical cunning of his historical narrative—specifically, his strategy of defining 'New Zealandness' by refusing to describe it in substantive terms.

The operation may well owe something to Pound—as critics they share the same kind of jubilant negativity. In Curnow's hands, however, it produces a more cogent historical narrative. The Pound of the early manifesto essays defines the requirements of modern poetry in part by lampooning the flabbiness of his immediate predecessors. The simplest thing to say about his position is that it's anti-Victorian. A more ambitious social and political critique is implicit, but only later will it blossom into the grandiose cultural history of *The Cantos*. In Curnow's settler context the relationship is tighter from the outset. The 19th-century versifiers whose reputations he will so mercilessly deflate (Domett, Bracken, C.C. Bowen) were amateur poets but professional politicians, quite literally the same people who were carrying out the material enterprise of colonialism. As postcolonial critics have learned to do more recently, Curnow saw poetry as an integral part of the colonial project: 'Wakefield's notion of a planned society [. . .] took for granted the easy transference of the English cultural tradition'.[52] And as allied expressions of the imperial impulse, they express the same failure of imagination. Having migrated 'bodily but not in spirit', the 'colonist-poets' brought to the task of settlement the same refusal of actuality that we now find embalmed in their gentlemanly versifying.[53] Whenever we hear Curnow letting the air out of one of these colonial titans—Bracken's voluminous assorted works are 'the weightiest objects of rhyme in the nation's cupboard of worthless keepsakes',[54] and so on—we hear his disdain, not just for the self-importance of Victorian amateur poets, but for the delusional over-reaching of Empire.

In both capacities, then, as poets and as statesmen, the distinguishing vice of Curnow's Victorians is inflation of scale. As 'ambitious men of action on a diminutive stage',[55] they are incapable of making the necessary adjustment from 'the large and comfortable illusion' to 'the small and painful reality'.[56] Curnow, though, is only too happy to help them. And this down-sizing gesture (nation by deflation) becomes a signature, not just of his criticism, but of his poetry of the nationalist period as well. He doesn't often quote himself. But the refrain from 'The Unhistoric Story' (1941) appears at least twice in Curnow's essays. Plainly it's a poem that matters to him, and it's easy to see why:

> Whaling for continents coveted deep in the south
> The Dutchman envied the unknown, drew bold
> Images of market-place, populous river-mouth,
> The Land of Beach ignorant of the value of gold:
>   Morning in Murderers' Bay,
>   Blood drifted away.
>   It was something different, something
>   Nobody counted on.

> Spider, clever and fragile, Cook showed how
> To spring a trap for islands, turning from planets
> His measuring mission, showed what the musket could do,
> Made his Christmas goose of the wild gannets.
> Still as the collier steered
> No continent appeared;
> It was something different, something
> Nobody counted on.[57]

Wherever these vast expectations appear (the mythical Land of Beach, the imagined southern continent, a Pacific empire), we know that Curnow will puncture them. Again and again his poems administer this New World reality check. This is the crux of his anti-myth, a habitual deflation of narratives of settlement. Crucially, however, the poem doesn't offer concrete alternatives. What appears in place of the explorers' grand surmises is nothing more than the *difference* that confounds their expectations. And not only Tasman and Cook, but all of the poem's successive protagonists in a capsule history of settlement that reaches to the present and beyond: 'And whatever islands may be / Under or over the sea, / It is something different'.[58] Where exactly are we? We still don't know, except that it's not where we thought we were.

Critical preconceptions about Curnow's alleged realism have helped to obscure the subtlety of his anti-mythology. Already his realism is that of a modernist: language and representation are inadequate, and reality is correspondingly elusive; the poem makes a drama of this problem, but doesn't resolve it. The result is a discourse about New Zealand that depends remarkably little on affirmative or substantive assertions. Fifteen years later, in his elegy for Wallace Stevens, Curnow salutes the poet who has become his master:

> Capable to detect where reality was not
> And scrupulous what to put in place of it.[59]

The same can be said about his own approach to history and myth. As an anti-myth, Curnow's account of settlement leverages off existing representations. But it doesn't supply the deficit; it doesn't supplant the illusion with a concrete reality. Anti-myth, from this point of view, becomes something more subtle than an alternative myth or counter-myth. In place of the illusory narrative, the *anti*-myth is designed to construct not a better story, but a hollowed-out space. It is this cleared space, this 'something different', that emerges at the core of Curnow's nationalist narrative. The ground is cleared over and over again, until New Zealand feels less like a place than like an ongoing process of consciousness.

Anti-hero: From Whitman to Prufrock

Reluctant nationalist though he is, for Curnow there is nowhere to hide from 'the problems set by his birth'. The formation of new nationalities is now a danger; it may also be an anachronism. But he has to make the best of it:

> Unless he is a new and altogether less passionate variety of social man—I wonder, is that possible—the New Zealand poet is unlikely to escape wholly the character of prophet to his people, some trace of Whitman and other Americans, the Polish Romantics, or the Irish poets of the revival.[60]

Curnow's response to this untimely assignment is to tackle the problem of Time head on.[61] The future has a great deal of work to do in Curnow, but its function is to complicate, not to predict. He adopts the prophetic future tense as a means by which to challenge the myth of achieved progress, as well as to unsettle the 'present condition' out which his own generation speaks. The future washes back into the present, invading the space opened up by critique, not with the promise of national self-discovery, but with the knowledge that we don't even know what we're looking for:

> The good poem is something we may in time come to recognize New Zealand by, not something in which we need expect to recognize obvious traces of the New Zealand we know.[62]

> 'New Zealandness' might follow; but was not what had been so much talked about.[63]

> Strictly speaking New Zealand doesn't exist yet, though some possible New Zealands glimmer in some poems and on some canvases. It remains to be created—should I say invented—by writers, musicians, artists, architects, publishers; even a politician might help—and how many generations does that take?[64]

The future is a critical corrective. It is also, for Curnow, a consolation. In an epigraph he quotes Matthew Arnold: 'That promised land it will not be ours to enter, and we shall die in the wilderness: but to have desired to enter it, to have saluted it from afar [. . .] will certainly be the best title to esteem with posterity'.[65] Only the future can redeem those injuries suffered by the poet who confronts our disowned history. And only in the future, as it continually recedes, is it safe to conjecture the anachronism of an emergent national identity.

Yet even this safety is compromised. The concluding couplet

of 'The Skeleton of the Great Moa in the Canterbury Museum, Christchurch' deserves its fame. Among the many writers to have referenced it is Glover, who rewrites it just a few years later in 'Sings Harry':

> Not I, some child, born in a marvellous year,
> Will learn the trick of standing upright here.
> —Curnow[66]

> Not I but another
> Will make songs worth the bother [. . .]
> —Glover[67]

This negated first person is a signature vehicle for critical nationalist subjectivity. There's something dissembling about it, of course—we needn't take its laying down of arms at face value—but the speaker isn't simply being bashful or self-deprecating. In Curnow, if not in Glover, there is a characteristic anxiety. Lacanian critics use the notation $\not{S}$ to represent the 'divided subject': a subject barred, or discompleted, by what Lacan calls the 'insistence' of the unconscious. In language we are divided against ourselves. The unknowable determinations of the unconscious, always with us in the 'otherness' of our own speech, imply that we can never hear exactly what we're saying or know precisely what we desire. Curnow, too, knows about this unsettling 'otherness'; he locates it in the future, as its shadow falls on the present. Curnow's aspirations to speak the language of national identity are conferred on a crossed-out, self-cancelling subject who is unmanned—diminished in standing—by an 'as yet' towards which he labours but whose meanings he cannot master. The consolation of an imaginary future is lined with symbolic, and real, threat.

When Curnow refers to 'Whitman and other Americans'

he's probably thinking of Emerson. Conceivably he might have in mind Robert Frost, or perhaps (though he didn't much admire him) Williams. But to find a convincing analogue for Curnow's own vein of prophesy, we need to canvass more laterally. The nearest ancestor, I would suggest, is Whitman's modernist anti-type, Prufrock. The 'I' of Whitman's 'Song of Myself' is perhaps the most unabashed subject in the whole of Romantic literature. In his tireless physical and spiritual ebullience—'manly and free', 'proud and erect'[68]—he embodies the principle of New World self-assertion. In contrast to Whitman's hysterical expansiveness, Eliot's Prufrock is the definitive obsessional neurotic: furtive, fastidious and crippled with doubt, he is incapable of action because it is *never the right time.* He has seen the future and he has been afraid. He is 'always already' depleted by it. When he pictures himself in prophetic mode, he envisions his balding head on a platter.

I don't mean, of course, that Curnow literally mimics Prufrock. But his down-in-the-mouth tone is more Eliot than Whitman. It's here, in the language of modernist disenchantment, that Curnow finds the makings of a viable nationalist subject, an anti-hero and anti-prophet to front his critical anti-myth. Admittedly, this wounded subject, with his gloom, his vigilance, his sheer bloody-mindedness, is apt to paint Curnow into corner. He himself will concede as much: 'I had to get past the severities, not to say rigidities, of our New Zealand anti-myth.'[69] There's a great deal to say, as we'll find in Chapter 5, about the emotional inhibition that marks this structure of feeling. The bandwidth is narrow, the manliness brittle and unyielding. On the other hand, the challenges at play are prohibitive: the challenge we've explored in terms of Romanticism and timeliness, and the even greater challenge—to which this chapter now turns—which is the settler's implication in the violence and greed of Empire.

Obsessional that he is, as a prophet of nation Curnow never quite begins. He acts out what feels like a settler defeatism. But in this deferral there is both a prudent historicism and a chastened, sophisticated realism—an awareness, that is, of the way in which the future will inevitably rewrite both present and past. The self-abasing attitudes that follow from this can never expunge the embarrassment of conquest. In Curnow's resourceful treatment, however, they do allow him tentatively to address it.

'the dead thing at our heart'

> he who sleeps in a conquered land beds himself with a corpse[70]

Robin Hyde's *The Book of Nadath* is a poem like no other of the mid 20th century. In Chapter 6 I will discuss the many ways in which Hyde is at variance with the nationalist paradigm. But first, the burning question is the one she presents above. Hyde, by my reckoning, is one of only two literary writers of the mid century (the other being Roderick Finlayson) who is willing to look candidly at the implications of settler conquest.[71] As a journalist Hyde was a passionate advocate for Māori, in particular over the alienation of Māori land at Ōrākei (a.k.a. Bastion Point), and her enthusiasm for Māori culture often seems closer to the spirit of our own era than to the 1930s. Not being committed to the nationalist movement, she is not bound by the movement's constitutive blindnesses. In the sequence from *Nadath* entitled 'The Greenstone Shadow', quoted above, she engages in a thought exercise that puts the boot on the other foot; the conqueror has in turn been overrun by an unspecified Asian occupier, referred to simply by colour: 'the yellow man'. As the colonised people of Nadath languish, finding their only dignity in silence and withdrawal, the new imperial masters run the gamut of familiar attitudes and experiences: they rape, they patronise, they romanticise, they envy. Finally they sicken of their own enterprise: 'the dead thing at our heart poisons us all [. . .] We cannot be ourselves, we cannot know ourselves, for shame'.[72]

If *Nadath* had been published in Hyde's own lifetime (instead, written in 1937, it lay in the archives until 1999), it's a safe bet that 'The Greenstone Shadow' would have been ignored, in particular by Curnow and his nationalist confrères. At the core of their cultural nationalist enterprise was a dilemma of apparently insurmountable proportions: how was settler literature to find a voice that felt local and natural—a voice that *belonged* here—when the settler belonged here only by right of conquest? There were limits, in other words, to just how much of the disavowed past could be taken on board. History had to be made real, but if a national culture were to get off the ground it couldn't be made *so real* that the settlers' descendants choked on their own imposture. Recently, of course, postcolonial criticism has been doing to the literary nationalists precisely what they themselves did with their own critical historiography: that is, confronting nationalism, belatedly, with its evasions of 'actuality'. Curnow's generation, we now tend to assume, simply ignored the inconvenient legacy of conquest. But the ideological manoeuvres that they resorted to are subtler and more various than this would allow.

In Cresswell's confrontation with the future, his awakened settlers will discover 'where they lie, and what realm it was they so rudely and rashly disturbed'. What exactly is that 'realm'? Cresswell, Wordsworthian Romantic that he is, probably intends no more than 'Nature': that 'sombre and savage landscape',[73] he calls it, despoiled by the ravages of mechanised agriculture. But the letter, if not the spirit, of his text reads otherwise. Thus the very next sentence leads off a new numbered paragraph: 'Their history begins with no certain aim, but haphazard. The first there of whom there is any record were Maori'.[74] And so on, through a reasonably forthright account of the New Zealand Wars. When Curnow demands a reckoning with historical actuality, he certainly doesn't mean to foreground a history of military conquest. But he knows it's there—just as surely as he must know (he quotes it seven times!) exactly where his favourite passage in Cresswell takes the reader next. Conquest travels in the shadow of his generation's revisionism, impossible to ignore, and yet equally impossible to negotiate candidly. Hyde puts it well: it is the 'dead thing' at its heart, the fact that promises ultimately to poison an enabling settler fiction.

The South Island myth

In the early 1950s a dispute broke out over what has since been referred to as 'the South Island myth'. Its context was the growing antagonism between Curnow and the younger Wellington writers grouped around Baxter and Louis Johnson. A particular flashpoint would be the second edition of the Caxton anthology in 1951, from which Curnow omitted a number of the Wellington cohort, including Johnson and Alistair Campbell. Labelled variously the Curnow–Baxter feud, or (with Curnow's shift to Auckland in 1951) the Auckland–Wellington feud, the quarrel would rumble on through the rest of the decade. The factors at play were many: there were the particular personalities involved; there was a broader intergenerational (as well as regional) *ressentiment*. The argument about a regional myth is one detail in a larger pattern. But it's a threatening detail: it presses on a weakness, a legitimate sore point. Behind this debate about 'region' and 'myth' is the spectre of prior occupation and the disabling facts of conquest.

No one states the core premise of this myth in more crystalline form than William Pember Reeves, in 'A Colonist in His Garden':

> We stand where none before have stood
> And braving tempest, drought and flood,
> Fight Nature for a home.[75]

It's a bombastic poem, still firmly colonial. But it captures the displacement that is the ideological core of this regional mythology, a feat of substitution through which the violence of colonial settlement takes place, not between peoples, but rather between Man and a hostile landscape. 'None before have stood' here because Nature forbids it: the land is uninhabited because it is effectively uninhabitable. Curnow, who quotes these lines more than once, is not deceived by this imperialist sleight of hand. But the fact that it does 'little justice' to Māori[76] will not deter his own generation from reinventing the same trope. A ceremonious rendering of New Zealand geography in terms of an intimidating Romantic Sublime—far-flung and alien, windswept and ice-bound—lays hold of a territory which it systematically depopulates. What suited the South Island to this expedient fiction was not just its geography but its specific colonial history. A smaller initial Māori population, a costly period of warfare in the 1820s (both within and between iwi), and the overwhelming European deluge generated by the southern gold rush, led to the situation where Pākehā ascendancy was achieved in the South Island without military force.[78] It was 'almost' as if there was nobody here. And why? Well, you only had to look at the mountains. By projecting the outcomes of this regional history onto a grimly Romantic landscape, it was possible to write as if landscape itself had set the stage for Pākehā occupancy.

'We reach here the very principle of myth: it transforms history into nature.' So states Roland Barthes in the mid 1950s.[79] The anti-myth of critical nationalism is a case in point. Confronted with the seemingly impossible dilemma of how to model a native idiom in a colonised territory, the nationalists fasten on the South Island landscape as a way to try to naturalise their foreclosure of prior occupation. The island is configured as a frozen desert, historically uninhabited because sublimely uninhabitable. The task of the settler is simply to tame it. This, once again, is what Mary Louise Pratt calls the 'anti-conquest'.[80] By displacing contestation onto landscape—a landscape which supposedly repelled prior settlement—the nationalist writers 'secure their innocence' in the very gesture of imaginative seizure.[81] An empty, inimical southern terrain, which a manly settler heroism is only now subduing, naturalises European occupation and mystifies its historical mechanics. Myth and locality are bound inextricably in fashioning the settler nation on the model of the South Island.

The imputation of such a regional myth made Curnow irritable in the extreme. 'Myth,' he protested, was 'a curious term [. . .] for what is simply a way of looking at history'; and, 'As for the "South Island" particularity it just doesn't exist'.[82] On the surface it's not clear why 'myth' should make him so jumpy; it was he himself who had written in a preface to *Island and Time*, 'the need is for legend rather than for "realism".'[83] But as theorist-in-chief of the nationalist project, Curnow knew where its weaknesses lay. In the 1945 introduction he writes:

> The idea that we are confronted by a natural time, a natural order, to which our presence in these islands is accidental,

> irrelevant; that we are interlopers on an indifferent or hostile scene; that idea, or misgiving, occurs so variously [. . .] that it suggests some common problem of the imagination.[84]

An 'idea' (the South Island myth 'idea') leads through this sentence to an unstated 'problem'; the idea is secondary, a symptom which points to ('suggests') the underlying dilemma. And one had only to look critically at those tropes of depopulation for the underlying problem to become all too manifest. Curnow himself would never be caught in the naïve postures that embarrass Charles Brasch: 'The plains are nameless and the cities cry for meaning'; or, 'Waiting for our songs the woods are still, / The stones are bare for us to write upon.'[85] But that didn't cure the anxiety that prompted them. In his verse he would struggle valiantly, but the problem wasn't going away. While nobody spelled out the kind of critique that I've outlined in the preceding paragraphs, Curnow knew exactly what he couldn't defend, and this knowledge saturates his poems of the early 40s.

Unhistory

It bears repeating: Curnow is not taken in by this myth of the South Island as *terra nullius*. Admittedly in *Island and Time* we're confronted with 'the *unpeopled* diffident scene' (emphasis mine).[86] And it's true that his poems never pass up the chance to stress the severity of their island locality, or to remind us how the bleakness of an Antarctic neighbourhood conspires against any habitation, let alone an articulate one: 'Hands reach north for warmth, out of the south / Come storm and silence like a blow on the mouth.'[87] To this extent his poems may well imply that their claim is on a territory that no one else wants. But Curnow isn't interested in the terrain of what he calls 'pre-history' ('a scale in which we need feel no smaller than men are')[88]—as if the problems of settlement could be explained (away) by the primal, implacable force of indifferent Nature. His poems insist grimly on a human scale, in which geography is the setting for repeated failures of consciousness. The key term, therefore, is not so much 'unpeopled' as *diffident*. Curnow's sense that everything is yet to be done has nothing to do with the land being empty. It's a consequence, rather, of colonial history: of the tentative, frequently risible quality of the settler imagination in its efforts to inhabit it.

To this end, the most effective play is historical diminishment. As we have seen, Curnow's modernist ground-clearing bundles together two lumbering targets—Victorian poetics and colonial politics—so often conveniently embodied in the same actors. Above all, his critical sarcasm fastens on the disproportionate scale of their ambitions in both fields: 'ambitious men of action on a diminutive stage', their verse records 'the management of small affairs in the language of great consequences'.[89] At once we can see how convenient this is in finessing the legacy of prior occupation. Rather than summon his forbears to justice, the more cunning strategy is simply to belittle them. It isn't that conquest is actively denied; when it can't be avoided, Curnow will name it. But he relegates it always to that world of 'small affairs'—a history that he wants us to see as trivial in scale:

> Green slashed with flags, pipeclay and boots in the bush,
> Christ in canoes and the musketed Maori boast;
> All a rubble-rattle at Time's glacial push:
> Vogel and Seddon howling empire from an empty coast [. . .][90]

'The Unhistoric Story' recounts not history, not pre-history, but *unhistory*: a history continually erased by the moving hand that writes it.[91] Uppercase (or mythical) Time, harnessed to the swift march of stanzaic form—and with the poem's refrain ('it was something different') to emphasise the repetition—reduces a record of military subjugation to just another petty instance of colonial self-inflation.

Not in Narrow Seas, from 1939, is the first of Curnow's genuinely nationalist volumes, and his most unrelentingly satirical. It is here that he goes furthest in exploiting his forbears' triumphalism. A case history of the Canterbury settlement—'a natural point from which to begin a study of the birth, life and growth of a nation now nearly 100 years old,'[92] as the poet announces, with heavy irony—it treats prior occupation with a sardonic reticence:

> Not leap of capture theirs,
> But as who safely dares,
> Seizing without sword
> Front garden and backyard.[93]

Only as an afterthought, in a Blake-inflected 'Epilogue', does the sequence speak directly to the embarrassment of conquest. Once more, however, the recognition of prior settlement is the occasion, not for remorse or conciliation, but for national self-mockery:

> *Bring me an axe and spade*:
> For this is insolent country,
> James Cook's pig-farm
> Without rule or road.

> *Bring me a winding-sheet*:
> For the brown singing people
> Affront with death our triumph, an
> Unangry death without fight.[94]

Thomas Bracken in *Musings in Maoriland* (1890)—Calder once more supplies the example—uses the gallantry of Māori resistance to glorify, and justify, the colonial land-grab; as Calder puts it, 'these shabby proceedings are embellished by the chivalry and bravery of a vanquished race, a worthy foe [. . .] military resistance of Māori [. . .] would excuse the large scale and indiscriminate confiscation of land.'[95] Curnow inverts this heroic image, reducing Bracken's 'wild untutored chivalry' to 'an / Unangry death without fight', not to deplore the event, however, but to downsize an earlier language of nation. On subsequent reflection, he may have deemed the gesture too bare-faced; in any case, he rewrote the second of these stanzas at a later date.[96] But in 1939 these lines are in keeping with a treatment of colonial history, not as atrocious, but simply as feeble.

'islanders / All'

> Now all the history that did not happen
> Begins, and stings like an unfrozen wound [. . .][97]

This couplet from Curnow's sonnet 'To M.H. Holcroft' revisits that most pivotal of critical nationalist topoi, the belated encounter with 'where we lie' which should have, but has not yet, taken place. In the wartime context of *Sailing or Drowning* (1943), however, these lines take on a more specific resonance. The next line records that 'beaches are barbed'; it's the war that is making this history awaken, a war that has now moved into the Pacific, reviving the memory of earlier conflicts, no longer so readily diminished or disavowed. An insistent point of reference throughout the volume is *Macbeth*. From here comes an epigraph for 'Pantoum of War in the Pacific', the gilt/guilt pun in 'Rite of Spring', and in 'The Navigators' a running motif of bloody hands that will not wash clean. Discernible now on the Pacific horizon is a postcolonial sense of guilt that begins to anticipate the more candid version familiar from a much later era of Pākehā self-criticism.

But while this disavowed encounter is starting to press more painfully, the settler nationalist project still demands that it be contained. In Curnow's verse the immediate effect appears to be a change of tactics; with this wartime awakening comes a cautious cross-cultural identification. In a common environment, beset by a common peril—'Always to islanders danger / Is what comes over the sea'[98]—successive waves of Pacific settlers begin to shed their differences: 'Surf is a partial deafness islanders / All suffer from, committed to the land.'[99] Curnow will never venture as far down this path of identification as Brasch does in his war book, *Disputed Ground* (1948): 'The earth holds them [. . .] their unprotesting memory [. . .] surrounding us with perspective / Offering soil for our rootless behaviour.'[100] Nor will he follow Robin Hyde into a full-scale effort to imagine what it would feel like to be conquered. Consistently, though, in *Sailing or Drowning* universals like 'all' and 'always' invoke a shared, transhistorical experience.

The volume ends with a trio of sonnets, 'Attitudes for a New Zealand Poet'. The first reflects on how far the poet has come from the satirical stance of a poem like 'New Zealand City', or even from *Not in Narrow Seas*:

That part of you the world offended so
Has atrophied, or else your strategy
Has changed, or else you have so much to do
The simplest way is seeming to agree.

The falling cities, bones and brutal sky,
And Eliot cactuses do not recur.
Now, it is not an easy question why
You were ashamed that things were as they were.[101]

These lines appear to resile, not just from the modernist décor that we observed earlier, but from the (self-)excoriating tone that went with it. The urge to try to kick-start the culture by shaming it is apparently receding. In the meantime, however, in the third and most familiar of these poems, reconciliation with 'things as they [are]' competes with an earlier language of censure and belittlement.

The Skeleton of the Great Moa in the Canterbury Museum, Christchurch

The skeleton of the moa on iron crutches
Broods over no great waste; a private swamp
Was where this tree grew feathers once, that hatches
Its dusty clutch, and guards them from the damp.

Interesting failure to adapt on islands,
Taller but not more fallen than I, who come
Bone to his bone, peculiarly New Zealand's.
The eyes of children flicker round this tomb

Under the skylights, wonder at the huge egg
Found in a thousand pieces, pieced together
But with less patience than the bones that dug
In time deep shelter against ocean weather:

Not I, some child, born in a marvellous year,
Will learn the trick of standing upright here.[102]

This version of the poem (the one we all know) contains one minor change from the original; in *Sailing or Drowning* the second line begins with a nod to Eliot, 'Figures in no waste land'.[103] However, even without the explicit allusion, we know we're back among the 'bones [. . .] / And Eliot cactuses.' The stress once again is on historical diminishment: the 'private swamp' on which the city is built is neither the 'great waste [land]' of European culture nor the better Britain of Wakefield's planned settlement. And in the famous peroration a delusional 'elasticity of pride' is stood on its head—Antipodean—in this *locus classicus* of the nationalist anti-self. If Curnow is taking leave of this 'attitude', he is certainly not apologising for it. With its model of a reconciled, acclimatised subject built on the model of this gigantic local 'failure', the poem reads instead as a belated 'anti' climax to his pursuit of settler identity through self-abasement and critical severity.

It also gives us *Sailing or Drowning*'s last word on the wartime effort to refashion the settler as a Polynesian 'islander'. The early years of the war had seen dramatic events in moa archaeology. The 'huge egg / [. . .] pieced together' was recovered from the Pyramid Valley site in North Canterbury.[104] Discovered in 1938, and excavated over the next three years, Pyramid Valley would prove the greatest of those 'swampy deathtraps' which to date had given moa science its richest resources.[105] While the Canterbury Museum were digging at Pyramid Valley, researchers from the Otago Museum were working at the Waitaki River Mouth, excavating a hunting camp at which it is now estimated as many as 100,000 moa may have been butchered and processed.[106] That humans had hunted and eaten moa had been known since Europeans first arrived. But the issue, often hotly contested, was precisely who these people had been. Were they forbears of modern Māori? Or were they, as German geologist Julius von Haast had insisted, an ancient ('Palaeolithic') group who had disappeared along with the birds themselves? It was Haast who coined the term 'Moa Hunter', and the idea had never gone away. But then, in 1939, in what Quinn Berentson calls 'the greatest archaeological discovery in New Zealand history',[107] came the find that would answer the question definitively. At the mouth of the Wairau River, near Blenheim, digging with his father's potato fork, 13-year-old schoolboy Jim Eyles unearthed the country's earliest known burial site. It was immediately apparent that the people of the Wairau Bar had hunted moa. And the detailed archaeology that followed would finally establish beyond doubt that they were the forbears of contemporary Māori.[108]

Moa bones were in the news. But the real news, from the Waitaki River Mouth, and even more from the Wairau Bar, was less about the bird than about its fate at the hands of the people who hunted it. To talk about the moa's 'failure to adapt' in terms of bird versus swamp, bird versus Nature, or bird versus island geography—and to identify in the process as indigenised islander ('Bone to his bone, peculiarly New Zealand's')—by Curnow's standards seems oddly obtuse. For once, the poem doesn't so much finesse the presence of Māori as elide it, or, better, *repress* it. And so, inevitably, what the poem doesn't want to know about 'returns'. We can hear it, for example, in that potent word *fallen*. While Curnow may have abandoned the Church, he hasn't lost his sense of foundational sin. The legacy of conquest weighs down the settler as surely as the knowledge of 'man's first disobedience'. Specifically it weighs on the poem's voice; it insists in the downtrodden tone, the abject 'attitude'. Most of all, though, it resurfaces in the space that Curnow clears with his favourite tense: conquest returns from the Other, from the 'as yet', a knowledge that shadows the disabled settler subject. What it means to fail, what it means to have standing, what it means to see history the right way up: these are all questions that the poem's 'Not I' hands over to the future, as it crosses itself out.

Blushes

Curnow is not an easy writer to love. I'm reporting here on my own feelings—my intuitive, affective response to his work—but also returning to a theme I broached earlier: how difficult I've found it to get his virtues across to others. He's gnarly and often difficult. He offers no help in the way of personal charm. He is frequently harsh, sometimes cruel, sometimes defensive, almost never confiding. But recently, the more time I spend with his work the more I find myself rehearsing gestures of praise and gratitude. Behind this lies the pleasure I've had in trying to tease out the nuances of his modernism and his nationalism. There is also a sense of regret, of compunction: like many, I now see, I have been guilty of underestimating him.

Over many years I have done my best to teach Curnow to undergraduates. He is, after all, the most articulate member of our most influential generation of writers. And yet I wonder now if his nationalist position was ever really 'teachable'—or is it simply too crafty, and too historically contingent, to be broken down in the classroom without reducing it to near-parody? In any case, I can see that it has defeated me, and that I have never managed to get across the subtlety of his mid-century project. In particular, I know that I have caricatured what I have sometimes called (inelegantly) his 'Pākehā-centrism.' I belong to a generation for whom this issue has been defining; we have spent a great deal of energy summoning settler writing to the bar of postcolonial justice. My mistake, it seems to me now, has not been in identifying the monoculturalism of mid-century nationalism—it *is* a monocultural endeavour—but in imagining that Curnow would be surprised:

> After all re-ordering of old elements
> Time trips up all but the humblest of heart
> Stumbling after the fire, not in the smoke of events;
> For many are called, but many are left at the start [. . .][109]

There's a wonderful passage in *The Pleasure of the Text* where Barthes describes what he calls the 'blush' of ideology. There is no text, says Barthes, that is not in some way coloured by it (adding with a characteristic flourish, that 'only Mallarmé, perhaps, is master of his skin').[110] Curnow has embarrassing moments, without doubt, particularly in relation to gender. But when it comes to negotiating settler conquest, I fail to see how we could ask much more. The problem was literally insuperable. No one could offer, in the same moment, a programme for a settler nationalism *and* a full and final reckoning with colonial rapacity. I have argued, then, that Curnow doesn't confront the problem so much as *finesse* it: he tables it, names it, and endeavours to keep moving, but always in the knowledge that it isn't going away. Today when I read Curnow's work, and the poems in particular, it seems to me outstandingly aware of what the future has in mind for it. His fallen settler nation comes already freighted with the knowledge of why, as surely as the moa, inevitably it is going to find itself on the wrong side of history. It's the same understanding that, in the most civic-minded poem that Curnow ever wrote, 'Landfall in Unknown Seas', informs his own indelible trope for the blush of ideology in its local and special form. He calls it: 'The stain of blood that writes an island story'.[111]

Chapter 5

Taking poetry seriously?

Manliness in Fairburn and Glover

'poetry for ladies'

When Joyce read *The Waste Land* in 1923 he applauded it in the language of the day: 'T.S. Eliot ends idea of poetry for ladies.'[1] It's a notebook entry, but the signs are not private. Any literary reader would have known what he meant: indeed, the remark has become notorious because it crystallises so much of its high modernist moment. Joyce greets the poem as a mortal blow in a contest over literary values—a contest in which the terms are ineradicably gendered. He doesn't mean that Eliot ends writing by women (or even by upper-class women: ladies as opposed to gentlemen). He is alluding, rather, to a constellation of literary vices which the period associates so strongly with femininity that a gendered shorthand can denote the entire complex.

The history of 20th-century poetry begins with a moment of radical compaction. Ezra Pound's manifesto essays of the period 1910–15 are the most influential documents in poetic theory since the heyday of Romanticism, and like the Big Bang the resulting explosion continues to send ripples through the farthest reaches of the poetic cosmos. The imagist precepts that Pound lays down—'Go in fear of abstractions', 'Direct treatment of the "thing"', 'Use no superfluous word', 'compose in the sequence of the musical phrase, not in sequence of a metronome', and so on—formalise an ideal of density and economy that will become the default tuning of 20th-century verse.[2] From the outset this minimalist rhetoric is incipiently gendered. One of Pound's choicest pejoratives is 'flaccid'. The poetry he's looking for will be—well—the opposite. Poetry needs to harden up. It needs to be 'difficult', as Eliot insisted, to address the complexity of 20th-century life. It also needs to become more disciplined—compact and lean, like a well-drilled masculine body:

> As to Twentieth Century poetry [. . .] it will be harder and saner, it will be [. . .] 'nearer the bone'. It will be as much like granite as it can be [. . .] austere, direct, free of emotional slither.[3]

In terms of Pound's career, and of modernism's, this is only a passing moment: there's the minimalist Pound ('In a Station of the Metro'), and the maximalist (*The Cantos*). But this initial compression will resound with such force that everything that follows in Anglophone poetry will come to read either as an endorsement of, or a departure from, these initial settings. Anything that ignores them entirely simply doesn't sound 'modern'. And so the modernist moment writes into the century's poetics a gendering of aesthetic values according to which the only way a poet can sound modern will be to sound masculine.

No surprises here, of course, for any reader versed in New Zealand's mid-century nationalism. Curnow would speak later of the impact of Eliot and Pound as he discovered them in the early 1930s.[4] There is also his reference of 1937 to modern English poetry as a 'technical research laboratory'. Pound, as I've said, would have loved this metaphor ('Consider the way of the scientists rather than the way of an advertising agent for a new soap').[5] And it's evident that at some stage in his early adulthood Curnow took on board the manifesto essays of the imagist period. Whether it's flagellating the Victorians, sneering at hobbyists, outlawing rhetoric and ornament, or insisting on precision, economy and density, there is so much in Curnow that sounds like Pound that one gets the impression of a language that has been completely internalised. 'Jejune poeticalities', 'lazy verbal flourishes', 'literary swathings', 'booksy vulgarity': any of these wounding phrases could be Pound's; in fact they're all Curnow's.[6] Or again, when Curnow complains of a 'degraded aestheticism' informed by 'no inward or outward fact of experience', the echo of Pound's '"thing", whether subjective or objective' intimates how closely Curnow's 'actuality' tracks Pound's insistence on concrete data.[7] Inevitably, then, Curnow's aesthetic discriminations are gender-coded in the same way as the original article. There's nothing especially occult about this; it can be as obvious as an admiration for 'the masculine erudition of Stevens'[8] or a contempt for a colonial manner that sounds like 'the voice of Alfred Lord Tennyson, thinned and grown womanish'.[9] But it also informs, more subtly, a host of other evaluative distinctions—dramatic/theatrical, seriousness/whimsy, toughness/self-flattery, intensity/archness, actuality/substitution, confrontation/evasion, discipline/impulsiveness, adult/child—where in every case it becomes as easy to identify the feminine-coded term as to identify the negative one.

As Joyce salutes Eliot, then, Charles Brasch will duly salute Curnow. The 'hard frost' of the Caxton anthology does precisely the same job that Joyce ascribes to *The Waste Land*. As Eliot had finished off 'poetry for ladies', Curnow's anthology 'killed off weeds'—where what constitutes a 'weed', and what characterises the 'sound growth' promoted by its extermination, are explicit in the governing terms of the metaphor. A reinvigorated New Zealand poetry will lean towards *hardness* in all its senses: difficulty, severity, and, to use an ugly but wholly apposite term, phallicism. It's writing that will aspire to a kind of crystalline (frosty) clarity, with a geographical slant, and likely as not a South Island one. There will be a strong, residual pastoralism. There will also be a code of emotional restraint: nationalist poetics will be not only rigid but in large measure *frigid*.

The conditions that, as we saw in Chapter 3, would prove so hostile to women writers between the world wars, implied something different entirely for their male contemporaries. The advantages they experienced appear self-evident. The nationalist paradigm was forged by men, who wrote according to its parameters, were validated by it and have continued to be valued in light of it. At the centre of this chapter are the two male poets who most explicitly illustrate this argument. The canonical profiles of Glover and Fairburn rest on bodies of work that in each case are slender and uneven; but they wrote the kinds of poems that the moment made possible, and in the fantasmatic economy of literary reputation they have been richly rewarded. By any obvious reckoning the situation is unfair, as the belated restitution of Robin Hyde's critical status helps to remind us. And yet it's wrong to assume that, as blokes, they enjoyed nothing but an armchair ride. They too were subject to the severity of the mid-century climate. They too could have their tender tips burned by the frost. Difficult though it is to keep sight of this—swept up as we so readily are in the zeal of retrospective equity—the poetic testimony of these mid-century hard men is also a record of shame, inhibition and self-censorship. The small amount of fully achieved verse that survives was produced out of complex emotional pressures. Beyond doubt their fame is the privileged effect of an era of gung-ho masculinism. But their work also reads as the record of a struggle with a structure of feeling, only partly of their own making, and hostile to much of what made them think and feel like poets.

Modernism on the Left

Whatever Curnow did for New Zealand literature, he didn't do it by himself. Critical nationalism was a team effort, and while Curnow provided the intellectual backbone, the establishment of the Caxton brand was the work of a formidable alliance. Neither Fairburn nor Glover would prove in the end to be Curnow's equal as a poet. And as thinkers about literature and history they were not in his league. But in their own way they were almost as crucial to the movement's impact as Curnow himself. I'm not speaking here of Glover's printing and publishing, instrumental though these were.[10] My concern is with what I will call, provisionally, Glover and Fairburn's 'populism'. Modernist severity was good for many things, but it didn't foster the mood of inclusiveness that a nationalist discourse demanded. Modernism tends to be individualistic, indeed atomistic: its default subject position is an isolated and alienated first-person singular, visiting its (often disdainful) analysis on a culture that the writer stands outside of and above. If this can be described as a *vertical* position, nationalism calls for a *horizontal* feeling: collectivist, demotic, audience-friendly. Whitman writes in the first-person singular, but his 'Song' proposes to speak for everyone: 'what I assume you shall assume, / For every atom belonging to me as good belongs to you.'[11] Curnow's literary voice extends no such invitation. It doesn't try to get alongside us and elaborate its 'I' into a convivial 'we'. The astringency of Curnow's thought left a gap between the movement and its imaginary constituency, a divide that Curnow could not surmount on his own. The impulse needed reinforcement from writers who had worked their way through recent British literature on a different trajectory.

A convention has arisen that treats 1922 as the official high-water mark of Anglophone modernism: the year of *The Waste Land* and Joyce's *Ulysses*, of *Bliss and Other Stories* and of Woolf's first experimental novel, *Jacob's Room*. If the Caxton group's most dynamic moment is around the beginning of World War II (say, 1939–41), then almost 20 years (a literary generation) separates the high point of modernism from the equivalent phase of literary nationalism. To put this another way, what lay between them was the European history of the period between the wars: the Depression, the rise of fascism, the emergence of the Popular Front, the Spanish Civil War (1936–39). At the same time a new wave of British writers were processing these events in Europe as they happened. The so-called 'Auden generation' were the same age as Curnow, Fairburn and Glover; the New Zealanders, however, were not strictly their poetic contemporaries, being thrown out of sync by the delayed (and diluted) impact here of first-generation modernism. Auden, for instance, had first encountered Eliot's work in 1926 and been immediately overwhelmed. Curnow, as we've seen, went through his major engagement with Eliot perhaps a decade later. In the interim, Britain had begun to feel the impact of writers Curnow's own age—writers who had dealt at first hand not just with modernism but with what came immediately on its heels: Eliot's conversion to Anglicanism in 1927 and the volume which marks it, *Ash Wednesday* (1930);

and Pound's disastrous lurch to the Right (he first met Mussolini in 1933). In New Zealand, then, writers of the same generation faced 'results' coming out of the 'technical research laboratory' faster than any single writer could process them. While Eliot and Pound remained largely unassimilated, there was now a left-wing reaction to be integrated as well: the rise of the MacSpaunday group, and Auden's move leftwards and away from Eliot (from about 1930); the two Michael Roberts anthologies, *New Signatures* (1932) and *New Country* (1933); the creation of the Left Book Club (1936); Orwell's *The Road to Wigan Pier* (1937); MacNiece's *Autumn Journal* (1939); and so on. In this sense the Caxton writers' British contemporaries were half a generation ahead.

Confusing as this must have felt, it played out to the nationalists' advantage. As they processed two successive waves of change, the Caxton poets took inspiration from both. Critical nationalism, in other words, is a hybrid of modernist hieratics and 30s left-vernacularism. It makes for a difficult formation to see clearly, because jostling together in it are two antithetical impulses. The forms that Left writing took in New Zealand in this period have been explored in definitive style by Rachel Barrowman in *A Popular Vision*. My own focus here is the yoking of that radical discourse to an inchoate modernism. This is where Glover and Fairburn become crucial. Not that either was a dedicated servant of the Left in the manner of, say, Mason or Winston Rhodes. But the socialist turn in 30s writing sat with them better than did the mandarin tones of high modernism. Each had a no-nonsense, populist streak—in literary terms, at least, a kind of common touch. And together they, along with Frank Sargeson, would help to ground the nationalist movement in a version of literary populism.

In some ways it might seem a tenuous confederacy. Curnow's intellectual severity is a long way from anything in Glover,

Fairburn or Sargeson. Privately, Sargeson would admit that Curnow's cerebral qualities intimidated him.[12] Fairburn and Glover were both in sympathy with objections to modernism that were being heard in Britain—from Michael Roberts, for example, in *New Country*, demanding that poetry 'clear itself from the complexity and introspection, the doubt and cynicism of recent years.'[13] It was either Glover or Winston Rhodes who wrote in a foreword to *Verse Alive* in 1937, 'Poetry has failed because it has become too detached, too remote from the interests of the people.'[14] Fairburn, after flirting superficially with modernist poetics, would gradually reject not only Pound and Eliot but also Joyce, Proust, Stevens and, for good measure, Picasso (Fairburn's hostility to abstract painting—including McCahon—would be unrelenting). Between them, indeed, Fairburn and Glover introduce an element of anti-intellectualism: ingratiating, perhaps, to a middlebrow audience, but an unlikely fit with the elevated tone of Curnow.

Marching under the nationalist banner, then, are quite divergent literary temperaments. Yet they share not only the challenge of the local but a hefty investment in the discourse of masculinity.[15] While the 30s sees a backlash against the more recondite aspects of modernism—formalism, abstraction, gratuitous difficulty—other forms of 'hardness' persist unchallenged. In fact the masculine orientation of the modernists will, if anything, be exaggerated. Modernism's heroics of risk—where risk was a purely formal proposition (the 'dangerous' work of avant-garde experiment)—is supplanted in the 30s by more literal, more obvious instantiations: war reporting, fighting fascism, or, if you're Hemingway, game-hunting, boxing and bull-fighting. Hemingway, of course, is the archetype of this 30s modulation. Though in terms of strict chronology he's an intermediary figure—born in the 19th century and publishing his most important work in the late

20s—with his minimalistic prose, his obsessive masculinity, and the seamless mesh of one with the other, he represents the template of 30s literary machismo. For the values consigned to history in Joyce's reading of Eliot—embellishment, luxuriousness, periphrasis, sentiment: anything 'soft' or 'Victorian' or 'ladylike'—there will be no chance of a comeback, in Hemingway any more than in Curnow. Even as the new decade retreats from high modernism, it distils and refines the incipient manliness of modernist aesthetics. And just as that masculine emphasis mediates between two generations of 'moderns', so too does it help to reconcile contending priorities within nationalism itself, informing Curnow's intellectualism as surely as it does the vernacular flag-waving of Glover, Fairburn and Sargeson.

Reality is sexual

Of the nationalist hard core, no one cares less about the doctrine of 'making it new' than Glover.[16] While he certainly engages with the Auden group, and particularly with Cecil Day Lewis,[17] to the mystique of Pound and Eliot he appears quite indifferent. He owes more not just to the Georgians but to the then-unfashionable 18th century. Part 30s truth-teller, part Augustan wit, Glover is no one's idea of a modernist. And yet, riding the groundswell of modern masculinity, even Glover can find common cause with early Pound.

Pound's 12-line lyric 'The Garden' was published on the eve of the World War I.[18] The poem describes a woman of the upper social orders wandering in Kensington Gardens. The embodiment of fag-end class inanition ('In her is the end of breeding'), she is said to be 'dying piece-meal / of a sort of emotional anaemia.' In Edwardian terms she would be described as 'neurasthenic'; she is so out of touch with her physicality that, as always in this gendered scenario, the speaker understands it better than she does. She would like to be approached, and yet fears to be approached ('is almost afraid that I / will commit that indiscretion'). Meanwhile, human life swarms around her in the form of the 'unkillable' vitality of the poor. Were she not so bloodless, she would be able to respond: to her social environment, as to her own sexuality. Instead she remains cut off from both, adrift in her enervated unreality.

A poem by Glover from 1941 could almost be a rewrite of Pound's.

A Woman Shopping

Beauty goes into the butcher's shop
Where blood taints the air;
The chopper comes down on the block
And she pats her hair.

Death's gallery hangs ready
Naked of hair and hide,
But she has clothes on her body
And a heart inside.

What's death to the lady, pray?
Even shopping's a bore.
—The carcases sway gently
As she goes out the door.

But death goes with her on the way:
In her basket along the street
Rolls heavily against her thigh
The blood-red bud of the meat.[19]

Here, too, the woman at the centre of the poem is insulated from the world around her—in this case, the gory reality that underwrites her consumerism. Again, in her unseeingness she is subject to the deeper perceptions of the poet-speaker. The poet's is a kind of X-ray vision. He *sees through* her, almost in a physical sense: sees through her basket, and by extension through her clothes, laying bare those 'facts of life' that the woman-as-shopper prefers to ignore. From Pound's Kensington to Glover's local High Street, the class implications have been diluted. But the gender dynamics of the scenario have, if anything, been amplified. The confrontation now is more sexually aggressive, the poet's gaze more salaciously knowing. While the 'truth' to be confronted is ostensibly mortality, the grisly double entendre presents it in the shape of the woman's 'sex'.

So, when Glover was writing this unlovely poem, was he actively aware of 'The Garden' as a precursor? Or is it no more than an unpleasant accident that Glover's *red meat* rhymes so neatly with Pound's 'emotional anaemia'? To me, the best answer lies somewhere in between. I doubt that Glover is consciously in dialogue with Pound; the connection doesn't fit with either his reading or his literary temperament. Instead, I would argue that the synchrony between them arises out of a shared idea, a deep and pervasive modern assumption about the matrix of knowledge, gender and sex. It is this that allows them to speak man to man, avant-gardist to curmudgeonly Georgian.

There is a moment in the 1960 Penguin introduction when Curnow, bemoaning 'the shadow-show of a poetry' that flourished towards the end of the 19th century, fixes on Anne Glenny Wilson's *Themes and Variations* (1889). Wilson's verses, Curnow writes, are 'effusions decocted from a variety of Victorian spillings; the chaste Muse of the Albums unviolated by any touch of the actual and the colonial.'[20] By now I expect we know this territory well enough to recognise that this is not simply an 'unfortunate' metaphor. In fact the gender semantics get nastier the more closely we look at them. On the one hand, we have (female) chastity; on the other, colonial reality. According to this logic, the looked-for confrontation with 'the actual' inevitably implies sexual 'violat[ion]'. It's an ugly formulation but it isn't exactly new. What we hear Curnow channelling—and the same precept informs both 'The Garden' and 'A Woman Shopping'—is that fundamental modernist belief whose emergence we traced in Chapter 3: reality is sexual, and women must accept that reality.

As the 1920s give way to the 1930s, as Eliot turns to God and Pound turns to fascism, there are facets of the modernist adventure that begin to shed their lustre. Modernist sexuality, however, is not one of them; on the contrary, it becomes more embedded, more explicit, more extreme. And it helps to hold the Caxton project together: an aggravated heterosexualism that mediates between two generations of 'moderns' (Pound and Glover), as it does between different voicings of literary nationalism (Glover and Curnow). We are dealing, of course, with a structure of feeling in which women have no speaking part. Sexual modernism constitutes women as objects of heterosexual knowledge; it enlists them in a discourse, exchanged between men, in the service of masculine homosociality. As if there were no other way to be real, women are force-fed the truth of their own sex. What it means for women to try to *write* from such a place is the melancholy story of the chapter after this one.

Demotic speech and settlement

Meanwhile, back in the public bar, it was Wordsworth who warned in the preface to *Lyrical Ballads* that his readers would find 'little of what is usually called poetic diction.' His object, he claimed, was to write 'as far as was possible, in a selection of language really used by men.'[21] On this question of 'real' or 'actual' language Pound strikes an almost identical note: 'Poetry must be *as well written as prose* [. . .] departing in no way from speech save by a heightened intensity (i.e. simplicity). There must be no book words, no periphrases, no inversions [. . .] nothing that you couldn't, in some circumstance, in the stress of some emotion, actually say'.[22] Consciously or otherwise, he must have had Wordsworth in mind ('Read as much of Wordsworth as does not seem too unutterably dull', is his backhanded compliment in 'A Few Don'ts').[23] But this vernacular impulse—the wish to bring poetry closer to spoken language—has been around for as long as there have been poets to jockey for position. Because ordinary language keeps evolving, and because no poetry can ever fully and finally evacuate the 'literary', the urge continually renews itself and lends itself to new strategic functions. For Pound it translates into a modernist imperative: less aesthetic baffling to 'imped[e] the shock and stroke of it.'[24] In Whitman, on the other hand, the same demotic imperative takes a nationalist turn. To jettison Old World literary norms, argues Whitman, is to repudiate the class relations from which they sprang: 'monarchies [and] priestly conventions [. . .] notions of gentlemen and ladies, founded on the idea of caste.'[25] For the settler nation to assert its difference, its writing has to embrace the kind of scaled-down aesthetic properties that affirm a non-hierarchical culture. In Whitman, then, poetic form and language are answerable to America's democratic experiment. And this, with appropriate local variations, is an argument that will translate through all settler literatures. If Jack is to be as good as his master—and few beliefs are more fundamental to New World ideology—then Jack's language needs to be good enough for poetry.

For New Zealand writers of the 1930s the vernacular imperative comes doubly determined. When Holcroft complains of an 'undigested Marxism [that] lurks in the minds of our younger poets' and of the way in which their British contemporaries have 'infected [them] with a desire to write tenderly of the working man,' he identifies fairly (for all his condescension) a major international vogue.[26] From James T. Farrell to George Orwell to Xavier Herbert and Jean Devanny, the decade of the Depression and the Left Book Club marks a high point for what is ambiguously called 'proletarian literature'. Curnow will object that the impact has been overstated, defending Glover against Eric McCormick's charge of writing 'facile tributes to the proletariat'.[27] But however judiciously Glover and others may have filtered the international groundswell, they could hardly be unaffected by it. In fact, contrary to all those other indications that made an inter-war nationalism feel so 'untimely', 30s proletarianism ran in its favour. The working-class subjects and vernacular language mandated by the literary Left required only a slight local recalibration to meet the Whitmanesque demands that come with New World egalitarianism.

Of course a working-class or vernacular literature was never a proposition to be taken too literally. It was one thing to endorse the experiences and language of 'ordinary' people, but another thing entirely to engage them in the outcome. Mason discovered as much in 1936–37 when the People's Theatre group that he had been instrumental in organising took Clifford Odets's *Waiting for Lefty* out into the heartland. Barrowman records that in suburban Avondale, and again in Hamilton, the audiences stayed away; but in the coal-mining stronghold of Huntly they showed up in droves—only to take umbrage at what the *New Zealand Herald* labelled the play's 'foul and blasphemous' dialogue. As a local observer put it, 'They don't like their own language thrown back at them.'[28] We shouldn't make too much of this incident, however: it doesn't so much negate the vernacular impulse as clarify its proper, which is to say strictly formal, scope. The demotic aspirations of nationalist writing were never about the audience it gestured vaguely towards reaching. As the volumes that rolled off the Caxton Press made clear—small editions, beautifully made—it was literary writing, for literary people. Its vernacular inflections, in form, language and subject matter, were a means by which it telegraphed, to a middle-class audience, the particular kind of 'imagined community' that it favoured.

Large as life

To defer to what Wordsworth called 'common' life was in keeping with the horizontal difference of the New World. It was a complex imperative, but it was rendered more approachable by a nationalist imaginary that for 'common' read 'masculine'. For a start, you could learn from Hemingway and Pound. With their terse, no-nonsense minimalism, they showed how to tone things down, and in masculine terms; if ordinary men wrote literature, this was what they'd sound like. When Fairburn, in a letter to Curnow, extols a poetry of 'brains, bile, guts', he plainly imagines that this is the way that real men talk about real things.[29] When Curnow concedes that Glover 'sometimes misses his point through a ruthless flattening of diction',[30] we scarcely hear it as criticism. We know that Glover's only fault has been to take a good idea too far, that 'ruthless' is a term of approbation, and that 'flattening of diction' is a sure indication of a poet in tune with egalitarian New World ideals.

But a hard-bitten literary language was not the whole

story. In 1947, when Fairburn visited the South Island for the first time, Curnow greeted the occasion with a tribute in the Christchurch *Press*:

> More than any other New Zealand poet, Mr Fairburn has value for what he is, as much as for what he writes [. . .] His apprenticeship included Rugby football, tournament golf, and a Byronic delight in sea swimming [. . .] His painting is more than a hobby. His audiences here [. . .] will see a man some inches more than six feet tall, wearing his forty-three years as lightly as twenty-one, a poet quite as large as life.[31]

It hardly ought to matter that he's more than six feet tall, and yet plainly it does. As Jensen has shown, the endorsement of popular norms is expressed as indelibly in the nationalist *habitus* as in anything that Glover, Fairburn or Mulgan actually wrote.[32] Their repertoire of manly behaviours—drinking, war service, boxing, breeding, gardening, shabby old clothes and the rest—broadcasts a conception of writing indifferent to received ideas of what Whitman calls 'caste'. No pale loitering in salons and libraries, no 'slack, "poetry-loving" frame of mind'.[33] We can spot the acclimatised settler writer by his likeness to the ordinary New Zealand bloke.

And so the nationalist movement draws a supplementary dividend on the public personae of its war heroes, its marathon swimmers, its boozers; however, to buttress itself in this ad hominem way is not without cost. The anti-intellectualism of New Zealand culture has been detailed in subsequent commentary from at least as early as Bill Pearson's essay 'Fretful Sleepers' (1952).[34] 'Farmers,' Fairburn is supposed to have said, 'are the real intelligentsia of this country.'[35] It's reported speech, and the audience that heard it was a Taumarunui meeting of the Farmers' Union. But it's worth taking seriously all the same, because what the person who recorded it conveys to Fairburn's biographer is a sense of the poet's genuine esteem for his rural audience. Fairburn worked for the Farmers' Union for several years in the mid 1930s, travelling extensively through the upper North Island, attending meetings and taking minutes. He knew how his members thought and spoke; he respected them, and was at ease in their company. The ability to 'pass' in non-literary society was precious to Fairburn, as it was to the larger movement. And while it's plain enough that Fairburn's comment is tailored to his particular audience (he'd come without the minutes of the previous meeting and was trying to ad-lib his way out of trouble), there is also a sense in which nationalist writing is *always* shaped towards that audience. Not, once again, because that audience would read it, but rather because respect for that vernacular world was so fundamental to the movement's sense of the difference of settler culture. So whether or not Fairburn *really* thought of farmers as the nation's intellectuals, he would never, as a poet, write in a way that suggested otherwise. We are speaking, in other words, of a habit of self-censorship. It is the price for an assimilative tendency in literary nationalism, and one which New Zealand writers have spent a long time paying off.

It was all very well to be a real Kiwi joker. The more difficult thing was to stand tall *as a poet* at the same time. This is the challenge that Curnow (mistakenly) believed had been answered by Mason and Cresswell, insisting that '*because* they were poets' they were therefore 'responsible adult New Zealanders':

> This was new; it was 'taking poetry seriously' [. . .] The early work of both [. . .] committed the whole man to the poetry.[36]

As we saw in Chapter 2, this judgement means more as a statement of aspiration than as a statement of fact. Cresswell took poetry seriously and himself entirely too seriously with it. He 'committed the whole man' and he remained committed, but this says as much about his questionable sanity as about coming to terms with poetry in a 'responsible adult' way. Not only was Mason gifted, he was 'responsible' to a fault. Unfortunately, though, for Curnow and his narrative of progress, by the time he reached this judgement Mason had long ceased writing verse. Neither Fairburn nor Glover would fare much better. Neither could manage the trick of being a poet, and feeling manly, at the same time. In Fairburn's case we can detect this problem already, as Curnow does himself, between the lines of the latter's 1947 encomium. The poet may be a fine figure of a man, but that welter of extracurricular activities is at odds with the ideal of wholesale commitment. Curnow warns: 'It is not for all to follow, and a time for the example of seclusion and concentration may come—if it has not come already.'[37] But for Fairburn the warning already comes too late. Within a couple of years his career will be effectively over.

Fairburn and Glover are the mid-century poets who act out most plainly the pathology of self-conscious masculinity. In Glover's case, this dubious good fortune is also at the root of his singular distinction. Where the best of Glover's work becomes complex and affecting is where the poems internalise his own deep unease about poetry as a form of expressive behaviour. Glover's career will degenerate into alcoholic fiasco, but the pressures and insecurities on which his life appears to shipwreck are apprehended, at least intermittently, in terms that are genuinely poetic; they appear as an aesthetic dilemma, not just a personal one. In this sense, in my reading, Glover comes closer to writing the poems he is capable of. In Fairburn, however, the outcome is less fortunate. As the most warm-hearted of the nationalist poets, Fairburn suffers most from the era's masculine self-consciousness. Where Glover, on occasion, is able to combine his wit, his ear and the full scope of his emotional ambivalence, Fairburn tends to oscillate more wildly between a compromised Romanticism and a self-protective disdain for his own best qualities. He leaves behind just enough to show what was lost, and *how* it was lost, to the tyranny of nationalist self-censorship.

Self-strangulation

Fairburn's career begins in earnest with an iconic exercise in masculinist self-criticism. In the final piece from his debut volume, *He Shall Not Rise* (1930), the 26-year-old repudiates everything he has previously done—including the youthful poems that fill the rest of the book.

Rhyme of the Dead Self

Tonight I have taken all that I was
and strangled him that pale lily-white-lad
I have choked him with these my hands these claws
catching him as he lay a-dreaming in his bed.

Then chuckling I dragged out his foolish brains
that were full of pretty love-tales heighho the holly
and emptied them holus bolus to the drains
those dreams of love oh what ruinous folly.

He is dead pale youth and he shall not rise
on the third day or any other day
sloughed like a snakeskin there he lies
and he shall not trouble me again for aye.[38]

The poems that Fairburn is tearing up here belong, as Curnow puts it, to 'the pearly twilight of the newspaper versifiers'.[39] Fairburn even merits (and presumably must have accepted) inclusion in the anthology that the nationalists so loved to hate, Quentin Pope's *Kowhai Gold* (1930). Curnow, of course, applauds this emergence from the opalescent haze 'into broad New Zealand daylight'. But he also admits that such a complete apostasy of self is on the one hand inherently Romantic and, on the other, faintly implausible: in Curnow's words, 'it is romantically more than any man can say of himself'.[40] The repudiated self, as Curnow goes on to argue, is not really dead, but only 'chastened and changed'.[41] Like some virulent growth it will keep coming back and require to be strangled again and again, until ultimately the creative urge will wear itself out in the interior struggle.

It's not as if Fairburn doesn't talk tough, or that he sounds unconvinced when striking harsh and critical attitudes. His reputation as a literary hard man doesn't come from nowhere. His most durable monument, *Dominion* (1938), grows directly out of his experience of the Depression.[42] Returning from Britain in 1932, he found himself, like so many others, chipping weeds on a relief gang. While Fairburn coped with the experience, even reading his way through *Das Kapital* in the down times, he saw men he worked alongside literally destroyed by it, and the fury of the language directed at legislators and 'bureausites' dates back to these events.[43] The immediate scene of the Depression occupies the bitterly satirical opening section, 'Utopia'. The second section, 'Album Leaves', takes a longer view of New Zealand settlement, presenting a history less subtly argued but no less disenchanted or 'critical' than Curnow's.

At the time that Fairburn began writing the poem, in the lead up to the 1935 election, he was also speaking at public meetings against the Reform government of Gordon Coates. Not that he viewed the Labour administration that swept it from power as any great improvement. Fairburn's cause was Social Credit; he had met the movement's founder Major 'C.H.' Douglas in England (introduced by Mansfield's former publisher at the *New Age*, A.R. Orage), and returned to New Zealand an ardent convert. Inevitably Fairburn's complaints about 'usury' echo, as Curnow noted, the same sentiments in Pound (and specifically the famous Canto XXX).[44] Early readers also spotted, in the poem's assemblage of five discontinuous movements, a debt to the way that Eliot had—with Pound's decisive editorial help—managed the fractured materials of *The Waste Land.* Eliot in fact read *Dominion* at Faber, and although he rejected it, wrote encouragingly and claimed to have enjoyed it.[45] However, Fairburn is one of those 30s poets in whom what appear to be modernist sympathies are exaggerated by the rhetoric of masculinism. His demand for a poetry of 'brains, bile, guts' inevitably calls to mind Eliot in 'The Metaphysical Poets' where he tells us to look, not 'into our hearts', but 'into the cerebral cortex, the nervous system, the digestive tracts'.[46] When Glover published *Dominion* at Caxton, he bound it—out of necessity, but aptly—in brown butcher's wrapping paper.[47] And yet the visceral rhetoric is not all it seems. Certainly Fairburn attacks *gentility* wherever he encounters it, including in his own work. But gentility is not the same thing as Romanticism: it makes a much softer target, and it's here that Fairburn parts company with modernism.

For Curnow, the New Zealand 'condition' is a failure of recognition endemic to the project of settler translation. The object of, or incitement to, poetic inquiry is 'something different' that defeats expectation; it eluded the first settlers, and it continues to confuse their descendants, of whom the best that can be hoped is that they learn to look squarely and stoically at their fallen circumstances. For Fairburn, too, settlement is a kind of fall: 'Haven of hunger; landfall of hope; / goal of ambition, greed and despair.'[48] But it doesn't evacuate the settler present in the systematic way that it does in Curnow. The problems that preoccupy *Dominion* are either more immediate (bad economics) or more diffuse and metaphysical (alienation from Nature) than those that motivate Curnow's historical anti-myth. Potentially they can also be solved: in the first case, by visionary economics; in the second, through a renovated compact with 'earth'.

In its third movement, 'Elements', *Dominion* addresses the physical world.

> In the summer we rode in the clay country,
> the road before us trembling in the heat
> and on the warm wind the scent of tea-tree,
> grey and wind-bitten in winter, odorous under summer noon,
> with spurts of dust under the hoofs
> and a crackle of gorse on the wayside farms.
> At dusk the sun fell down in violet hills
> and evening came and we turned our horses
> homeward through dewy air.[49]

The sweetness of these New World memories ('O lovely time! when bliss was taken / as the bird takes nectar from the flower') is blackened by the fell breath of the Old: 'Smoke out of Europe, death blown / on the wind, and a cloak of darkness for the spirit.'[50] But the spiritual darkness can still be annealed in a return to Romantic first principles:

> Fairest earth,
> fount of life, giver of bodies,
> deep well of our delight, breath of desire,

> let us come to you
> barefoot, as befits love,
> as the boy to the trembling girl,
> as the child to the mother [. . .]
>
> Fair earth, we have broken our idols:
> and after the days of fire we shall come to you
> for the stones of a new temple.[51]

In Curnow, Arcadia is an error of perspective: an effect of laying the wrong kind of reading over the difference of the physical scene. But in Fairburn, it is the stuff of Wordsworthian memory, with a 'renovating virtue' that can still be appealed to even in the teeth of material calamity.

Fairburn could do, almost as vehemently as anyone, the language of masculine brutalism and nationalist asperity. And yet the main currents of modernism were alien to him, both emotionally and intellectually. Whatever *Dominion* owed to *The Waste Land*, Fairburn would duly repudiate Eliot, just as he would Stevens and Joyce. Of the influence of Eliot he would write in 1948, 'There seems to me to be a lack of vitality, an old-maidishness, a too insistently scholarly attitude, and a whole lot of straightout damned obscurity.'[52] More to the point still is an undated notebook entry:

> What a blight has fallen over this literary age in Britain! Its presiding genius, T.S. Eliot, has never, so far as one knows, written a love poem.[53]

For Fairburn, Romantic that he is, the second cardinal remedy for the depredations of modernity is—alongside Nature—'the brief eternity of the flesh'.[54] Fairburn's love poems are among the least apologetic anywhere in our verse before the 1970s. It's notable, however, how often his lovers are shown in a state of siege, as in 'To Daphnis and Chloe in the Park':

> You have desired each other among crowds
> lost in a blackened forest of voices
> and a glance or a whispered word
> has transfigured that desolation.
> You have dreamed yourselves alone in the world
> coming to each other singing,
> under the sun's carnal eye, the great hot flower
> burning in the azure negation,
> over mountains bright with the blood of spring
> and all time and creation
> ripening to that moment of delirium
>   *but you're going to get hurt.*[55]

At a first approach, the causes of unease are quite conventional: a surrounding context of envy and small-mindedness, a recognition of time and mortality. And the note of furtiveness need not surprise us in a poet habitually unfaithful in his own marriage. But I can't help but wonder if there's something else, too, that says less about the fear of getting caught, or about puritanism, than it does about the strictures of the hard frost.

Fairburn wrote more and better love poems than any male poet of the 30s and 40s—which is not saying much, since they're almost the *only* love poems of that frigid era. The 'presiding genius', Curnow, was almost as niggardly with his love poems as Eliot was.[56] There's a scattering in Glover, but his most sustained (though not especially successful) efforts come much later, as do a small number of poems by Brasch. More telling is Glover's verdict from 'Polonius's Advice to a Poet', a stanza quoted approvingly by Curnow in his 1981 introduction to Glover's *Selected Poems*:

Love poems if you like. But keep them short.
It's all *vieux jeu*, unless you're crude and stark.
She won't, we needn't, read them. Sport,
Tell her you love her, and tell her in the dark.[57]

Fairburn might have laughed at the boyish joke (for 'tell her in the dark', read *actions speak louder than words*), but what could he possibly have made of the sentiment? It's hard to imagine a more direct rebuke to the fervent, al fresco eroticism ('under the sun's carnal eye') of Daphnis and Chloe.

The poems for which Fairburn is remembered today date from a period of about 15 years: say, from 1935, when he began *Dominion*, to 1949 ('To a Friend in the Wilderness'). There's enough there to prove that he was, at his best, the most ebullient poet of his generation—and yet little enough to show that something went wrong, that a barrier came down between the writer and the expansive corpus that it was in him to have written. Instead we are left with the surrounding rubble: the squibs and epigrams and *jeux d'esprit*, the frivolous broadsides, the endless disputation that was enough to draw a veiled rebuke even from Glover;[58] and beyond that again, the genuinely ugly things—the confused, belligerent writing on women; the damaging and disfiguring homophobia. It's easy to think of Fairburn as a self-defeated poet. And yet, what beats him—strangles him—is not himself, but the internalised prohibitions of the frosty mid century. While Fairburn exemplifies nationalist masculinity, in certain respects he also contravenes its strictures. Hard-mouthed, bloke-ish, argumentative, he can also be exuberant and gregarious—a lover (however fecklessly) of women, an extravagant enthusiast for family and children. He is the poet who sees the ponga as 'the shape of a coiled spring':[59] a poet of energies, a vitalist. His biographer, Denys Trussell, records how in a fit of exuberance Fairburn once shoved Clifton Firth's head through the ceiling.[60] But he also observes that as performer of his own poetry he was reticent and 'strangely inept',[61] and that the same inhibition extended to any discussion of his serious work. Public nudity wasn't a problem—he couldn't be relied on not to open the door naked—but to play the public role of the serious poet evidently was more intimidating.

In recent times, Fairburn's homophobia has probably received as much notice as his poems. It has angered critics looking back from the point of view of today's sexual mores; it has also confounded those who loved him most, and who have struggled to reconcile it with their feelings for someone they valued for his warmth and conviviality.[62] Sadly for the small North Shore literary community, it destroyed his relationship with Sargeson. In my view, it also undermined his creativity.

Glover and Geoffrey Fairburn (younger brother of Rex) did the poet no favours with their posthumous edition of his prose writings. *The Woman Problem* takes its title from an essay of 1947. Fairburn himself never published the piece—an unlovely stew of misogyny and homophobia—and anyone who first comes across him in this guise is unlikely ever to get as far as reading his verse. The essay, however, does at least offer an insight into the way in which his homophobia compromised his poetry. The year 1947 brought the establishment of the State Literary Fund. Fairburn thoroughly disapproved. He argued instead for an organicist ideal both of the creative process ('Art is something that happens, like the shoot of grass bursting the concrete pavement')[63] and of the writer's relationship to society: 'I can't accept the idea of the "artist" as a special being: abstracted from his human context of working, paying taxes, cricketing, boozing, tupping'.[64] State funding of writers offended these organicist principles. Worse, it encouraged an alternative understanding of the writer as 'a specialist in art-production'.[65] And according to Fairburn it was this 'aesthetic' attitude that played to the advantage of (his term) 'the homosexuals': people who didn't have family and children and who 'in a deep and tragic sense' were 'isolated from the full human context'.[66]

The sum effect of these ideas was deeply destructive. Publicly it was the issue of state funding that precipitated the break with Sargeson. Privately the hardening of Fairburn's prejudice was part of what choked his poetic process. Without doubt this homophobic feeling was something he internalised. I don't mean that Fairburn was secretly gay. I mean that the issue made him feel insecure; that inevitably he policed himself; and that, according to these strictures of his own devising, it was imperative that he not take poetry *too seriously*. By stigmatising the 'specialist' he painted himself into a defensive corner, where the acting out of what he mistakenly called wholeness ('working [. . .] boozing, tupping') displaced the creative performance that it was meant to contextualise. When we get to Sargeson in Chapter 7, I'll have more to say about the ways in which this process works itself out. Homophobic effects can't be isolated or quantified. But it seems to me that homophobia has its hands around Fairburn's throat, and that in terms of his writing, by a curious logic, it may in the end damage Fairburn more than Sargeson.

Poet or pork butcher?

Curnow, Fairburn, Glover: the three names clump so readily together that it's easy to mistake them for a single entity, a kind of Kiwi 'MacSpaunday'. Throughout this book my focus is on the ways in which nationalist writing expands as we unravel its structural underpinnings; accordingly, I'm as willing as anyone to write of them collectively, to aggregate. At the same time, however, there is a value in prising them apart (that is, I also wish to *disaggregate*). The longer I spend with these three poets, the more I become aware not just of how distinct they are, but of how differently I feel about them. Curnow is the poet I have no choice but to admire: relentlessly intelligent, exacting, formidable. He is far and away his generation's most accomplished poet and critic. But Curnow is a difficult writer to feel warmly about. The emotional palette is too restricted. Curnow, as much as anyone, suffers from the governing severities of the climate—not just that sometimes he can be spiteful or vengeful (there is at least energy in that) but that so often, for me, his positions feel excessively fortified. He lacks not only warmth but vulnerability. Fairburn, by contrast, has both those qualities: the first very explicitly, the second not far below the surface of the masculine rhetoric. As a poet, I think Fairburn achieved the least of the three, and the least part of that of which he was capable. But to me, in some imaginary sense, it is Fairburn who seems the most likeable. In some ways, of course, Fairburn can't be defended (there's the homophobia, and more); but in other respects it's Fairburn I'd be happiest to find myself stuck in a lift with, or in some swampy public bar. And Glover? I wouldn't enjoy drinking with Glover, and I don't envy his friends and family. The truly successful poems—I agree with Bill Manhire—are not much more than a handful: 'Sings Harry' and a few others. But those are the poems for which I'd reach into the fire. Of the three, Glover is the poet I love.

Glover is present in the earliest recesses of my childhood experience of poetry—certainly the first New Zealand poet I ever knew by name. I have written elsewhere of my teacher, Jack Taylor (an Australian, tuned into the bush ballad tradition), who played us recordings of Glover, at prep school in Christchurch, when I was nine or ten years old.[67] Among an audience consisting largely of the children of South Island sheep farmers, I may not have been the only one with whom the poems struck a chord. But as I got to know Glover better, the connection became more complex. By now I was a teenager, at the poet's alma mater and forcing house of the Canterbury upper-middle class, Christ's College. And I found that in my head I had Glover confused with my father. I couldn't have explained it then—I'm not sure I can now—but there were several quite transparent connections. Though my father was 11 years younger than Glover, he too scraped into the war generation, and though he didn't dine out on it like Glover, he was inevitably marked by it. Both were city-bred College boys who identified with the sheep-farming establishment. Both were blue-eyed inebriates: irascible, intermittently charming, a danger to themselves and others. My father didn't write, but he had a cultivated tongue and a gift, which others feared, for the sardonic *bon mot*. Unlike Glover, my father had actually gone farming—viably during the wool boom, and then with increasing difficulty as tougher times on the farm, and his own depression and deteriorating health, took over. I could add a good deal more, but my confusion around Glover must already be evident. In short, I have transferred onto Glover my feelings about someone else. He was never going to be just an ordinary poet, or a poet whom I experience purely through what he wrote.

No mid-century writer suffered more severely than Glover from a sense of inhibition around the practice of poetry (or as he himself insisted on calling it, *verse*). To Sargeson many years later he would write: 'You may recall that the orgulous pride of a "poet" always appealed to me less than that of a pork butcher.'[68] 'Orgulous' means something like 'prideful'—a tautology, to make the point doubly clear. Poetry isn't a job for a man, let alone a 'whole' man. In a pattern with which we're already familiar, Glover will present himself as anything else—sailor, printer, boxer, drinker—rather than admit to 'taking poetry seriously'. An account of a public reading from the mid 1970s describes him clowning drunkenly, reaching into his pocket for a handkerchief and pulling out a brassiere. 'Why did he have to fool?' asks the journalist Jill McCracken, and 'Why did it all seem so sad?'[69] This is the poet who once declared, 'No son of mine plays the violin.'[70] Just as in Fairburn there *is* something sad about the pressure to disown high sensibility.

But where Glover, in my view, fares better than Fairburn is in his ability to translate this struggle into writing. I'm thinking of Yeats's famous dictum: 'Out of the quarrel with others we make rhetoric; out of the quarrel with ourselves we make poetry.'[71] Glover has less to say than Fairburn. For the most part, he strikes me as an opportunistic poet who could make a finely crafted job of whatever task presented itself: anti-myth poem ('Centennial'), pylon poem ('The Road Builders'), topical satire ('The Arraignment of Paris'), and so on. But he does have one recurrent theme, and that is his internal struggle with musicality and feeling. Like Fairburn, he didn't just write about this, but also acted it out in extra-literary or para-literary activities (drinking, light verse, various kinds of foolery). And again like Fairburn, he does his best work within a brief compass, and there's little enough of it. However, where the two differ is that, far more than Fairburn, Glover is able to make of that self-censoring impulse an antagonist to grapple with *inside the poems*. The richest single vein in his work is the ongoing quarrel between his fear of poetry and his lyricism. His gifts are both lyrical and comic, and it's the play of one against the other that makes Glover at his best such an engaging experience.

As a comic poet, Glover has a natural affinity with the critical nationalist urge to downsize and debunk:

Centennial

In the year of centennial splendours
There were fireworks and decorated cars
And pungas drooping from the verandas
    —But no one remembered our failures.

The politicians like bubbles from a marsh
Rose to the platform, hanging in every place
Their comfortable platitudes like plush
    —Without one word of our failures.[72]

At his best, Glover could thread his language effortlessly between the 'literary' and the vernacular. A constant inflation and deflation of register, regulated by his unfailingly musical ear, mimics the drama of pomp and inanity that the poem satirises. And Glover's laconic comedy domesticates—'humanises', even—the critical animus. It is an altogether more homely version of anti-myth than Curnow could ever manage: more demotic in tone and more inclusive of its audience, all the way down to the politicians wafting up like farts. But Glover didn't write very many of these poems. Lacking Curnow's passion for history, Glover's criticality is a matter of fleeting jabs. His more ambitious work is more lyrical in intent, and here the role of comedy becomes more complex and ambivalent.

Curnow was Glover's close friend and always his most admiring reader. But he understood the problems that Glover was up against: the suspicion of hieratic voicings can lead to 'wilful flatness or banality'; the 'humorist in Glover' who would 'turn the whole thing into a joke' is not entirely a trustworthy ally.[73] With a subject like the jingoism of the 1940 Centennial, the deflationary urge is entirely salutary. But it's capable of making trouble when Glover is trying to find other registers. Where Fairburn's problems with the high calling of Poetry manifest in extracurricular frittering, Glover's are apt to lead to a defensive intrusion of the comic impulse where it doesn't belong. 'A Note to Lili Kraus' is best remembered for the couplet: 'Lili, emotion leaves me quite dismayed: / If I'm on fire I call the fire brigade.'[74] Gordon Ogilvie calls this 'Glover at his absolute worst'.[75] Where the voice turns facetious it can obliterate other registers jostling for attention.

The tendency of comedy to hijack a poem can produce more nuanced effects than this. In 'Landing Field', a piece of war-flavoured 'pylonese' (as Sargeson describes it),[76] the poet salutes planes and pilots in lightly elegiac tones. But by the third section things are getting a little sombre: planes crash and men die or await their death 'sitting upon a floating wing, lighting / a last cigarette.' And so by way of compensation, the fourth (last) section becomes whimsical, with planes transformed into butterflies, and Romanticism's favourite heavenly body into a dirigible:

> and soon
> rises above those housed and settled wings
> like a great balloon, the lighter-than-air
> serene sky-filling moon.[77]

While in 'Landing Field' playfulness steps up to trump lyricism, in 'Holiday Piece' it is lyricism that ambushes comedy. In keeping with the premise of the poet on vacation (though of course the poet in Glover is *always* more or less on holiday) the poem refuses to make an effort. It comes across as an aimless doodle, the kind of thing you might scribble on a bus, full of low-budget rhymes and coy syntactical inversions:

> Now let my thoughts be like the Arrow wherein was gold,
> and purposeful like the Kawarau, but not so cold.
> Let them sweep higher than the hawk ill-omened,
> higher than peaks perspective-piled beyond Ben Lomond;
> Let them be like at evening an Otago sky
> where detonated clouds in calm confusion lie.[78]

But after three stanzas governed by these same ephemeral 'thoughts', there comes a change of subject ('that snowfield') and a shift in tone:

> Lastly, that snowfield, visible from Wanaka,
> compound their patience—suns only brighten,
> and no rains darken, a whiteness nothing could whiten.[79]

It's as if at the end the poet can't help himself. Or as if, assured that the throwaway quality of the previous stanzas has lulled the reader into inattention, he has seized the chance to make the briefest 'raid on the inarticulate' while nobody's listening. Complex rhymes both in pattern and sound; sophisticated syntax (the only place where the poem departs from simple compound sentences); and magisterial Nature greeted with an unmistakeable heightening of register: all these effects help to cast over this final stanza at least a passing shadow of solemnity. There are hints here, 'lastly', not only of the sublime, but even, in all that whiteness and brightness, of the gravity of 'last things'.

Losing the farm

I am not suggesting that beneath that gruff exterior there might lurk some kind of closet Anglican. The nonchalant front, though, is certainly protecting something: a more ambitious poet, a more lyrical poet, a poet who wants not just to amuse but also to engage us emotionally. By common consent, this more elevated voice gets its most complete outing in 'Sings Harry', published finally in 1951, though begun as early as 1940. Glover's personal breakthrough here was the discovery of the persona poem, which offered him, as Manhire puts it, a way of 'expressing obliquely what he felt, without obliging him to answer for his feelings or opinions'.[80] With a mask safely in place there was less need for other forms of defence. There are fewer jokes. The persona is permitted not only to 'feel' but explicitly to *sing*.

The feelings that 'Sings Harry' lets off the leash are Romantic: the poems sing of memory and loss. And this melancholy music evokes an imaginary experience of settlement that the critical path mapped by Curnow is not designed to access:

I Remember

I remember paddocks opening green
On mountains tussock brown,
And the rim of fire on the hills,
And the river running down;

And the smoke of the burning scrub,
And my two uncles tall,
And the smell of the earth new-ploughed,
And the antlers in the hall,
Sings Harry.

Then Uncle Jim was off to the wars
With a carbine at his saddle
And was killed in the Transvaal
—I forget in just what battle.

And Uncle Simon left the farm
After some wild quarrel,
Rolled his blanket and rode off
Whistling on his sorrel.

My father held to the land
Running good cattle there,
And I grew up like a shaggy steer
And as swift as a hare
While the river ran down.

But that was long ago
When the hawk hovered over the hill
And the deer lifted their heads
And a boy lay still
By the river running down,
Sings Harry.[81]

What Harry does in these poems—it is virtually his only action—is to remember. Invariably this involves dwelling on loss, but Harry's sense of loss is also his sense of continuity. Something I have not forgotten about my very first experience of this poem—this is me aged ten, once more—is responding to, but puzzling over, the strange word 'sorrel'. A sorrel, I learned, is a reddish-brown horse; someone else might have called it a chestnut. But the poet, of course, prefers sorrel for the rhyme—not just the full rhyme with quarrel, but the intricate network of slant rhyme and assonance, so typical of Glover, that travels with it: hills, tall, smell, hall, saddle, killed, Transvaal, battle, wild, rolled, whistling, hills, still. And his ear prefers sorrel for a further reason—for something more that it carries with it—the word, half-concealed in its lexical shadow, that names the thread drawn by these aching cadences. *Sorrow*: not just the poem's theme, but the poem's act, what it does; it sorrows. Sorrow is the feeling that, running through memory, running through family, holds Harry in place.

I'm guided in this reading by the late Barry Barclay, distinguished Māori filmmaker, and a difference that he posits between Māori and Pākehā feelings towards the land.[82] Watching the work of aspiring young film and video makers, he is struck by what he takes as an iconic Pākehā motif—disembodied feet on a pedestrian crossing, which he reads as an image of alienation. This 'drifting feet syndrome' Barclay takes to be strictly a Pākehā phenomenon. Māori, of course, are greatly concerned with where their feet stand. But Māori anxieties about themselves and the land are experienced, Barclay writes, not as *alienation* but as *dispossession*. I'm not sure we have to take all this as gospel. But it does seem plausible to me that those Pākehā filmmakers with their unsettled feet (Barclay is writing in 1990) are legitimately descended from their nationalist forbears of the 30s and 40s. I can't help thinking of Charles Brasch: 'none knows where he will lie down at night'.[83] Alienation is the mood of settlers who don't yet know where they stand—only that their place has been misrepresented, that their standing is shaky, that 'standing upright' belongs to the future. And this mood, in turn, tells us something important about the quite different attitude struck in 'Sings Harry', a poem that turns its back on the rhetoric of alienation, and lays claim instead to the sorrow of dispossession.

The sequence begins with a cancelled first person ('Not I but another / Will make songs worth the bother') that, as I have observed, sounds a lot like the 'Not I' of Curnow's moa poem. But in one sense the similarity is deceptive. Yes, it's a disclaimer—Harry is no rimu or kauri, only a cabbage tree. But it doesn't disclaim, or empty out, the present in deference to the future. Harry's consolations derive from the past.

The present is occupied, not with dismantling or evacuating settler history, but with grooming it into a musical, mythical shape. It's a more naïve gesture than Curnow permits himself. Curnow's nationalist anti-myth is far more accountable to the 'real' history of settlement. Glover simply steps over colonial usurpation, and in doing so conjures up a sense of settler occupancy which, far more readily than anything in Curnow, answers to received expectations of nationalist sentiment.

'I Remember' was first printed in 1946 under the title 'I Remember, Sang Harry'; in this version both title and refrain appeared in the past tense: Harry *sang*.[84] But the rearranged tenses of the final version make a more emphatic emotional claim. Glover's persona sings in the present in order to articulate the achievement of a past. Settlement now has a history—it remembers—and the core of that memory is dispossession:

> And I was a fool leaving
> Good land to moulder,
> Leaving the fences sagging
> And the old man older[85]

Harry remembers what he has lost. And the more grief it costs him—or the more that Glover is able to touch us with that grief—the more persuasive is the poem's claim to an imaginative habitation of place. Harry's memories crystallise in images of South Island countryside—known, loved, owned and then foolishly neglected. But the sense of loss that inheres in these images insists on a claim to imaginative occupancy. Harry may have *lost* his place, but he *knows* and *feels* his place, as his melancholy tells us.

In 'Sings Harry', nationalist writing has its Romanticism restored to it. Behind the shelter of the mask, and more than on any other occasion, Glover risks in this poem the expression of concentrated feeling. It's a poem which, for once, *invests* in feeling: it commits itself to its pastoral sorrows to claim, in return, an imaginative belonging. And it's surely not coincidental that it's Glover, in this Romantic mood, who more than any poet of his cohort has touched the Pākehā imagination.

Recently I stayed a couple of nights at a bed-and-breakfast in Havelock North—a delightful place: stylish, contemporary, laid-back, gay-friendly. In the communal kitchen–dining area there's a decent library of New Zealand books, and on two impressive plate-glass windows the owners have sandblasted a pair of matching texts. On the south side the visitor can read the opening lines of the Ngāti Toa haka, 'Ka Mate'; on the north, the refrain from Glover's 'The Magpies': 'And *Quardle oodle ardle wardle doodle* / The magpies said.'[86] How appropriate, I thought, looking out on the deeply settled pastoral prosperity of Hawke's Bay. If Pākehā writing offers anything to put beside 'Ka Mate' as an iconic 'folk' text, then surely it's Glover's poem. Manhire describes it as 'the single New Zealand poem to have achieved a kind of "classic" status'. He also points out that—so aptly in a Glover poem—the magpies are struggling, laconically, perhaps clownishly, towards music: that, while they *speak* their iconic chorus, somewhere in that ardling and doodling there's a voice trying to *warble*.[87] I'm not sure these lines are 'determinedly unpoetic', but I understand why Manhire describes them this way. The poem would never have achieved its folk status were its music not dry enough for the Kiwi palate. But musing on this settler 'classic', face to face with Te Rauparaha's haka, I realised I'd never really thought about the story, and what *that* might say about the poem's iconic value. It occurred to me, then, that this best-loved, most deeply *settled* of New Zealand texts tells in six stanzas the same foundational story as 'Sings Harry': the story of Pākehā dis/possession, of Tom and Elizabeth, and how they 'took the farm', and then lost it.

Chapter 6

'Caught on the hinge of an opening door'

Hyde and heterosexuality

Between traditions

Close under here, I watched two lovers once,
Which should have been a sin, from what you say:
I'd come to look for prawns, small pale-green ghosts,
Sea-coloured bodies tickling round the pool.
But tide was out then; so I strolled away
And climbed the dunes, to lie here warm, face down,
Watching the swimmers by the jetty-posts
And wrinkling like the bright blue wrinkling bay.
It wasn't long before they came; a fool
Could see they had to kiss; but your pet dunce
Didn't quite know men count on more than that;
And so just lay, patterning sand.

And they

Were thin pale people, not often clear of town:
Elastic snapped, when he jerked off her hat:
I heard her arguing, 'Dick, my frock!' But he
Thought she was bread.
                                        I wished her legs were brown,
And mostly, then, stared at the dawdling sea,
Hoping Perry would row me some day in his boat.

Not all the time; and when they'd gone, I went
Down to the hollow place where they had been,
Trickling bed through fingers. But I never meant
To tell the rest, or you, what I had seen:
Though that night, when I came in late for tea,
I hoped you'd see the sandgrains on my coat.[1]

Section VI of 'The Beaches', from the late sequence 'Houses by the Sea', comes loaded with iconic freight. There can hardly be a more vivid rendition of the classic Kiwi topos that treats the beach as the arena of a passage from innocence to experience. It is among the few nearly perfect things that Robin Hyde wrote. And unlike so much of her uneven and (to me, at least) often frustrating body of work, it belongs incontestably to its modern literary moment. In its low-key prosody,[2] in the precision of its imagery, in its laconic modulation of candour and restraint, it's a poem that for once seems entirely uncluttered by the moth-eaten trappings of Victorian and Edwardian 'poetry speak'. It resonates almost like a Sapphic fragment, or like the stage-managed remnants of 'Kubla Khan'. It speaks of the poet Hyde *might have become* had she not died so early, had she travelled in better company, had she—as her least forgiving critic, Curnow, put it—'found her appropriate discipline, or realized her need of it.'[3]

Why couldn't Hyde find this idiom earlier? Why was

she so reluctant to learn from those poets whom she knew, dismissively, as 'the moderns'? Her male contemporaries, Curnow and James Bertram, portrayed her as a victim of colonial disorientation.[4] Revisionist critics, no less predictably, have reframed the problem in terms of gender; it's impossible now to read Hyde without reference to the misogyny of literary nationalism, and without in the process recasting her deviations from its masculine norms as a form of deliberate protest. Inevitably my own approach derives from this revisionist context. But in asking what's at stake in Hyde's refusal of nationalist aesthetics I want to shift the emphasis just slightly: from gender to *sexuality*, and from the masculine bias of literary nationalism to the broader horizon of what I have been calling, after Christine Stansell, *sexual modernism*.

The primal scene, as Freud conceived it—the child's observation or intuition of adult coitus—confronts the subject, not just with the Freudian metaphysics of 'castration' (lack, exclusion, the deficit that creates desire), but with the fundamental question of where the viewer stands in relation to this discovery. How does the subject, emotionally, erotically, assimilate both the fascination and the trauma of what Lacan calls this 'factitious fact'?[5] To the watching child in Hyde's poem, the lovers in the sand dunes pose the same question. And as surely as they might do in an analytic case history, the poem's responses resonate throughout Hyde's work. The indispensable term is ambivalence. The speaker is both disconcerted and fascinated. The tryst is perceived in terms of aggression and coercion (the arguing, the snapping elastic, the woman devoured like a picnic lunch); but it also provokes the viewer to quasi-erotic daydreams (Perry), to identification with the woman ('I wished her legs were brown'), and to an ultimate identification with the scene as a whole. In the 'hollow place' left behind by the lovers the young girl situates herself.

She comes away not only marked by the scene (sand from the 'bed' that she trickles through her fingers) but desiring now to be *recognised* as a sexualised subject: 'I hoped you'd see the sandgrains on my coat.'

To grasp how Hyde understood her position sexually, we need to introduce into this ahistorical 'scene' her awareness of the historical specificity of her own situation. In *A Home in This World* this sense of contingency provides one of the narrative's governing metaphors:

> It seems to me now that I am caught on the hinge of a slowly-opening door, between one age and another. Between the tradition of respectability, which was very strong in my household and had cut me off from all real family love the moment I infringed it, and the new age, foretold by Nietzsche and some others. Just as Presbyterians who now get up in congress and heatedly discuss the effects of dancing, and of one glass of claret-cup on the bloodstream and subsequent purity of the race, seem to most of us a little droll, so in time will an Iris Wilkinson, knocking her head on the ground and her bleeding knuckles on the door, seem extremely queer to those who have learned to be happy without self-consciousness [. . .] Just the same, I will carry my skinned knuckles and sometimes abject countenance through life, and so will a good many other women.[6]

Sadly, she was right. Her work reads today like a compendium of all the ways that women between the wars were being squeezed. Hyde is part of that cohort whose careers coincided with a wholesale reinvention of the sexual expectations of women—both their own expectations and what was expected of them—and it's this as much as anything that marks her as a modern subject. (What woman before Hyde ever wrote a poem about watching sex?) However, it's not a passage of history that is well understood, or even well documented—partly because, as we saw in Chapter 3, it's also a period in which writing by women is more fugitive than at any other time in the 20th century. And so the ways in which Hyde's career *hinges* on sexuality offer a key to understanding not just her difficulties, but her singular distinction. Dispatched in haste from that scene of upheaval, her work supplies a rare account of how it felt to be on the sharp end of the century's first sexual revolution.

After the Hyde revival

The last 30 years have seen an impressive growth in Hyde's reputation. When I first read Hyde in the late 1970s, the only work in print was *The Godwits Fly*. But as Mary Edmond-Paul explains, the upswing in feminist publishing from around this period initiated a veritable explosion of Hyde publications.[7] Between 1984 and 1991 all her significant prose works would be reissued, most with hefty critical introductions. The year 1984 also brought the first *Selected Poems*, edited by Lydia Wevers, and the first appearance of the previously unpublished autobiographical text *A Home in This World*, edited by Hyde's son Derek Challis. A second phase of archival restoration from the mid 1990s has been largely inspired by Michele Leggott. Leggott's variorum edition of an unpublished poem *The Victory Hymn* (1995) was followed by the lost prose poem *The Book of Nadath* (1999) and the lavish and meticulous *Young Knowledge: The Poems of Robin Hyde* (2003). Meanwhile, a long collaboration between Challis and Gloria Rawlinson finally resulted in *The Book of Iris: A Life of Robin Hyde* (2002), opening the way for further archival material to appear as *Your Unselfish Kindness: Robin Hyde's Autobiographical Writings* (2011), edited by Edmond-Paul, who has also given us the scholarly round-table *Lighted Windows: Critical Essays on Robin Hyde* (2008). This welter of activity has transformed Hyde from the most neglected writer of her generation into the most intensively published and most widely discussed. She now appears as central a mid-century figure as Curnow or Sargeson; indeed, in critical terms, she might be said to stand currently as *the* iconic writer of the interwar period.

The hegemony established by the nationalist tradition—its largely untroubled dominance until as late as the mid 80s—lends this rediscovered Hyde an incomparable strategic value. But while 'someone like Hyde' may be a kind of structural necessity ('if Robin Hyde hadn't existed it would have been necessary to invent her,' as the cynical rendition has it),[8] the scope and the singularity of her work are not critical fabrications. If Hyde makes the programme of her masculine contemporaries seem narrow and obsessional, it's because her own oeuvre is genuinely capacious—in its scale, its variety, and the reach of its interests and sympathies. Her feminism, of course, is key, but it isn't the only thing that sets her apart. Her social canvas is broader than that of any other 30s writer; her work records more of the kinds of lives that are being lived. In terms of urban experience, proletarian experience, and of the horrors and the ongoing ramifications of World War I, only John A. Lee covers anything like the ground that Hyde does. Again, she is virtually on her own in her explicit sympathy with Māori—the only other fiction writer or poet who comes to mind is Roderick Finlayson—and in her alertness, as we saw in Chapter 4, not just to the history of Māori dispossession, but to what that history means as a condition of settler culture. Meanwhile, looking through the other end of the telescope, she also challenges the Caxton writers' localism with her emphatic internationalism: her awareness of the Pacific, her commitment to China, her insistence that '*Now* when internationalism seems most dangerous we should play that card for all we're worth.'[9] Wrap all this up in a sprawling and still emergent body of work, a glamorous legend and a history of belittlement at the hands of male critics, and it isn't hard to see why 'Hyde studies' has been blossoming.

But what of this question that Leggott poses in a landmark essay of 1995:

> Can the genius of Duggan, Hyde and the others touch us, a readership long since trained in the pleasures (and prestige) of formal difficulty?[10]

The prestige of 'formal difficulty' refers of course to modernism, and the problem of negotiating Hyde's poetic, approaching as we do from the near side of the modernist paradigm shift. Plainly *something* is reaching across to us. Her recent apotheosis speaks volumes about it. The Hyde oeuvre is thick with information, and steadied by the protocols of a governing historical relativism (an alertness to what Leggott calls, judiciously, 'previous competences')[11] yields it up freely to contemporary critical discourse. However, the urgency of the political meta-narrative doesn't deal with all the difficulties presented by the poems. Leggott, for one, wants more than this, hence her appeal to 'genius' and 'magic';[12] she is speaking as a feminist cultural critic, but also as a modernist poet. What happens, then, if we insist on reading Hyde not just for the politics of centre and margin, but for poetics—whether in pursuit of what Leggott calls 'foundation' (lineage, modelling, useable skills)[13] or simply out of hunger for a high-voltage experience, for the shock, the excitement that can make reading poems feel almost like writing them? What is the reader to do in this context with Hyde's own determined refusal of modernist values?

Leggott's response to this dilemma is exemplified in the poems of her 1995 volume *DIA*, a work which her author's note frames explicitly as an act of homage and historical recovery. The predominant tactic is citation or sampling: 'picking out white-hot lines [. . .] and recombining them with an ear for the heart, complexity, and engagement with which they were written.'[14] By this means, Hyde is re-tooled for modern conditions. These 'white-hot' fragments of a disaggregated text are shaken free of the received literary language and moribund poetic forms in which, at source, the contemporary reader so often finds them embedded; under the pressure of modernist formalism, the poem's latent energies are liberated. Hyde's texts are 'recombined', not just among themselves, but with the language of her contemporaries (Duggan, Bethell), with later women poets (Dinah Hawken, Bernadette Hall), and with the modernist pantheon that informs Leggott's own poetic idiolect. Elsewhere Leggott will bring Hyde into dialogue with such different modernist poets as H.D. and Robin Blaser. The effect is like a sci-fi alternative history (what would have happened if . . . ?). Rehomed with Leggott's poetic family, Hyde embraces the encounter with the modern that she refused so determinedly in her own practice.

For Leggott this has proved highly enabling. However, it doesn't solve the problems that Hyde's verse presents in its unimproved state. Restoring those fragments to their original context, we still face the impediments that Leggott's modernisation of Hyde has strategically shorn away: the syntax shackled to received poetic forms, the archaisms, the dreary ornamentation. How can her work 'touch' me, as a modernist-trained reader, through the clouds of her anti-modern poetic and the cobwebby dreck of her image repertoire—the 'pre-Raphaelitish junk, milliner's imagery, bloody topazes & opals & argozies,' to invoke, as one can hardly avoid in this context,

Curnow?[15] For this is the conclusion to which these reflections are inevitably directing me: that even after all this industrious revisionism, I am forced to admit that many of Curnow's objections—gratuitously mean and over-determined though they may be—resonate still with my experience as a reader. When I read her poems alongside the best of Curnow or Glover, of Mason or Fairburn, of Bethell or Baughan, they feel, with relatively few late exceptions, like museum pieces; they may be interesting, but they're dead to the touch. Were it my job now to anthologise Hyde, my choices would be almost entirely conventional: the best of Hyde, for me, is still in 'Houses by the Sea' and the China poems. For the rest, I can seldom get past the effect of her refusal of the poetics of her own century.

The reader, I'm sure, will discern my unease, and I raise this evaluative flag here explicitly to highlight it. The question of Hyde's 'value' is so eminently political that to query the reassessment of her verse defies all one's better instincts. And yet, I would argue that to override these modernist objections is also to ignore a historical cue; that it's easier now to engage with Hyde's poetry if we admit that a good deal of it is effectively 'unreadable'; and that those regressive elements that disable so much of the verse have most to reveal if we accept them as such. Hyde's is an oeuvre in which, as Curnow said of Cresswell, the meanings do not 'lie [. . .] all at one level'.[16] There are places where the symptomatic meanings may be richer than the purposive ones. All the same, I'm not trying to lower Hyde's colours (Hyde, after all, is *not* Cresswell). On the contrary, I believe that if we read Hyde less solicitously we may find she counts for even more than we thought.

From this angle, Hyde's most significant theme is sex in transition in the 20s and 30s. Her texts present the testimony of a sexualised subjectivity in a way that no New Zealand writer before her even approximates (not even Mansfield).

From the unflinching record of male sexual adventurism in the Starkie books, to the fantasy serial monogamy of *Wednesday's Children*, to the romantic longings and unromantic agonies of Eliza Hannay in *The Godwits Fly*, Hyde's most substantial protagonists are always sexually conscious beings; and this is to say nothing of the candid autobiographical texts that have appeared posthumously (*A Home in This World*, *Your Unselfish Kindness*). Writing to Pat Lawlor she feels the need to defend herself, though not to apologise:

> Yes, I write about sex—either as the tragedy it is, or the free and clean thing I want it to be. Of course in practice and experiment it doesn't work out like that, and of course I know it and have been made smaller by sex in most years of my life—not in all. But I don't see how that alters the objective.[17]

Hyde is never shy of utopian politics, and the progressive ambitions of the sex reform movement are to a large extent her own. But she knows as well as anyone the demands involved in the modernisation of sex. She is caught, as she puts it, in that opening door—she is not free simply to walk through it—and being *in* this moment, she can't always describe it lucidly or analytically. Her career, then, also bears witness to the moment's challenges in less happy, more involuntary ways. As an unmarried mother and solo provider she lives its contradictory demands at the most brute material level: quite literally, she *embodies* them. But she also records them, as a writer, in a kind of *acting out*. This is where I situate her recoil from modernist poetics, an aversion in which is inscribed, as I will argue, an inchoate protest at aspects of modernist sexuality.

When Virginia Woolf was warning listeners at Cambridge about the menace of masculinity on the defensive, she was speaking to an audience of women exactly Hyde's age. As I explained in Chapter 3, it was this generation, born in the lead-up to World War I, who would bear the full impact of those 'sex-conscious' interwar decades. In New Zealand, thanks to Leggott, Jensen and others, the resulting decimation of women's writing has been persuasively documented. As far as I am aware, though, no one has yet framed this local 30s wipe-out in an international context. With the usual suspects so readily to hand—pioneering, puritanism, the Kiwi bloke and indeed literary nationalism—it is easy to assume that we are dealing with a local singularity. However, the moment we look for analogous figures—to whom might Hyde profitably be compared in order to ask how she could have positioned herself differently?—we discover that alternative models are extremely thin on the ground. It wasn't only Robin Hyde who couldn't find a place in the modernist 1930s; it was her entire generation. Just before World War I was a very bad time to be born as a woman writer, not just in New Zealand, but anywhere in the English-speaking world.

In this there are major implications for how we estimate Hyde. Plainly this context has a bearing on her problems, her struggle. But it also has a bearing—and it may be substantial—on those delicate questions of 'value' and 'significance'. Hyde is a woman writer speaking out of a silence against which precious few others prevailed. When we look at the decimation of women's writing in her era, the flawed and uneven quality of her oeuvre begins to seem less remarkable than the fact that she wrote at all. And not only that, but this mid-century eclipse underlines the importance of her analysis of her own situation. Of course her work is patchy. But to allow Hyde her weaknesses—and to investigate them—is part of a process of attending more carefully to those specific historical pressures to which her work bears witness. Where the record is so sparse—where there is so little (anywhere) to testify to women's experience of this moment—what Hyde's text can tell us about her struggles as a woman writer begins to look even more significant than we had imagined.

Chest trouble

War hero and reprobate Douglas Stark, known to one and all as Starkie, inspired two of Hyde's most important works of fiction. By the time she first encountered him in 1932, on a newspaper assignment at Mt Eden prison, Stark's reckless bravery, along with his inveterate drunkenness, violence and petty crime, were already the stuff of legend. Later Hyde extracted his larger-than-life story during two series of interviews in 1935 and 1937. Pacy and violent, *Passport to Hell* (1936) is for many readers her most accessible work in prose. Described by Alex Calder as a 'novelised biography',[18] it follows Stark from childhood through to the end of World War I. The sequel *Nor the Years Condemn* (1938) details his troubled return to civilian life in the 1920s. This second work is more conventionally a novel: longer, more digressive, with a wider cast of fictional characters. For readers who have the patience, it also contains perhaps the fullest articulation of Hyde's social vision.

Passport to Hell was immediately acknowledged as a noteworthy feat of imaginative realism. Former servicemen like William Downie Stewart and John A. Lee attested to its veracity.[19] Lee applauded the way the writer 'submerged herself in the psychology of the experience', while a British reviewer described the battle scenes as 'more realistic than any written'.[20] But another kind of realism is also evident, a verisimilitude that owes less to the horrors of warfare and to Hyde's ability to identify with her informant's experience, than it does to her own sense of (gender) history. Interleaved with the violence of the battlefield we read equally vivid episodes from the war between the sexes. In London there is the basement, preserved like Miss Havisham's room, where a newly married couple are said to have poisoned one another over their wedding breakfast.[21] In Cairo, the Anzacs run amok through the brothel district—a cloudy historical incident known as the 'battle of the Wazza'.[22] And on the Western Front there is the soldier who, jilted by his fiancée, enlists his comrades as a firing squad:

> They went with him over the top of a little hill, and there, nailed to a tree, was his much prized photograph of the girl [. . .] He'd nailed it up very carefully, so that the nails didn't damage the young throat, laughing eyes, soft hair.
>
> 'Get to a range of fifty yards,' he ordered, 'and shoot the _____ to bits.'[23]

We needn't supply the elided noun to read the semantics of this ritualised vengeance: 'Then the rifles cracked, one after another, and when they'd finished Jack Benshaw's girl was nothing but a black grinning hole against the tree.' The war between the sexes doesn't let up just because there's a shooting war. On the contrary, the 'great' war exaggerates the more subtle one, and its after-effects will resonate in much of Hyde's work.

The war is a prelude to the years of her own adulthood, and to new shades of conflict between the sexes that define her understanding of the 20s and 30s. The departure of a generation of men for Europe leaves an injury that will never heal. As Starkie on board the troopship observes the mass grief of those left behind, Hyde remarks: 'How could the men on the ship expect to come back to the same women when, departing, they had destroyed them?'[24] If there is an answer it is on the second-last page of the book, where a returning soldier waits at the deck-rail until New Zealand is clearly in view before slipping over the side and drowning himself.[25] For those who make it back, 'after a four years' break which they would never be able to explain', it is to 'the immense uncalculating jealousy of the world, largely a woman's world, which had not been able to take part in their four years, and which had at last learned to drag along without them.'[26] The alienation of the returning soldier has become a truism, but we should remember that Hyde experienced it at close quarters, watching her father return like a tramp ('sneak-bold past the kennel')[27] to a family among whom (like John Hannay in *The Godwits Fly*) he was now superfluous. The ubiquitous 'men without a country' who shamble through *Nor the Years Condemn* are no doubt descended indirectly from George Wilkinson, as perhaps are elements of Hyde's identification with the most 'derailed' of them all, Douglas Stark.[28] But the shattered veterans, their brides and families—these are only part of the picture. As troops prepare to leave in *Passport to Hell*, Hyde reflects on the young women (perhaps 12 or 15 years older than herself) caught up erotically in the drama: 'Some of the men left their mark on the young bodies in crepe de Chine and China silk, and babies were born. But that generation of New Zealand girls, and the next, were to learn that there are worse things than babies.'[29] The comment is not explained; on its own it remains enigmatic. However, Hyde's exploration of the post-war era supplies the context to make sense of it. 'Worse than babies', for Hyde's generation, will be coping with the gender economy that emerges from the wreckage of the war.

In this analysis, Hyde concurs with Woolf and with those more recent feminist historians whose work I referred to in Chapter 3. The damage inflicted on the war generation will be parlayed into a new mode of hyper-masculinity:

> Those that came back from the war had ventured over the hills somewhere, restless, trying for adventure; or they had picked up chest trouble at the front, or worse. You could get engaged, triumphantly, to a good-looking, fine-faced returned man, give trousseau parties and indulge in the pride of showing your silk and semi-silk things to your girlfriends. Then, perhaps on the eve of the wedding, there would be an incoherent note, a policeman around in the morning, and an inquest on a man who had put a bullet through his head. Somebody would explain that he had been badly shell-shocked at Ypres, badly gassed. Poor old Jack, everybody said. Yes, but nobody thought, in the same degree, poor young Laura or Mavis, wrenching on a new hat over her bedragglement, piecing together the bits of her suburban pride and of her genuine uncomprehending sympathy, which could only say, in darkness and in light: 'Oh, however could you do a thing like that? [. . .]' It was no good: bright light, thick dark, the gulf between men and women existed and widened, and after their first shiverings they got used to it, and decided they hated one another. The girls said they were content with their jobs, and took expensive beauty treatments. The men lounged together, telling stories, pretending a vague homosexual philosophy, toying with an equally vague day of love and wrath, when, banded together, chesty but very forgiving once they had satisfied their dignity, they would put the women back in their place.[30]

'Chest trouble' comes in two forms: the damaged masculinity that returns from the war, and the muscle-bound version ('banded together, chesty') that puffs itself up, trying to reassert its dignity and put the women back where they belong. The threat of retaliation is 'vague', like the 'vague homosexual philosophy' behind it, but remembering the photograph of Jack

Benshaw's girlfriend, and the Anzacs rioting in the Wazza, we can safely guess that the 'day of love and wrath' implies a sexualised aggression. Hyde's generation—as Woolf had foreseen—will bear the full force of this masculine restoration. As that long day unfolds through the 20s and 30s, it will take forms more subtle than explicit vigilantism. Subtle, but also more systematic. Women will be restored their accustomed place outside patriarchal power, and yet contained in that place by a fundamentally modern mechanism.

Homosociality, it is important to note, does not prohibit heterosex. In fact it's just as likely—as is certainly the case with the homophobic masculine culture of the mid century—to insist on a heterosexual norm. But it regulates heterosexuality's scope. The celebration of same-sex relations delimits the relationships of men and women; genuine trust and intimacy are reserved for homosocial relations between men. While women's place has always been outside power, in the interwar period the determination of that place by 'family' and 'home' (think Coventry Patmore: the Angel in the House) begins to give ground to a definition of women's place by sex. I refer here, of course, to the discourse of sexology. But remember, too, Pound and Glover ('The Garden', 'A Woman Shopping'). There, as well, a woman's sex is in each case the poem's telling discovery. It has the evidential value of the thing she doesn't know (that she has repressed) and therefore must be confronted with; and the tactical value of the thing she cannot speak of (she must be *spoken for*). As that which she embodies, but cannot articulate, sex becomes not just the woman's truth, but the ground of her ignorance, and of her silence. In the long game of post-war reconstruction, woman is not just invented as a heterosexual being but is reduced to that being. She is good enough for sex, but not for solidarity. Sexuality excommunicates her from friendship, from knowledge and from writing.

Networks

In a happier story—an alternative (fantasy) history—the painter D.K. (Dorothy) Richmond (1861–1935) might have been someone important in Hyde's life. Her death is recorded in the autobiography that Hyde writes for her psychiatrist Gilbert Tothill. Hyde recalls Richmond's house in York Bay, which the Wilkinsons rented for a month one summer, as 'the first really bookish house I ever inhabited—shelves and shelves of books in almost every language, out of which I particularly remember the Koran, some exquisite verses of Oscar Wilde's'.[31] This is Katherine Mansfield country (Wilde, Wellington's eastern bays) and a glimpse of something richer than the genteel poverty and benign philistinism of the Wilkinson household. It has all the makings, in other words, of what Freud called 'family romance': the alternative, ideal family that you wish was your own. But Richmond will never be Hyde's imaginary mother:

> She was kind to me, she knew I was shy, so she never made me uncomfortable or awkwardly shy. She was a beautiful sunset. She never married—like me. But she didn't beat herself against the transparent cool glass.[32]

Richmond may be a painter, and unmarried, but she is not beating her 'bleeding knuckles' against the barriers of gender respectability. In the elderly spinster's model of a creative life, Hyde sees nothing to affiliate with. In fact Richmond's other appearance in her writing is as a source of potential threat. Travelling incognito on the Cook Strait ferry, smuggling home to Wellington the infant she has recently borne in secret, she spots her 'creamy-haired, black-sticked figure' strolling on deck and hastily takes cover: 'to have explained to her that she mustn't mention to anyone that I was travelling with a new baby [. . .] seemed to me at the time an undertaking of which I was quite incapable.'[33]

In this episode there is both a failure of recognition and a failure of transmission; it is a missed connection not so much personal as historical. *Like me*, Hyde says, Richmond never married. And yet in this they are really not alike at all, for they take the unwed option under quite different sexual regimes. Richmond belongs to a generation for whom it had been possible to sustain a creative or political career from within the space of intimate relations with other women. Her romantic friendship with Frances Hodgkins (1869–1947), with whom she travelled and painted extensively in the first decade of the century, was not a lifelong partnership like some; nonetheless it reminds us of an option that for Hyde's generation appears to have closed down entirely. For women like Bethell, Mackay and Duggan the companionship of other women offered love, security, encouragement, material assistance—that is, all those enabling functions that wives before and since have played in the lives of creative husbands. Moreover, not only did they share these one-to-one partnerships, but these in turn were part of a more extensive, largely homosocial fabric. They were likely as not to be networked, not just into the political energies of first-wave feminism, but into a premodernist literary culture as well.[34]

By contrast, how isolated Hyde will be. The post-war era, with its sexual science, eroticised marriage and anti-lesbian homophobia, has collapsed the homosocial space in which her predecessors were able to function so productively. In the passage where Hyde remembers Dorothy Richmond's house, she also recalls acting scenes from Shakespeare with the woman who was probably her most intimate female friend, Gwen Hawthorn. But what she records is loss: 'Gwen who is buried, buried, buried in her marriage and brats, and with all the bright gold gone from her hair'.[35] This is the friend who, as Simone in *The Godwits Fly*, had promised Iris/Eliza that 'they would have lovers when they were grown up, but not too many babies.'[36] Now the sway of heterosexualised marriage has lured her away from that homosocial pact; sequestered with husband and 'brats', she is 'buried' beyond reach. Among other female friendships, only Hyde's relationship with the Rawlinsons seems to have had anything like the same force, although at present that three-way relationship is tricky to interpret, given its complexity and the problematic role of Gloria Rawlinson as co-author of the only biographical account of it that we have. Otherwise, Hyde's orientation is overwhelmingly towards men.

For Richmond, to remain unmarried meant a cultivated existence, uncomplicated by heterosexual entanglement and by children. For Hyde, as a sexual modern, it means almost the opposite. As we know, Hyde became pregnant twice, and carried both confinements to full term. The first ended in a still birth, in her first serious breakdown, and in the self-reinvention of Iris Wilkinson as Robin Hyde, in memory of the dead child. The second resulted in the birth of Derek, after a furtive, sequestered pregnancy, which in turn led to the endless financial and emotional struggles of managing his care, and to ongoing subterfuge and grief with her family (Hyde's father would never learn of the child's existence; of her three sisters, two would learn eventually, the third not until after her death).[37] It is not clear if Hyde ever seriously contemplated marriage as a solution to her material difficulties. What we do know, however, is that for a woman of Hyde's vintage there was almost no precedent for combining writing with marriage and motherhood. The alternative she faced was to earn enough money (in a discriminatory wage economy) to support both herself and her child,[38] while at the same time attempting something equally improbable: to make herself a place, as a heterosexual woman, in the homosocial masculine culture that takes hold with literary nationalism.

With the emergence of the Caxton writers in the 30s came a decline in fortunes for a more senior group of taste-makers. These are the writers whom Chris Hilliard has dubbed 'the bookmen', men like Alan Mulgan, Pat Lawlor, O.N. Gillespie, and, most emblematically in this context, Charles Marris, who as the editor of *New Zealand Best Poems* was the target of Glover's 1936 lampoon 'The Arraignment of Paris'. With their routine anti-modernism and their stronghold in the daily press, they stood for precisely the kind of book-loving gentility that the nationalists were determined to eradicate. Glover in his 'Arraignment' caricatures Hyde as a follower of the detested Paris, and it's true that the bookmen admired and supported her, as they did Eileen Duggan. But Hyde didn't throw in her lot with them exclusively. She also had a good deal to do with the opposition. The literary scene was tiny, so it's no surprise that she came across the Caxton writers in person. More than this, however, she seems actively to have cultivated their friendship. In Auckland she was on good terms with the printers Ron Holloway and Bob Lowry, and to some extent with Mason and Fairburn. Briefly, at least, Hyde shared Fairburn's enthusiasm for Social Credit; Fairburn and Mason were both allies in the campaign against the Ōrākei evictions; and all four men were at a party to celebrate the launch of *Journalese* in 1934.[39] Also in 1934–35 she pursued an intense correspondence, on poetic and to some extent spiritual matters, with Allen Curnow. Cresswell, whom she had long looked forward to meeting,[40] was another whom she got to know in Auckland in the mid 30s; she proposed him as a delegate to a PEN conference in London, and it was through Cresswell that she met the Stronach family and came to stay in their beach cottage at Castor Bay. In fact, of all the nationalist writers, it is only around Glover that Hyde seems consistently wary. And still she offered him poems for *Verse Alive* and for the 1937 *Caxton Miscellany*, while it was even believed in the nationalist camp that Hyde had talked Marris out of a libel suit over Glover's broadside.[41]

What did Hyde get in return? Very little. It is not enough to say that she was kept at arm's length. For the nationalist hard core (Glover, Fairburn, Sargeson, and more formally, in his critical essays, Curnow), Hyde and her work are an object of scorn. Almost invariably the forms this takes are gendered; often they are explicitly sexualised. As the nationalist writers close ranks against Hyde, it is her presumed sexuality that condemns her as irrevocably 'other'. Of particular note in this context is Sargeson. Complaining to Glover, he dismisses Hyde's poems as each 'a sort of orgasm in 3 stanzas', adding: 'I wouldn't mind so much if they weren't so obviously masturbatory orgasms.'[42] In one sense this is all too familiar: pre-emptively reduced to her sexuality, the woman writer is discounted accordingly. But what does it mean—this aggressively erotic language—when its author has no sexual interest in women? Why is a gay man posing as an expert in the varieties of female orgasm? It isn't an isolated example. Consistently Sargeson writes about Hyde in the language of heterosexual pursuit, boasting (again to Glover): 'We had a tender goodbye under a vine growing down an alleyway behind the Regent Theatre [. . .] I went over big with Iris over the last few days.'[43] Whatever is at work here in Sargeson's discourse, it doesn't appear to be sexual desire. And the same confusing cross-currents flow back and forth in the distressing account of Hyde in Charles Brasch's *Indirections*.

Hyde's situation during her last months in Britain encapsulates her dilemma as a woman writer. Her nearest friends in this lonely episode are the two men who, as editors, bookend the nationalist movement: James Bertram, founding editor of *Phoenix*; and Brasch, the soon-to-be editor of *Landfall*. Hyde describes Bertram to Rosalie Rawlinson as a 'godsend',[44] and in her ill and solitary state she seems to have relied on him heavily. After first encouraging Hyde to move into the same boarding house, Bertram was also able to arrange for her admission to Middlesex Hospital.[45] They shared a fascination with China (they had first met by accident in Hong Kong, though they had corresponded earlier), and he helped polish the manuscript that became *Dragon Rampant*.[46] They dined together frequently around London (sent a fiver by John A. Lee, Hyde spent it taking them to a French restaurant); and she would climb the stairs to Bertram's attic room to read him her poems. In a letter to Bertram on the day that he returned to China, Hyde makes little secret of her feelings for him: 'I do like you so much—yes, and love you so much. Partly gratitude, but that's not all'.[47] Yet, while it seems as if Hyde was at least half in love, Bertram's condescending summation of her life in *Landfall* in 1953 ('a rather embarrassing record of dangerous living and over-stretched ambition') strongly implies a mismatch in their regard for each other.[48]

It was Bertram who, shortly before returning to China, introduced Hyde to the person who would eventually publish these ungenerous comments, Charles Brasch.[49] The two men had behind them a deep, romantic friendship reaching back to their teenage years at Waitaki Boys' High School.[50] What occurred now with Hyde was effectively a transfer of responsibility; as Brasch recalls, 'I liked her, was interested in the new poems she was writing, and felt anxious about her, as James was. After he left England and she was discharged from hospital [. . .] she came to stay with me at Bishop's Barn.'[51] But his guest demanded more of him than 'rest and quiet and good food'. Brasch describes Hyde making a sexual pass at him, and when rejected ('I could not respond more than in friendship') cutting open her arm with a razor blade and making a showy presentation of the injuries.[52] A more improbable sexual conquest than the chaste and fastidious future editor is difficult to imagine. 'Physically she repelled me,' Brasch records, and nothing we know of his sexual tastes and his romantic comportment would lead us to expect otherwise. But how could Hyde fail to recognise this? Most probably, I would suggest, because sexual desire itself is not the issue: if Hyde turns to sex, it is as a plea for acknowledgement, a futile endeavour to force her way into the intimacy shared by her male contemporaries. Sex appears to be the only means by which Hyde, as a woman writer, can imagine penetrating that circle. And yet no matter whom she sleeps with, she is never going to be a Waitaki Old Boy. Sex supplies the terms in which she feels herself defined, and yet from a masculine point of view it defines her exclusively as an outsider.

Ghosting in the background of this dismal scenario we can once more discern the figment of an alternative, matrilineal history. A couple of weeks before her death Hyde addressed a meeting at the New Times Bookshop, reporting on her experiences of the war in China. The New Times Bookshop and its weekly meetings were the brainchild of suffragist and anti-fascist campaigner Sylvia Pankhurst (1882–1960).[53] Pankhurst was immensely impressed by Hyde. Herself a second-generation suffragist (daughter of the famous Emmeline Pankhurst), she would later describe an immediate sense of connection across the generations: 'Her thin little hand clasped mine with a confiding pressure, which seemed to say she knew how sharply I was grieved for her, assuring me we would struggle together for the same ends.'[54] Pankhurst responded protectively, inviting Hyde to her home, insisting that she visit her osteopath, and proposing that the younger woman come and live with her as soon as she had a spare room; meanwhile, she would arrange for Hyde to stay with one of her network of women friends. Despite being told, 'No, I must be alone to write', Pankhurst immediately messaged a colleague, seeking her assistance in 'mothering Robin Hyde'.[55] A few days later she had a spare room of her own, and wrote to Hyde inviting her to stay. Receiving no reply she sent a second invitation, but Hyde had killed herself the previous day. 'Like a trail of mist,' writes Pankhurst, 'she had slipped through the hands stretched out to her.'[56]

The episode reads like an allegory of the misconnection between feminist generations. The residual networks of suffragist feminism open towards her, but Hyde is looking the other way. The prospect of being 'mothered' fails to resonate; the language of an older mode of homosocial nurture no longer speaks to her, any more than the vocational model of a Dorothy Richmond. For Hyde, that feminine homosocial culture no longer supports either her sexual or her literary identity. Instead, on the very day she insists on being 'alone to write' (Hyde by now is living in a one-room flat in Notting Hill), she proposes to D'Arcy Cresswell that she move in with *him*. Cresswell, whom Derek Challis describes as her 'only remaining literary friend in London' after the departure of Brasch for the United States, is unreceptive. He fears that Hyde will 'involve' him in 'an uproar'. And besides, he's keeping a room free for *his* old school friend, Ormond Wilson.[57] To a network that might have mothered her, Hyde is indifferent. To the end, her demands remain resolutely focussed on a masculine homosocial network to which she is extraneous.

Guts and sawdust

'We think back through our mothers if we are women,' writes Woolf in *A Room of One's Own*.[58] And yet, even as she was sharing this enabling thought, the process of 'thinking back' was being interrupted. For Hyde's generation—the generation of what Showalter has called the 'feminist crash'[59]—the achievements of their 'mothers' would prove intransmissible. Hyde's career, fraught as it is both from a personal and creative point of view, exemplifies this mis-affiliation. For all her impassioned feminism, Hyde is an intellectual orphan who can't imagine herself mothered. Setting out 'to build the house of woman', as she puts it in a sequence from *The Book of Nadath*, it's as if she has to dream the entire edifice from scratch. Just as the homes of those older women offer no form of shelter that Hyde can recognise, in Woolf and her cohorts (the great generation of women modernists) she can find no foundation that she wishes to build on.

As readers have noted over the years, there are parallels between Hyde's career and Mansfield's: a Wellington connection, a focus on children, a perhaps deliberate echoing of 'Prelude' in the first chapter of *The Godwits Fly*.[60] It's hard to ignore the painful similarities in their career trajectories—Mansfield dead at Fontainebleau at 34, Hyde in London at 33. And there's the gratifying argument that our two major writers of World War I (for Hyde in her own way is a writer 'of' the war as much as Mansfield is) both happen to be women. But while Mansfield's response is demonstrably that of what Vincent O'Sullivan calls a 'contemporary mind',[61] Hyde's response, a generation later, in many ways is not. Hyde has a good deal to say about those writers she calls 'the moderns'. It's a label she uses inclusively—it may be Pound and Eliot, it may be Edith Sitwell, or Auden and Spender, or her local male contemporaries—but whoever is in her sights, her opposition is unrelenting: Hyde's anti-modernism is a key motif of the critical position she stakes out for herself. Inevitably she pleads for the Romantic values that modernism condescends to. She decries what she sees as a dearth of feeling; she complains of excessive formalism, intellectualism and obfuscation. Pound, she writes, though 'scholarly and able', is also 'over-intellectualised and a little stupid'.[62] Curnow (she has just read his *Three Poems*, published 1935) 'has a genuine gift and sense for poetic beauty, and if he ever bothers to feel for a little without attaching the chemical analysis, may write something of great merit'; in the meantime, however, 'he is too abstruse and too obscure.'[63] More off-putting still for Hyde is her sense of her contemporaries' social inertia, and she is quick to progress from aesthetic objections to upbraiding modernist political quietism. Poets 'who seek most ardently after revolution in form' turn out to be 'strangely averse to any sort of living [sic] their principles';[64] while of the local literary nationalists ('the Mob') she observes: 'Shelley gave them the entire and simple outline of a plan of action, and they haven't music enough in them to read it, nor guts enough to use it if by chance they did.'[65]

Partly through her popular association with Mansfield, Hyde is sometimes mistaken for an inward-looking, subjectively oriented writer. It is not a judgement she would have welcomed. Despite her intense feelings for her psychiatrist Gilbert Tothill—she may well have been the first New Zealand writer to have significant experience of psychotherapy—she was wary of too much self-contemplation. She disliked the ready pairing with Mansfield,[66] and she loathed what she saw as the introspection of so much contemporary fiction: 'Woolfs, Wests, O'Flahertys, Sitwells, all spilling their guts and sawdust according to which their beings are stuffed with'.[67] (So strong is the objection that in *Wednesday's Children* it emerges entirely out of context: 'Maritana's Maori boy friends [. . .] used to turn [octopuses] inside out like gloves, revealing the fact that they had baggy cream insides. Wednesday couldn't bear to see them like that, she said they reminded her of modern novelists.')[68]

As a novelist Hyde is at her most impressive in the panoramic world of the Starkie novels: large casts, historical sweep, critical social record, and chiefly external modes of narration. Her fictions are not psychologically minded. *Wednesday's Children* may take place largely in the chief protagonist's head, but the aim is to write a political allegory, not a subjective case study. Even *The Godwits Fly* is far broader in its social canvas, and clumsier in its negotiation of subjective states, than anything Mansfield would have permitted herself.

Hyde's response to the war, I have suggested, is not 'contemporary'. And yet, doesn't the writer I have just been describing exemplify the politically minded outwardness of the 30s? Up to a point the objection is valid. As we've seen, the decade brought a conscious repudiation of what *New Country* editor Michael Roberts called 'the complexity and introspection, the doubt and cynicism of recent years.'[69] The politics of the era drew writers to the Left, and away from the extremes of modernist formalism. In the company of the Auden group, Henry Green and Orwell (Hyde was a great admirer of *The Road to Wigan Pier*),[70] there is nothing historically aberrant in Hyde's socialist-friendly humanism, in her commitment to a broad readership, or in her readiness to bear witness in whatever form was available. Orwell was only one of those who moved back and forth between journalism and fiction. Isherwood and Auden made the same journey that Hyde did, to the conflict in China, to write *Journey to a War* (1939). To this extent, then, Hyde is a writer of the 30s. But the moment we turn from the prose back to the poetry, this sense of Hyde as a worldly and current writer dissolves. However much the poets of the Auden generation may resile from modernist formalism, none of them tries to write as if modernism never happened. Above all, none contests the central modernist precept that the rupture of the

20th century demands a renovation of literary language. Hyde becomes an outlier by refusing to accept that premodern ideas of 'literariness' have lost their currency.

Not that she is unaware of the changes a modernist poetic demands. She registers the modernist recoil from the emotional values of Victorian verse,[71] and she can see how her own work appears in this light: 'Crushing comment from the modernist critic's viewpoint: not only mournful but also dated.'[72] Hyde even parodies herself from a modernist viewpoint. 'The Singers of Loneliness', from *The Book of Nadath*, dramatises a number of contemporary poetic positions: there's a Cresswell figure (his misogyny, his Hellenism), a fruity South Island pastoralist, and some quarrelsome 'moderns' ('Hear us, oh people! Today we are the only singers').[73] But the first poet under the microscope is a woman identified by her over-ripe diction and her Pre-Raphaelite stage machinery:

> One sang, whose heart was full of an olden shore. She sang, 'Oh where are you fled, my purple companions?
>
> Where is it moored, that ivory barque whose sails drip honey, and what air do its perfumes sweeten today? For my soul remembers its voyages, I am sick to set out.
>
> Let the keen waves bring me a prow, and bear me away into another and softer wind, an island wind, where the vines run full of grapes. It is there I shall be satisfied.
>
> Who has stolen the myrrh and the cassia from my limbs? Who has broken my urn, and unlocked my spirit into this bare world?'[74]

The riposte that follows would not—at least in its gendering, and in its basic sentiments—be unacceptable to Curnow or Pound:

> You are the harlot of words: as a cunning woman draws the silks over her limbs, you have drawn words over your thought [. . .][75]

There are times when Hyde seems to be willing herself in a modernist, masculinist direction: 'have been feeling for some time past that my verse is far too frail and nebulous—jelly-fishy—so I'm trying to introduce a few vertebrae into the poor animal';[76] or, 'I am going to write a series of short stories as hard and tight and cold as I can make them.'[77] Moreover, tracking the issue back to its historical crux, it's clear from *Passport to Hell* that Hyde can articulate the relationship between modernist aesthetic imperatives and the carnage of the war—hence a passage making sport of the ghastly disconnection between a lyric from a pre-war classroom and the reality of the trenches.[78] But she won't take the lesson home with her. One thinks again of Mansfield, upbraiding Virginia Woolf: 'I feel in the *profoundest* sense that nothing can ever be the same, that, as artists, we are traitors if we feel otherwise: we have to take it into account and find new expressions, new moulds for our new thoughts and feelings.'[79] For Hyde, too, who grew up with it, the war defines her sense of where she finds herself in history, including where she finds herself as a woman, caught in the gears of that post-war remaking of sex. Yet somehow she never internalises the injunction that is literary modernism's most sweeping (one might say *hegemonic*) legacy, that the writer must 'find new expressions'—that post-war modernity must be addressed in its own language—and that whatever else that language might be, it will not be the language of Victorian high sensibility.

Poetry in the dug-out

> After reading your poetry and enjoying its music I sense a lack—of what. Of contemporaneity. There isn't about it the smokiness of industry, the clang and whirr of the age of speed and pain.
> —John A. Lee to Hyde[80]

How does Writer X belong to his or her moment? In one way or other, this is the question the literary historian is always trying to answer. With Hyde, however, it takes on a case-specific urgency. For of all the writers I spend time with in this book, none is so unsettled in her own contemporaneity. Hyde is not merely an oddity like Cresswell, whose anachronism feels like a private psychopathology. Hyde's out-of-timeness cuts deeper than this, for although she creates her own antiquarian world, the pressures that shape its construction are historical and legible.

When Lee presents his typically forthright critique, Hyde responds in good spirit. The challenge is not unfamiliar to her: she knows that she doesn't want to 'hang about manufacturing the literature of escape', and she's alert to the costs that come with 'another landscape, which is more than half a dream.'[81] But the challenge of the contemporary world is one that she hears differently as a poet and as a prose writer: 'In prose I know I can do it, and have, a bit, in [*Passport to Hell*] [. . .] But poetry's different—queer—I have almost no control over it.'[82] The date is 1936—Lee has been reading *The Conquerors*—but Hyde, even before China, has seen more than her share of the contemporary world's 'pain'. The evidence is there in her fiction and in her journalism; in prose, as we've seen, she makes a plausible 30s writer. And it might be argued that, page for page, Hyde is more successful in prose than in verse. Certainly she is less problematic. But it's poetry that matters more to Hyde: 'I love poetry as I could never love anything else.'[83] And it's her poetry that is so difficult to account for: so wilful, so outlandish, so complexly warped and distorted. This is why, despite talking in equal measure about her prose, I have tended to identify Hyde as a poet. For it's the poetry, I think, that in the end can tell us most about what it means for the writer to be trapped in that opening door.

Hyde's search for 'a home in this world' is not, she tells us, about 'four walls and a roof on top', but about 'a centre of equipoise [. . .] a place from which one can advance.'[84] She's looking for a place she can speak from and write from. But she's searching from inside a structure of feeling that acknowledges her only as an object, a problem, a demand. Hyde belongs to a generation of women who couldn't locate that place. Dislodged by the rising sexual tide of the 20s, they found a platform neither in the homosocial structures of suffragism, nor in the modernist spaces cleared by the Woolfs, Steins and Mansfields. Most, as the record suggests, were silenced. Hyde was not. But it came at the cost of her building in her poetry an antiquarian otherworld. She describes this poetic 'home' in a letter to John Schroder: 'like one trying to live a pre-war life, in a wartime dugout, with a strictly modern bomber poking about overhead'.[85] She was perfectly able to spell out the dangers. They are there in the ultimately lethal fantasies of *Wednesday's Children*. Or again, in that self-parodic sequence from *The Book of Nadath*:

> Finding your lovers of today ignoble, you have stolen a dead Pharoah's thighbone [. . .]
>
> Let the dead rest in peace, oh soft-haired singer, lest they take you at your word, and your voice echo forever in the airless vaults [. . .][86]

But her poetry, as she explained to Lee, had a will of its own. It homed in on the past. And in the pastiche and costume drama that resulted (an 'airless vault' describes it well), the bulk of her poetic output would be permanently entombed.

The poetic bunker that Hyde dug for herself was shaped in equal measure by her recoil from the emerging modernist consensus, and by the saturation of her own imagination in the mazy world of Tennyson and the Pre-Raphaelites. In terms of the formal protocols of the decade, Hyde's deviations are so exaggerated that even Schroder—certainly no modernist—was moved to try to tone down her rhythms and update her archaisms.[87] But Hyde doesn't simply 'fail' the dress code; she flaunts her transgressions, as if acting out, formally, her own exclusion from the masculine-modernist hegemony. Of course her prosody is also an intuitive fit for the image stock to which her imagination defaults:

> I'd like a house in the forest of Ys—isn't that two-letter word, Ys, pure Malory? Names were so lovely then—Camelot, Benoye, Broceliande, the Joyous Gard—strung together, not like jewels, like the more beautiful, waterworn pebbles out of any old sleeping river.[88]

The Arthurian legends (Malory, Tennyson) from which these signifiers derive are, of all the atavistic materials from which Hyde builds her imaginary 'home', probably the single source that calls most strongly to her—especially, as Megan Clayton points out, in the watershed period in Avondale Hospital.[89] In her version of medieval romance—with its chivalric codes and extravagant passions—the poet plays Guinevere to courtly apparitions who displace the 'ignoble' lovers of the disabling 1930s.

From a nationalist point of view the whole package is an

outrage. Camelot? Tennyson? Nothing could speak more plainly of a discourse upholding the 'pretended' against the 'actual'. This is even before one observes that the Tristrams and Lancelots of Hyde's Arthurian theatre are, beneath the costumes, already largely fictitious. Safely unavailable and highly idealised, Hyde's deceased teenage crush, Harry Sweetman, and her psychotherapist, Gilbert Tothill, are as lovers almost as fantasmatic as the fathers of Wednesday Gilfillan's (imaginary) children. So yes, the procedure is certainly regressive, and it's no surprise that Curnow, in particular, should make capital of Hyde's alibis. But what Curnow would later describe as Hyde's 'confoundment' has far less to do than he imagines with the specific history of settlement. Curnow and his colleagues are in no position to see it—they are part of it—but Hyde's romantic atavism betrays a disturbance between men and women that colours their own position as writers as indelibly as it does hers.

From Hyde to Plath

Finally, what can we say about the poet who wrote that passage from 'The Beaches' with which we began? How should we now interpret the gulf between the Camelot fantasia and the lucid objectivity of this 'other' Hyde? Traditionally—and again the convention begins with her male contemporaries—this gap has been plotted onto a graph of 'maturation'. In her very late works, the story has it—in 'Houses by the Sea' and the China poems—Hyde begins to cast off her 'literary swathings' (Curnow),[90] writing in a more restrained language and more directly from the world at hand: 'Her best new poems [. . .] showed what memory made of experience more fully lived, showed her at last becoming a poet' (Brasch).[91] It's hard not to fall into line with this narrative—which is also to say, with the nationalist meta-narrative of the growing up of New Zealand literature. But it's far from clear that Hyde herself saw it this way. As Leggott points out (Leggott who more than anyone reads against the grain of that nationalist growth narrative), Hyde was at work on the favoured last poems at the same time that she was writing the visionary pastiche of *Nadath*—her longest single poem, and a mile away from the stripped-back objectivity that made so much more sense to Curnow and Brasch.[92] Hyde isn't learning at last to be a modernist; she is simply trying out different things. Or, as Leggott concludes, 'There are always two versions': not just *Dominion*, but also Hyde's long poems; and not just the Hyde of 'Houses by the Sea', but the 'epic, prophetic' voice of *Nadath*.[93] If Hyde was discovering a new way of writing that was more in tune with nationalist demands, there is nothing to suggest that she was about to abandon everything else she knew in favour of it.

From a certain angle, the next three decades will vindicate Hyde's refusal to fall into line. At a first approach, yes, in its nuanced demotic tones, its imagism, its laconic drama of perception and narration, the mode of that 'primal' beach scene appears difficult to go past. Why on earth, in the 1930s, if you *could* write like that, would you *not* write like that? Nonetheless women poets didn't. If we ask, that is, how poetry by women will eventually re-emerge from the long winter of the mid century, it will not be by taking up the restraints and economies of 30s modernism. The only poet of Hyde's generation who springs to mind as working in that vein is Elizabeth Bishop—who, plagued by depression and alcoholism, appears to have lived a lonely and unhappy life, and who produced, with great difficulty, a very small body of work. Wonderful writer that she is, there is little in Bishop's example to countermand the bleak profile of Hyde's generation of women, or to suggest that the dryness that Hyde rejects is the missing ingredient that will help women write again. The women poets who will finally break through at the beginning of the 1960s will not be restrained and objective. Sylvia Plath and Anne Sexton, it seems to me, are the first women poets to discover a way forward in the aftermath of the sexual reordering of the 1920s. Theatrical and visionary, 'unbalanced' and suicidal, we can feel behind their extreme measures the weight of three decades or more of inchoate struggle. And though Hyde will not be there to see the birth of Confessionalism, in a speculative sense we can imagine it making sense to her. For she knows that it will take more than literary good behaviour (the masculine decorum of modernism) to claim for herself a speaking part in a discourse in which women are *spoken for* by their sex. Her desperate situation calls for something more radical: a poetics of prophecy, vision and theft.

In a poem that Leggott dates from 1937—contemporary with *Nadath* and the first drafts of 'Houses by the Sea'—Hyde rehearses an entirely different version of that primal scene with which we began. Not this time in the cool tones of imagism, but with the fervour of Romantic prophecy:

Prometheus

No anger now, no surging of desire . . .
Only the light waves fronding on the sand,
The grains of sand fine gold from breast to knees:
And only in my cupped hands burn the little
Red semen, harsh and brittle,
Borne downwards from these trees with hair of fire,
Borne from these slow and ancient rata trees.
Against the sand blue shadow quivers tall . . .
Once it was told that in another land,

Prometheus, hot-running from the caves,
Splashed to his thighs such licking milky waves,
Flourished against the sun his godly brand,
And in a second had the world aflame . . .
And burnt out littleness: and burnt out shame.[94]

The descendant of Shelley's, Hyde's Prometheus steals on her behalf not fire but sex.[95] The poem fits the brief that she described to Pat Lawlor: 'Yes, I write about sex—either as the tragedy it is, or the free and clean thing I want it to be.' She has mostly, she admits, 'been made smaller by sex', but here she summons an avatar to 'burn out' that history of diminishment. It's a poem, we could say, about *uplifting* sex: redeeming and transforming it through a seizure of subjective agency. It begins to sound like the kind of text that could make a happy ending out of this long narrative of sex-in-transition.

And yet, while Hyde can describe that transformative ending—can name it as a desirable outcome—she can no more enact it in this poem than she can in real life. The problem, to put it bluntly, is the poem itself, as it struggles half-heartedly to occupy its straitjacket form (*viz.* the underwhelming rhymes, the redundancies in lines six and seven). Did Hyde ever write a convincing sonnet? The constraints seem at odds with the scale of the vision; the proposition calls for a broader canvas, and a fresh, as yet undiscovered language. Trapped in this poem there is something more fierce: we can hear it in the indecorous splash of the pivotal metaphor. Rata bloom as *semen*? Now that could be something! And yet the mashing of codes is like the clash of two eras, neither of them contemporary, so that once more the trope enacts Hyde's isolation: transgressive and yet orphaned, it shrinks to an anomaly for want of an emergent form and idiom in which to situate itself.

'Prometheus' appeared among the 'later poems' of the posthumous *Houses by the Sea*, edited by Gloria Rawlinson and published by Caxton in 1952. Five years later, Allen Curnow restaged the sex-on-the-beach encounter, complete with his own extravagant version of the stamen/semen metaphor. Readers who knew Curnow personally insist that 'Spectacular Blossom' is a love poem, in which case I can only say that it's a strange and (surely?) disturbing one. Initially the poem sets the scene for a ritual sacrifice whose victim/object is at once a shoreline pōhutukawa and a woman stepping into the shallows. But as the scene unfolds it turns explicitly (hetero)sexual. There are now two victims, a 'girl' and an 'old man', three if we include the tree, commingling in a lurid, orgastic carnage: 'woody tumours burst in scarlet spray' while the slit throats of the lovers 'ejaculate' blood.[96] Did Curnow, then, consciously or otherwise, take his cue from Hyde's own ejaculatory figure? The question is intriguing. And yet finally it's not of much consequence. For what the dialogue between the two poems reveals is no more than Hyde herself already knows; we hear it in her gender analysis of the 20s and that grimly erotic urge to 'put the women back in their place', a mood that by the 50s may be decades old but on the evidence of this poem has not gone away. The extremity of Curnow's vision can't be historicised entirely; it's also his own particular thing, as is evident the moment we begin to track that 'stain of blood' through his long career.[97] But the poem also speaks (*continues* to speak, as late as 1957) from inside a structure of feeling. And that Hyde, too, can only speak from inside that structure—talking back to an embattled masculinity that in itself has no idea how to talk to women—explains why her own poem already feels defeated in its effort to envision an uplifted sexuality.

Prometheus gets his name from the Greek word for 'forethought'. Since he brings mankind the gift of fire (and hence metal-work), probably we can call him a modernist. But he is also a figure of Hyde's own untimeliness, and of her punishment for it. Hyde, like Prometheus, looks to the future where she sees a door opening for women, and yet she cannot pass through it. We might recall the passage that Curnow quotes from Matthew Arnold: 'That promised land it will not be ours to enter'.[98] And yet, for Hyde, to have 'saluted it from afar' will earn her only mixed rewards. Chained as she is to the rock of the present—trapped in that historical 'hinge' between two waves of feminism and two modes of feminine subjectivity—she will suffer, like the rest of her female cohort, for being ahead of herself. From inside that interwar structure of feeling, she can't find a language to describe where she is. Woman as a heterosexual subject does not yet speak in the first person. Christina Rosetti and Ruth Pitter don't write poems with semen in them; nor does Gertrude Stein or Elizabeth Bishop. No one has yet conceived a feminine poetic to push that door fully open, and Hyde, unable to conceive of poetry in modernising terms, treats it instead as a form of consolation. Her vision of uplifted sexual relations is relegated to an unreal 'other land', her language of default acting out her historical displacement. And all of this (call it the punishment of foresight) Hyde herself can see, at least in glimpses. She knows that, as the door opens further, inevitably she will come to seem 'quaint', even if it won't be till the early 1960s that others will arrive at a strategy less quaint than hers.

Chapter 7

Calling a spade a shovel

Sargeson's 'disguised poetry'

'My New Zealand'

When Frank Sargeson embarks on what will turn out to be his autobiographical trilogy, he contrives to give the first word to someone else:

> Glorious here, away back, on the swirling banks of the Waitaki, mountains all round. I have a comfortable cottage to myself near the homestead, and am writing mornings on a sunny verandah. This is *my* New Zealand! *Letter from a friend.*
>
> It disturbed me, that short paragraph D. had managed to squeeze into the last bit of space on his notepaper. From where I sat at my writing table, I looked out the window and saw nothing of my own New Zealand.[1]

Holding the door open for nationalism's most iconic fiction writer, we meet once again the iconic failed poet. For 'D.' is none other than D'Arcy Cresswell who, with his uncanny knack of insinuating himself—'present without leave', photo-bombing our literary history—will be as important to Sargeson in the defining of his position as he is to Curnow. In the narrative arc of 'Up Onto the Roof and Down Again', as this first instalment will be titled, Cresswell acts as prompt or incitement. The perception that the two inhabit different New Zealands (or 'have' different New Zealands, as the possessive pronouns imply) provokes Sargeson's construction of his own imaginative itinerary, a journey that finally will lead him back to the 'Third Class Country' of his uncle's King Country farm.

If Sargeson defines 'his' New Zealand against Cresswell's, it is worth asking what Cresswell's version entails. The answer supplied in his note is a familiar one: landscape ('the Waitaki, mountains all round'); solitude (a 'cottage to myself'); privilege ('a comfortable cottage [. . .] near the homestead'); and imaginative possession ('This is *my* New Zealand!'). Sargeson's point, if he doesn't exactly say it, is that Cresswell's lofty pastoral utopia is not so much national as regional. Revisiting the story of this letter in 1960, at the time of Cresswell's death, he makes the point more explicitly:

> [. . .] one may readily suppose that Nature would never have figured so greatly in all his writing if it had not been for his early experience of the Canterbury scene, 'world of vast rivers, high mountains, and great reaches of barren tussock-land.' For my part however, I was forever bound to the hilly stump farms of the King Country [. . .][2]

Sargeson finds no great fascination in the doings of 'South Island sheep-farming pukka sahibs,'[3] as he calls them disdainfully, reviewing a novel by James Courage. His own New Zealand, then, will be in many ways a corrective to the distinctly mainland Romanticism, not just of Cresswell, but more importantly of Glover, Brasch and in certain respects Curnow. The goal of imaginative possession remains in common. But the world of Sargeson's prose will differ notably from that of the South Island nationalist poets: working class to their upper-middle class; urban or suburban to their pastoral; romantically gregarious to their Romantically solitary.

None of which need surprise us by now. Literary nationalism is not *one* idea. It is the effect of an assemblage of writers exploring a range of related problems within a common structure of feeling but from diverse points of view. An effective nationalist movement, as I've argued, needs the reach of Glover and Fairburn, not just the acuity of Curnow. But it's fair to say, I think, that it needs Sargeson even more. In the story of the invention of New Zealand literature, only Curnow's role is as profound as Sargeson's. He's crucial because he writes prose fiction in company largely dominated by poets. More than this, he's vital for his refinement in that fiction of an idiom that will pass for local vernacular—the language which convinced Dan Davin, for example, when he first read Sargeson during World War II, of his 'perfect ear' for 'the patterns of thought and speech' of the Kiwi blokes in uniform with him.[4] If any writer brings to the nationalist brand a sense of being in tune with the man on the street, then it's Sargeson. What Glover achieves, in snatches, in the folksiness of his verse, Sargeson develops in a manner both easier to recognise and more tempting to imitate.

But where readers of the time, like Davin and Ray Copland, were excited by the demotic verisimilitude of Sargeson's prose, since the early 1980s critical attention has focussed more on its dissimulating qualities: on the author as a game-player, and on his low-key realist style as a mask protecting his closeted sexuality. Michael King's 1995 biography makes clear for the first time just how tightly his fortunes as a writer and his misfortunes as a gay man were bound up together.[5] Convicted in October 1929 on a charge of indecent assault on a male, Norris Davey (as he then was) retreated to the sanctuary of his uncle's King Country farm. When he emerged eighteen months later it would be as Frank Sargeson. With the passage of time, and thanks to a lifetime of dedicated work, this well-judged pseudonym has come to stand for the quintessence of a localised masculine realism. And yet the literary identity we know as Frank Sargeson doesn't so much embody a normative masculinity as *impersonate* it. It's a masculinity forged under the pressure of intense homophobic anxiety. Consequently, Sargeson's early fiction—reading it now 70 years after the event—is marked by effects that still seem audacious, but which also remain, in places, densely enigmatic.

Green potatoes

Cresswell makes a second appearance in Sargeson's memoir, this time right at its core—in the middle section of the middle volume, *More Than Enough*. The several thousand words that Sargeson bestows on him, as well as being the best portrait of Cresswell by any other hand than his own, also amount to the most detailed assessment of any other writer that the autobiographies offer. Titled 'To Live? To Write?', the chapter frames the breakthrough moment in the early 1940s when Sargeson writes the weightiest and most important of his early fictions, the 80-page novella 'That Summer'. As in the 'my New Zealand' gambit, Cresswell serves here as constitutive other—a model for Sargeson to define himself against. In the late 1930s Cresswell, like Sargeson, was living penuriously in a North Shore bach; as Sargeson puts it, he 'was the first person I met who in order to achieve his purposes had adapted himself to a manner of living which resembled my own'.[6] But there the similarities end, or so Sargeson would have it. He charts his position as an emerging New Zealand writer by rejecting, point for point, everything that Cresswell does or that he stands for. Rhetorically speaking Sargeson leans on Cresswell as heavily as Curnow does (even though Sargeson fends Cresswell off, while Curnow effectively identifies with him). But there's one crucial difference underpinning their respective manoeuvres, making the game for Sargeson more complex and more fraught. For Sargeson, Cresswell is not just a rhetorically convenient antecedent, as he is for Curnow. He is also a fellow gay man, with a history of public scandal to rival and exceed Sargeson's own, and with his own distinctive first-hand experience of exposure and disgrace.

For recent gay readers, the so-called 'Whanganui affair' of 1919 has become Cresswell's monument to infamy.[7] It could hardly be otherwise: on Cresswell's part, it reads as a story of mind-boggling iniquity. At its centre is the Whanganui mayor, Charles Evan MacKay, an intelligent and liberal-minded man and by all accounts a highly effective administrator. But MacKay was unpopular with members of the local establishment, and particularly the Returned Services' Association. Cresswell enters the story through a cousin, a member of the anti-MacKay faction. MacKay was known to be gay, and Cresswell was persuaded (just *how* he was persuaded remains unclear) to act as bait in an entrapment plot. The two were thrown together, MacKay took an evident interest in the younger man, and Cresswell then demanded his resignation under threat of exposure. MacKay's response—and who could blame him?—was to produce a revolver and shoot Cresswell in the chest. The poet, however, survived to tell the tale, while MacKay was duly disgraced, deposed and imprisoned; he would die in exile, in Berlin in 1929, shot by a policeman in a riot that he was covering as a journalist. Meanwhile the city for which he had done so much (among other things, building the Sarjeant Gallery) set about erasing his name from its records and monuments.

I have written elsewhere about whether or not Cresswell deserves recognition as a 'gay writer'.[8] Given the hypocrisy and cruelty of this affair, it's hard to quibble when the editors of an anthology like *Best Mates* decide to leave him out. But one thing needs to be acknowledged. We don't know exactly how Cresswell was persuaded to play his pusillanimous role: he may have done it gladly (he had enough cranky right-wing sympathies); he may have been paid; it's also possible that he may have been blackmailed himself.[9] Whatever the case, we can at least say this: Cresswell had seen up close what a vindictive homophobia could do to a gay man. Despite this, however, in his subsequent career as a writer he would be quite unabashed about his own sexual preferences. In particular, the autobiographies offer a candid account of his sexual adventures, upstairs and down (though mostly down), both in Britain and in New Zealand in the 20s and 30s.

For Sargeson, then, addressing the problem of how to live and write as a gay man, there is this fundamental difference between their two approaches: nowhere in Cresswell is there any attempt to couch his interest in men in terms of normative masculinity. Sargeson and Cresswell are both Romantics. But where Sargeson, as a nationalist and a humanist, celebrates interpersonal affinities (his 'I', we can say, is always trying to become 'we'), Cresswell's more grandiloquent and arguably paranoid strain of Romanticism glories in the gulf between 'I' and 'they'.[10] Poetry, for Cresswell, is an exercise in exceptionalism. His true companion is Nature itself, and if Nature approves of him ('a hare had remained quiet in a field and allowed itself to be stroked, a herring had leapt from the sea to lie quiet in his hand', Sargeson tells us)[11] then the judgement of what someone else might call a community could hardly matter less. For Sargeson, by contrast, assimilation into that local human environment is everything, in terms both of his personal survival and of his project as a nationalist writer.

Cresswell on board ship en route to New Zealand, 1928

At the centre of Sargeson's account of these differences is a gleefully sardonic set piece—a case study, it could almost be, in how *not* to belong to one's local community. Invited to eat at the poet's bach, Sargeson arrives to find an inebriated Cresswell ('he had fallen into unexpected company, and [. . .] had not cared to refuse drinks when they were so kindly offered'), with no food to be seen. His host, however, is undismayed; he has been 'cultivating the soil', and the pair set off to dig potatoes for dinner.

[. . .] at the top of the nearest cliff above the sea we discovered after searching among the coarse grass a few square yards which did indeed show some appearance of having been cultivated (although it seemed a rather long time ago). It was some moments before I understood that among the grass a different kind of vegetation, brown brittle and withered to almost nothing at all, was in fact what remained of potato tops. We had brought with us a fork and a bucket, and it was announced that we would now dig the crop; but the time of year was autumn, the soil had dried out and set like cement and the fork was useless. I asked how long the potatoes had been set, and how he had turned over the ground which I knew to be a trifling inch or two of topsoil over clay [. . .] Our strugglings with the cement would have been useless if there had not been cracks into which a prong could now and then be inserted; but we had to give up with only a dozen or so moderate-sized marbles coloured a deep greenish brown at the bottom of the bucket. But despite their disappointing size and appearance Cresswell said they would be excellent nourishment besides of a superior flavour since there had been no tampering with nature by the use of artificial aids to growth. Clearly, however, he had his doubts. And when he asked how it would be best to cook our potatoes I said (trying to make my voice sound offhand and indifferent) that when it was a question of possibly poisonous foodstuffs [. . .] the Maoris in their native wisdom would first partially boil, then finish in the oven, a method which was said to drive off the poison. There was afterwards silence about the potatoes, and we ate bread and butter and sheep's tongues from a tin. But these latter had required another walk—to the nearest store, which had by now closed; but it was explained to me that the man and his wife never minded being knocked up at any hour. Alas, ahead of me Cresswell chose the moment when he was

> beginning to mount the steps to the door to turn and ask me how I got on for credit with the local tradespeople. I hedged. I had seen the door at the top of the steps quietly opened by an unsmiling woman. Cresswell's words were, 'You should never worry, I have owed these people money for nearly a year, and they are *proud* to have me for their customer.' He turned and without a break or hint of dismay that I could detect continued with a good evening and a request for what was wanted—a request that was complied with without greeting or comment or change of expression.[12]

While Nature may be the presiding deity of Cresswell's luddite Romanticism, nonetheless he is obliged to admire, reports Sargeson, his own 'more practical relations' with it.[13] As everyone knows, in Sargeson's garden at Esmonde Road things actually grow. Indeed it's hard to overstate the importance of gardening to the Sargeson myth—to the way he personifies the stay-at-home New Zealand writer. His garden is the outcome of commitment and continuity, of being somewhere in particular and working there. It attests to that fundamental nationalist conviction that the 'local and special' will sustain the imagination. But sustenance and sustainability have more immediate (more 'practical') dimensions. Sargeson can feed himself—vital if he wants to avoid the distraction of other employment—can provide for himself, that is, without being a parasite. Since Cresswell believes firmly that the world owes him a living, he's willing to freeload wherever he can; he *asks leave* of nobody; he accepts patronage as no more than his due. Sargeson, by contrast, shows us the writer as a citizen like any other: Curnow's 'responsible adult New Zealander' in his case describes a genuine determination. His gardening is a routine suburban activity (manly, unthreatening). It also ties him into the local economy of gift and trade (he sells his surplus to the same local tradespeople Cresswell is so high-handed with). And it sustains his much-vaunted hospitality and conviviality. Almost anyone who remembers Sargeson will recount the meals produced from his garden; and the autobiographies themselves are also full of them (inevitably there's a story about feeding Cresswell, and another about Robin Hyde).

Sargeson with Christine Cole in his garden at Esmonde Rd

With his gumboots deep in the Takapuna soil, Sargeson is anchoring himself not so much in uppercase Nature as in that more 'practical' thing—an *environment*: physical, economic, social. To Glover he writes, early on in their friendship, 'I live mainly with the people I draw my material from'.[14] And in Sargeson's gardening is the most tangible meeting of his more unusual priorities and theirs. At stake here is not precisely 'credit' (with 'the local tradespeople', for example) so much as its intimate neighbour, credibility. If Curnow's contribution to the making of literary nationalism is to write its 'critical' history and curate its emergent canon, Sargeson's is partly to refine a language for a local fiction, but even more, perhaps, to embody writing as an achievable vocation. Sargeson is the writer who genuinely does 'commit the whole man' to the job. It's this that makes the autobiographies such a key text—the originary account of the making of a New Zealand writer—for it's Sargeson who proves that such a thing is indeed possible. To this end, he stresses the regularity of his routine. Every day, he tells us, he works: a page a day, no excuses. Then in the afternoon, the garden; in the evening, reading or entertaining friends.[15] The gardening is that 'practical' hinge without which—given that as a fulltime writer he has virtually no cash income—the rest of the routine would not be possible. It's also the activity that comes closest to making his own occupation look like anyone else's. Whether working the soil, writing his page a day, or preparing food in his tiny kitchen, Sargeson is always doing the same thing: he is trying to *naturalise* the vocation of the New Zealand writer.

All of which, again, is diametrically at odds with Cresswell, to whom it would no more occur to adapt himself to the way ordinary people live than it would to make concessions to the way other people write. About the second point, and about where it leaves Cresswell as a writer, Sargeson is quite undeceived: 'he remained as a poet indissolubly wedded to hide-bound notions about what he conceived the proper language for Poetry to be, unyieldingly hostile to everything that attempted new kinds of diction'.[16] In short,

Cresswell is vehemently anti-modernist, and the outcome, at least for his poetry, is fatal. At the same time, however, in the embodied conjunction of Cresswell's eccentricity and his archaic *literaryism* (to borrow Pound's phrase), Sargeson is able to sense the opposite possibility. When Sargeson weighs up the language of modernist minimalism—the laconic anti-expressivism of Hemingway, for example, or before him Sherwood Anderson—he appears to intuit that this naturalistic idiom is capable of concealing as much as Cresswell's performance advertises. This is the epiphany to which his long disquisition on Cresswell leads him: that by fashioning a narrative prose so plain that it 'might be mistaken [. . .] for documentary journalism', it may be possible in this disarming manner to effect 'a kind of disguised poetry'.[17] A left-leaning realism offers him the means to negotiate the fearful liability of his sexuality. The first requirement for the former Norris Davey, of course, is to conceal his orientation—his literary identity ('Frank Sargeson') is invented on that premise. But the stratagem of poetry in disguise offers more. In the space opened up by this dissembling prose—this closet, to give it its customary name—there is scope, while inventing a nationalist house style, to explore his own menu of meanings and pleasures.

Epistemology of the closet

We've seen how 'poetry for ladies' works. We know, in other words, that the value system that marks out the territory of literary nationalism is gender-coded at every fork in the road. Anywhere there's a choice to made, a direction to be called, a distinction to be drawn, there's always an option marked 'masculine', and it's always the favoured one. I have argued that behind these aesthetic discriminations is a reordering of sexual relations that overlaps with the modernist 1920s. And we've seen in the case of Robin Hyde what all this means for a writer on the wrong end of it, unable either to avoid or to identify with a militant masculinity by which she is both sexualised and minoritised. Earlier, I underlined three factors shaping this assertively masculine climate: the impact of World War I; first-wave feminism and the ensuing backlash; and, above all, the heterosexual science of the 20s. So far, however, I have not placed much weight on the implications of masculine homophobia. In Sargeson the problem of homophobia confronts us head on; we are reminded not only of how vicious it is, but of how widely its implications extend. Before we can fully appreciate the force of hard frost manliness, we need to come to terms with what Eve Kosofsky Sedgwick, in *Epistemology of the Closet*, calls a 'chronic modern crisis of homo/heterosexual definition'.[18]

The perception of this crisis as 'modern' is indelibly associated with the work of Michel Foucault and specifically the first volume of *The History of Sexuality*. Homosexual acts are not modern, of course; for centuries they were prohibited under the loose designation of 'sodomy'. But it's the late 19th century that converts these acts into what Foucault calls 'a new *specification of individuals*'.[19] The 'homosexual' (a term dating from 1869) is now, as Foucault puts it, 'a species'. From this point every individual will be assigned to one of a binary pair of sexualities: 'sexual identity', in its modern sense, is born. I have looked at the consequences for women and the effects of anti-lesbian homophobia in the 1920s. But on the masculine side the crisis sets in earlier. In the Oscar Wilde prosecutions of 1895 this new sexual 'species' is rendered instantly and spectacularly visible. The fallout will contaminate the new century. Indeed, for Sedgwick, so potent is this anxiety around sexual definition that it will operate in the discourse of the modernist epoch as a 'master term', or master binarism, to rival in its impact 'the more traditionally visible cruxes of gender, class, and race'.[20]

What is a 'master term' in this sense? As I understand Sedgwick, it's the kind of distinction that irradiates the language of an era, reinforcing other judgements which it draws into its discriminatory force field. Think again of some of those evaluative tropes familiar from the language of critical nationalism: hard/soft, plain/decorative, natural/artificial, dramatic/theatrical, actuality/escapism, seriousness/hobbyism, public/private (and so on). We know that if we take the distinction between the genders and run it down this list, the term we have been taught to value always connotes masculinity. As the saying goes, the privileged term is 'coded' masculine. But what if we apply to the same catalogue this new determination between gay and straight? If anything the coding is even more obvious. The negative term is invariably marked 'gay'. The evaluative language of nationalism (and before it, modernism) is informed and infected not just with a masculine bias, but with a homophobic one.

Of the many implications of this homophobic coding, let me briefly touch on three. First, the force of the nationalist aesthetics must in part be the force of homophobia itself. Imagine, for instance, the male writer who chose to write in a language that was, say, *artificial*, *decorative*, *theatrical* and *private*. To do so, he would have to push back against the entire weight of a homophobic culture. Homophobia lends to the rhetoric of critical nationalism an inertia, a surplus momentum, an accentuated vehemence. This is not to say that its proponents are always demonstrably homophobic; Fairburn surely is, but Curnow, it seems fair to say, is not. The question is not of individual attitudes and behaviours, but of the rhetoric that nationalism evolves out of modernism: a stacked deck, already inculcated with homophobic values.

Second, this homophobic bias bears down on everyone: it's not an issue for gay people only. The imaginary writer described in the previous paragraph might be gay or might be straight, but either way the proposal is still unthinkable. In one sense, of course, this must sound outrageous. I'm not suggesting, obviously, that for gay people and straight people the *stakes* are the same or the experience *feels* the same. But nor is it entirely a 'minority' issue—a problem within nationalist writing just for a notable gay contingent (Sargeson, Brasch, McCormick, Pearson). Sedgwick characterises homophobia as 'a mechanism for regulating the many by the specific oppression of a few';[21] as such, it infects the whole culture—it polices everyone. Nationalist writing profits from homophobia. It is part of what makes the movement so irresistible. But it also narrows the movement's range. Its signature is the kind of thing Virginia Woolf complained of: constraint and rigidity; a refusal of emotional 'androgyny'. And it's here, I would argue, that the question of homophobia bears on the case of straight but deeply inhibited writers like Fairburn and Glover.

Third, and here we reach the key point for Sargeson, the blatancy of this homophobic coding offers (paradoxically) a means of negotiating it. Because the homophobic weighting of nationalist rhetoric is so explicit—because each choice is already marked so clearly—formally speaking, it's a rhetoric that can be *simulated*. It makes itself available as a language of subterfuge, a language of concealment: a stylistic closet. And while the closet is a tyranny, it can also be a means of survival—in this case, not just for the individual writer (Sargeson), but for values and feelings that nationalist writing would otherwise be entirely bereft of.

This is the perception, or perhaps intuition, that Sargeson picks up and runs with in the 30s and 40s. In his fiction of this period he will refine a delivery to be known universally as 'the Sargeson style'. Masculine, plain, laconic, realist, local and resolutely inexpressive: it is a manner from which, to the utmost possible degree, every received marker of the 'literary' has been stripped out. Nothing could be further from the Cresswells of this world; nothing could be less pretentious, more 'natural' (or manly, or straight). In precisely these terms the Sargeson style will be welcomed, imitated and canonised. That such an idiom could serve as a vehicle for a romantic vision of same-sex love will prove so unthinkable an idea that almost no one among his contemporaries is ready to countenance it.

Cresswell (foreground, seated) and friends, Toc H bach, Milford, 1930s

Cross-dressing, cross-plotting

As Cresswell leaves for Britain in 1938, Sargeson sets to work on the novella-length fiction that will test his proposition about poetry in disguise.[22] Fittingly, 'That Summer' is directly concerned with concealed identities: it is among other things a comedy of misrecognition, a bedroom farce. It is also, as readers have agreed from the outset, the summit point of Sargeson's early career, as well as being that rare thing in the nationalist canon, an affirmative love story.[23] But it didn't come easily: it took four years to write (no wonder its author wants to call it a 'novel', though it's only 80 pages long). And nor has unravelling its disguises proved a simple matter. More than 70 years since its first publication, it reads as teasingly as ever.

By the standards of a Sargeson story, there's a lot of plot business in 'That Summer'. So the best place to start is with a thumbnail synopsis. The story is told in the first person by the naïvely good-hearted Bill. It opens with Bill quitting his job as a farm labourer to spend summer 'in town'—an unspecified port city—where he takes a room at Mrs Clegg's boarding house. He spends his days aimlessly, lying on the beach, going to the pictures and idly trying to pick up women. Boarding with him at Mrs Clegg's are the other two principal characters. Maggie is the flirtatious wife of an absent 'matelot', Bert (also known as Mr Popeye). Terry, plainly modelled on Sargeson's long-term companion Harry Doyle, is an elderly Australian: barman, betting enthusiast and former horse-trainer. When Terry loses his job, Bill insists on sharing his room with him; to provide for them both he takes a short-term job, and engages in minor scams and petty theft. The plot gathers pace when an abortive sexual encounter between Bill and Maggie is interrupted by the return of Bert. The next morning Bill is arrested, charged (presumably with sexual assault) and locked up. Terry, however, assures Bill that everything will be taken care of, and when the case comes to trial Maggie unexpectedly reverses her testimony. Freed from jail Bill discovers that Terry (who has always had a suspicious cough) has been moved to a sanatorium. Bill breaks him out in the middle of the night and ferries him home in a wheelbarrow to Mrs Clegg's. There he nurses him as his death approaches. In the course of an evening drinking beer with Bert and Maggie, Bill finally works out the obvious: that Maggie is a man. Terry dies, and we last see Bill talking to a taxi driver. In response to Bill's asking 'if he knew of any decent sheilas', the cabbie replies, approvingly, 'you surprise me'.[24]

Maggie's cross-dressing, and the plot that depends on it, confused and unsettled Sargeson's mid-century audience. Some readers simply couldn't understand it. 'Fairburn even mistook the sex of one of the characters,' Sargeson told a friend, with a certain grim satisfaction.[25] An early gay reader, Bill Pearson, was equally confused.[26] But the problem didn't end with coming to grips with this basic plot device. Even for an audience that understood the story's mechanics, there remained the challenge of fitting Maggie and Bert into the broader picture of homosocial nationalism. If this was a story about two male couples, how did the two couples, and the two plotlines, fit together? Even sympathetic readers struggled with this question. Eric McCormick, for instance, saw 'That Summer' as 'Sargeson's most satisfying story, beautifully proportioned and nearly always convincing'; and yet even so 'the homosexual sub-plot is clumsily devised'.[27] James K. Baxter went a couple of steps further. Complaining about 'a crude and sneering insistence on sexual abnormality', he averred: 'Even his greatest story is saved only by the intensity of its realism from becoming a bad homosexual joke'; and further: 'The story within a story about the sailor's "wife" who turns out to be his catamite seems to have no bearing on the main theme.'[28]

Baxter, though, makes an important point, and one that we need to take on board if we're to negotiate this work. As well as stating plainly that 'That Summer' is a love story, he can see that 'behind the sneer [about "sexual abnormality"] lies a deep and genuine valuation of the kind of friendship that merges imperceptibly into homosexual love'.[29] To Baxter's credit, then, he recognises the thing that homophobia insists we *don't* recognise: the shading, the imperceptible merging, that Sedgwick describes in terms of a 'homosocial continuum'. Homophobia, in Sedgwick's analysis, 'disrupts' the 'visibility' of this social/sexual shading: it doesn't uncouple homosocial continuity, but it recoils from it so violently that it becomes difficult to discern.[30] Baxter, who *can* see it, doesn't mean to be homophobic, but he finds it hard to place the two couples on the same page. The 'physical relationship of the Popeye couple' and the 'subtle emotional relationship of Bill and Terry' belong, in Baxter's reading, to different stories.[31] For Winston Rhodes, by contrast, they plainly run in parallel, and yet just as plainly require to be separated:

> [. . .] there would seem to be the deliberate intention of exploring both a normal and an abnormal hunger for companionship [. . .] It is noticeable that although the dramatic significance of 'That Summer' depends on the homosexual theme, its human significance depends on the relationship between Bill and Terry [. . .][32]

The couples belong in the same story, but only as the means to a salutary contrast: 'the homosexual episodes help to stress Bill's normality'.[33]

That readers as skilled and kind-hearted as Baxter and Rhodes insist on these distinctions tells us how deeply this homophobic reflex is embedded in nationalist literary culture.

Normal/abnormal; human significance/dramatic significance; (good) intensity of realism/bad homosexual joke: the homophobic cleavage of these binarisms—the slash-mark that separates one term from the other—is understood to segregate the story's two couples beyond the possibility of slippage or contamination. But is this really Sargeson's own choreography? What does a scrupulous reading support in terms of kinship, or, otherwise, between the two partnerships?

Reading with an anti-homophobic intent, the obvious place to start is with the court scene and the reversal of Maggie's testimony. For Sargeson, this has to be a charged moment, since it replays his own (or more strictly Norris Davey's) court appearance from 1929. That he 'escaped' (the term is relative) with a suspended sentence was the outcome of a pretrial arrangement. He agreed to pose as an innocent victim and to testify against his fellow accused, Leonard Hollobon; the latter was duly convicted and sentenced to five years hard labour. As Michael King argues, Sargeson/Davey's own feelings about this betrayal must have been devastating.[34] That Bill and Terry are a fictional version of Frank and Harry barely needs arguing. Frank is more worldly than Bill, of course, but Terry and Harry are virtually identical, while the tenor of their relationship, and numerous incidentals, confirm what we know of domestic life at Esmonde Road.[35] In the court scene, however, it's difficult not to conclude that Frank is also Maggie, and that in restaging the events of 1929, but with Maggie now recanting the betrayal, Sargeson is engaged if not in reparation then in some kind of post-dated wish-fulfilment. The author's stake in his own fiction is not confined to Bill and Terry. Consciously or otherwise, he is intimately engaged on the 'other' side of the narrative as well.

In another way, too, these allegedly separate plotlines cross and interlock in the events of Bill's trial. As far as the 'bedroom farce' is concerned, Maggie's reversal of her story marks its climax. Admittedly, Bill has not yet cottoned on (for him, the cross-dressing plot won't resolve until the end of the story).[36] But since the reader, or at least the alert reader, is already in the picture, the drama of Maggie's concealed identity is at its most intense with Bill's appearance in court—where for Bill to be cleared, we assume, Maggie's secret will need to be exposed. The same sequence, meanwhile, is equally significant in the terms of the relationship between Bill and Terry. Their friendship, after all, has not been without its vagaries. While Bill wants 'a mate that won't let him down',[37] and while there's no doubt of his loyalty to Terry, it's an open question as to how Terry really feels about him. Bill has been the provider and has made all the running. On their last day together before the arrest Terry disappears with a stranger who has just won big at the races. Bill, then, has plenty of grounds for doubt, and not the least notion of how Terry can help him. So when Terry comes through (by threatening Maggie with exposure), Bill has reason to be doubly relieved: not just at being freed, but at the verdict on their friendship. It's the one moment in the story where Terry vindicates his trust, which makes the scene as much a climax of the 'love story' as of the comic misadventures of the innocent among the 'abnormal'.

Love and sex

The 'homosexual subplot' is anything but incidental. The two main narratives and the two main couples interlock in ways that are essential to the story's meanings and to Sargeson's investment in them. And yet I'm not convinced that Winston Rhodes, when he discriminates so forthrightly between 'normal' and 'abnormal', between a valorised 'human significance' and a debased 'dramatic significance', is not taking up an invitation that the story itself extends. The distinction is homophobic, but it's possible that Sargeson authorises it.

A significant factor here is Bill's heterosexuality. Though we never see Bill succeed with girls, it's certainly not for want of trying. In fact, in this aspirational sense, he's probably the most priapic protagonist of a Sargeson story until we get to Michael Newhouse (read: *casa nova*) in *Memoirs of a Peon* (1965). For good measure, Bill is also conventionally homophobic: the cook at the Dally restaurant is 'a tonk', 'a real old auntie'.[38] These indications of his hetero-normativity are seized on by Rhodes with relief, in particular the parting exchange with the taxi driver who is presumably about to hook him up with a prostitute. His inquiry after 'sheilas' is for Rhodes 'the final comment on what some critics have all too easily taken to be a [. . .] homosexual theme.'[39] So what should we make (what does Sargeson make?) of the cabbie's ambiguous expression of surprise? Given all that's transpired between Bill and his cobber, a suspicious reader, too, might be surprised—might wonder if the author isn't signing off here with an arch 'homosexual joke'. But *is* he joking? Or does he seriously want to persuade us that Bill is straight in order to normalise his relationship with Terry? If the latter, then we have to judge the story complicit—at least up to a point—in the homophobic reading that Rhodes extracts from it.

One significant element implies that this may be justified. During Terry's declining days at Mrs Clegg's, Bill once again runs into Maggie, who attempts to apologise to him. Bill responds grudgingly, while still refusing to take Maggie's broad hints about her sex.[40] But Maggie asks feelingly after Terry, and a short while later she comes to visit, accompanied by Bert, who brings an armload of beer. The scene is thus set for what in a certain kind of fiction (comedy, bedroom farce) would be the casting off of disguises, the restoration of fractured couples, forgiveness, reconciliation. The feel-good, anti-homophobic resolution would see the two male couples discovering their solidarity: 'who was I to be interfering with anyone's pleasure in a world like this?' Bill reflects promisingly.[41] Maggie is still trying to unravel her disguise ('I'm sick of wearing these glad rags round my legs'). However, Bill's recognition ('I was a wake-up so far as Maggie was concerned') comes only when he and his friend are alone again. In the meantime, the party has degenerated into bickering and renewed threats of violence between Maggie and Bert. Peace and order—homosocial domesticity—are not restored until the other couple have finally been got rid of. Throughout the story, heterosexual couples (the farmer and his wife, Mr and Mrs Clegg, Ted and Mavis who steal Bill's cash) are shown in a state of continual conflict, both verbal and physical. In this they contrast utterly with the peaceable, largely non-verbal co-existence of Terry and Bill. The implicit misogyny of this distribution is not at odds with Bill's putative heterosexuality. If he's straight, then women are available to pursue sexually but not to be mates with; for friendship, there are men. Sargeson's handling of Maggie and Bert, therefore, is revealing. Rather than admit them to the world of homosocial love, he reduces them to a parody of a heterosexual couple, male and female, fucking and fighting: they are represented, that is, by their discord, and by the sexual specificity of their notionally 'perverse' arrangement. To this extent, Sargeson has done just what Rhodes suggests: he has assigned these unlike couples to opposite ends of the continuum, demonising the relationship marked explicitly by (homo-) sex.

If I'm reading him rightly, then Sargeson may well believe he can execute this move at no great cost. It is, of course, a closeted manoeuvre: the scapegoated sexuality of Bert and Maggie, and the putative heterosexuality of Bill, fence off an area of homosocial innocence in which to set Bill's relationship with Terry. However, it does remain a love story, as well as a 'gay' story in the most decisive sense. In other words, I'm not sure it's crucial to Sargeson that Terry and Bill should actually be lovers. After all, what is same-sex love? When Patrick Evans in his fine novel *Gifted* (2010) fictionalises the relationship between Frank and Harry Doyle, he decants their physical relationship into the intimate domesticity of caregiving and nursing. This strikes me not just as a tactful move, but as an emotionally convincing one. I am persuaded, in other words, not by *Gifted* alone but also by the relationship between Bill and Terry in 'That Summer', not just that this physical codependency was eroticised for Sargeson, but that in some degree it was essential to the feeling of loving another man. *Here* in some sense is where the 'action' is. To insist, then, that something must be lost if Bill and Terry don't have sex—that sex should, as ever, reveal the truth of their relationship—may well be no more than a homophobic presumption: *Where is the sex? It's what gay people do!* And yet any man, conceivably, can have sex with another man. To love a man romantically, on the other hand, is something more exacting.

Overreading: 'The Hole that Jack Dug'

Let us suppose, then—provisionally—that to Sargeson the narration of same-sex love does not of necessity imply representing genital sexuality. Let us allow, too, that Maggie and Bert may serve in this story as a normativising screen: that, reduced to a caricature of 'perverse' sexuality, they are sacrificed to the cause of making Terry and Bill's relationship appear 'normal' and wholesome. The two propositions together are plausible. But the question they leave in abeyance is this: what is the reader now to do with the erotic thread that, even so, weaves its way through the text—teasingly, yet insistently, even outrageously?

It was an essay by Simon During, from *And* 1 (1983), that first brought the eroticism of Sargeson's fictions out into the open. The centrepiece of During's 'Towards a Revision of Local Critical Habits' is an aggressively close reading (in During's terms, an 'overreading') of the first few pages of 'The Hole that Jack Dug' (1945). 'Aggressive' is During's own description. It's not that his intentions are hostile towards Sargeson; rather, the essay is a calculated attack on the 'habit' of reading only within the parameters of the text itself. This is what he calls 'underreading'—not so much a failure to read closely or to read 'what's there', but a failure to read for information that falls outside the text's frame of assumptions. Its antithesis, 'overreading', is of course During's remedy. Again, this is not a question of reading 'too much', but of something analogous to 'overseeing'—reading with a longer focal length. It doesn't treat the text as self-contained: it's concerned with historical and institutional contexts. And it doesn't assume the text to be a unified statement: it expects to find internal contradictions, and understands 'that fictions may be more knowing than they know'—in other words, that some of their meanings will be unconscious. If nothing about this sounds alarming today, in the early 1980s it was a different story. During's reading contained a number of provocations, of which the attention to homoeroticism was just one (the essay as a whole was a key intervention in terms of the overdue arrival of a local post-structuralism, a.k.a. 'theory'). But in the context of approaches to Sargeson specifically, it was the homoerotic theme that set the cat among the pigeons.

Not that anyone has ever doubted that the story favours the world of masculine mateship over the feminine and the domestic. As so often in Sargeson's stories, it is women (in this case Jack's wife, referred to as Mrs Parker) who are the bearers of puritan and petit-bourgeois values. What During does is simply to look more closely at the obvious: the insistent erotic charge that colours the perceptions of Tom, the narrator, when focussed on his friend Jack. Modelled apparently on Sargeson's friend Bill Anso,[42] Jack is the subject of a well-nigh lascivious gaze: we see him digging his hole 'with nothing on except his boots and his little tight pair of shorts'; we hear that 'he's a big specimen of a bloke, he's very powerfully developed' (no wonder the shorts are tight); and we see his outdoor labourer's suntan, glazed with sweat: 'he had a shine on as well'.[43] However, because During restricts himself to the opening pages we don't get as far as my favourite example, and surely one of the horniest moments anywhere in Sargeson's fiction. I am thinking of the scene in which Tom comes round in the evening and finds Jack labouring on by candlelight:

> I watched while he lit up and fixed the box so the light shone where he wanted to work. And for a few minutes I stayed watching, the shovel going in deep each time under his weight, the candle-light showing up the hollows and curves made by his big muscles, and the sweat making him look as if he was all covered with oil.[44]

What sort of hole is Sargeson trying to dig for himself with a shovel like that? Somewhere between the photographs of Herb Ritts and the line drawings of Tom of Finland, this is mateship all right, but not as we know it. Meanwhile, During doesn't just get us looking, but also listening: 'As for me, I'm ready to stick up for Jack any time.'[45] Or there's what he calls, rightly, this 'amazing sentence': 'Just about any man, I should say, would find it awfully trying to be a woman married to Jack.'[46]

During doesn't answer, or even try to answer, all the

questions he raises. In particular, he doesn't attempt to resolve what I'll call (perhaps unhelpfully, but I'll clarify this in a moment) the 'intentional' problem. Take for example the sentence about being married to Jack. This he identifies as 'almost without doubt a carefully contrived Freudian slip'.[47] Proceeding on the basis that in the Freudian unconscious there's no such thing as negation, During can then translate it: 'so what the odd grammar means is "Just about any man would try to be a woman married to Jack."' For my money, fair enough. But the nagging remainder is in the moment just prior: '*almost* without doubt [. . .] carefully contrived.' What is the reader to make of that 'almost'? Has Sargeson 'carefully contrived' this effect or not? Or as During himself asks:

> [. . .] what is the status of those sexual innuendoes? Are they just part of the narrator's unconscious, part of a desire in him to gloat over Tom's sexiness and so to be picked up by the implied reader? Or are they part of the text's unconscious, entering a reading over which it has manifestly no control, to be appropriated only by an extrinsic and overreading criticism?[48]

During's project here is to complexify—to complicate our interpretive habits—producing fragments of a specimen reading for a more or less pedagogical purpose. So the 'status' of this subtext needn't be resolved; it can simply be left to resonate as a productive ambiguity. This is enough for his fundamental purpose: to shake up the reading of local literature, to make us work harder.

The *And* intervention was dramatically successful. From this moment onwards, the critical game changed quite decisively. And it's a key moment too in the reception of Sargeson: the first glimpse, that is, of the refreshingly 'gay' Sargeson, whose image would be filled out by the King biography a couple of years later, and whose heroism would be celebrated by gay and gay-friendly critics like Peter Wells and Kai Jensen. As Jensen would put it in *Whole Men*, 'Sargeson's closeted sexuality [. . .] is a national literary treasure.'[49] Despite this, however, we are really no closer to answering the question that During leaves hanging—a question that is not the same matter of indifference to a historically minded, anti-homophobic criticism as it is to a polemical exercise in post-structuralist overreading. For During, everything can lie in one plane: complexity is all, while questions of intention and consciousness have no orienting value. But when the focus shifts to the question of homophobia, to the way it shapes nationalist culture, and the way that a writer like Sargeson negotiates it, then the writer's intentions become not just a legitimate matter of inquiry, but a fundamental one. If the 'game' for Sargeson—a desperate game, in which the stakes are fearfully intense—is to somehow write what he is prohibited from writing, then we need to attempt to isolate the conscious dimensions of his strategy. It's one thing to celebrate Sargeson as a gay hero. But if we are actually to understand his project, we need to ask whom he is writing for, and what he wants them to hear? To know what the sexual subtext 'means' we need a particular kind of thick description: that is, we have to make a call about what it means *to him*. This is the challenge I want to address as we turn our attention back to that paradigmatic concealment text which is 'That Summer'.

Squeaky wheels

The 'status' of Sargeson's winks and nudges is closely bound up with the problem of comedy. It's a complex, a knot, a textual ganglion that makes fearsome demands on the reader's sense of tact. So perhaps it's not surprising that readers of 'That Summer' who have broached the topic of comedy have then quickly backed away from it. For Baxter, we recall, the story as a whole teeters on the verge of becoming 'a bad homosexual joke'. It is 'saved', however, by 'the intensity of its realism', and so we don't get to find out what Baxter is (not) amused by. The same feint repeats in a later passage: 'Perhaps he intends an illuminating parallel between the physical relationship of the Popeye couple and the subtle emotional relationship of Bill and Terry. Or perhaps he is playing a joke on the earnest reader.'[50] To which I can only respond blankly, earnest reader that I am: *I don't get it*. Rhodes is equally coy: 'it is not difficult to discover a rich vein of comedy in his work, although some forms of wry humour that he is accustomed to exploit may occasionally jar or be misinterpreted by sensitive readers.'[51] The only clue we get about 'what's so funny' is that for Rhodes and Baxter alike the question of the comedic leads directly to Bill's time behind bars. 'The jail scenes,' adds Baxter, after the comment about 'the earnest reader', 'are certainly sensitive recording, and one would be loath to part with them.'[52]

At the risk of being tactless, then, we need to listen in earnest to Bill's naïve narration of his first night in prison.

> I may as well tell you that when you're in clink there's always a spyhole in your door. You can't see out, but if you keep your eyes skinned you can always tell when anyone has come along for an eyeful. And that first night I just happened to be watching when somebody came along and moved the slide, so I asked could I have a dab of vaseline to put on my piles. And mister peeping Tom said he'd have to see about that.
>
> Of course it was mainly a gag just to have somebody to speak to, though as a matter of fact my piles were hurting pretty bad [. . .] there I was in the dark and it didn't look as if

> the vaseline was going to turn up. So I thought I'd better turn in, and it sounded as if the jokers locked up alongside were doing the same thing because I could hear their beds creaking.
>
> And maybe it was because of the way those beds creaked that I couldn't get to sleep. They didn't stop creaking, and I thought maybe they were jokers like me who'd been locked up for the first time [. . .] I never thought about Terry or Maggie much. I just couldn't take my mind off the jokers that were locked up alongside me, because their beds never left off creaking all night.[53]

I find it hard to imagine what Baxter has in mind when he describes these scenes as 'sensitive recording'. Calling for a dab of vaseline to apply to his bottom (*Come and get me, boys!*)—is this really what the average Kiwi bloke does on his first night in prison? No wonder the bedsprings are creaking: it sounds as if lubrication is needed all round. And so on. It's not the most elevated humour; it might, according to taste, be called 'a bad homosexual joke'. But to my ear the camp absurdity of Bill's 'gag' makes the status of the subtext unequivocal. Sargeson is amusing himself.

The jail scenes are one of those crossing points where the couples and plotlines intersect. It is Maggie in drag who has had Bill locked up, and in prison the decorum of the 'bad' bedroom farce appears to prevail. Similarly—another crossing of Maggie into the homosocial domain of Bill and Terry—when the 'straight' couple receive a visit in their newly constituted shared bedroom:

> [. . .] when I went back to Terry there was Mrs Popeye sitting on the bed in her kimono-thing.
>
> Our Maggie's come to see us, Terry said.
>
> Good, I said. How are you Maggie?

> I'm feeling fit, she said, and the way she sort of slowly blinked her eyes made me think of a kid's doll.
>
> We know what you're fit for, Terry said.
>
> [. . .]
>
> Fancy you two boys sleeping here together, she said.[54]

Again, the comedy is broad, and more or less anodyne. It's not such a risk to make a joke about Bill and Terry sleeping together as long as the joke is spoken from the other side of the homophobic divide. That's just Maggie, in other words; bad jokes are her domain. However, what about this, from the night before?

> But when we got to the top of the stairs [. . .] all Terry's gear was in a heap outside his door and the door was locked [. . .] So while I made us a cup of tea he put his things in my room, and then we managed to get pretty comfortable in the bed even though it was a pretty tight fit.[55]

If Maggie had made this remark about the uncomfortably 'tight fit' then it might be easier to read its tone (to ascribe it a 'status'). But this is just Terry and Bill (and the text). So who are we to blame for this 'bad homosexual joke'? Or again, in the scene towards the story's conclusion, where Bill springs Terry from the sanatorium; here too there is no Maggie to take responsibility for the coded eroticism.

To transport his friend back to Mrs Clegg's, Bill lifts a wheelbarrow left overnight by a relief gang working on the road: 'We've got our taxi waiting, I said, and he said oh yeah, but he thought it was a great stunt when he saw the barrow'.[56] The caper is heavily overlaid with our knowledge of Terry's mortal illness. A barrow is also a funeral mound (a tumulus), and as Bill ferries his dying cobber through the darkened streets to the hospice of his own room there are undertones of a passage towards death. But if the barrow is a kind of bier, it is also a kind of bed—'He didn't need the blanket but he sat on it folded up'[57]—and the hijinks it gives rise to have a boudoir resonance, especially when we actually try to visualise what's happening, or if we dwell too long on the passenger's helpful comments: 'Terry joked about how I needed more benzine, and said horsey keep your tail up'.[58] Bill's busting Terry out of the confinement of the sanatorium repeats Terry's rescuing of Bill from jail. But there's a stronger (and stranger) link back to the prison scenes, when Bill, preparing for the night ahead, reprises his own extraordinary actions of his first night locked up: 'I went up to Mrs Clegg's and got her to lend me a piece of dripping, which I thought I might need in case the barrow wheel started squeaking.' Picking 'the one that [runs] easiest', he 'grease[s] her up'.[59] If the squeaky wheel is the one that gets the grease (the lube that might ease not just a wheel but a creaking bedspring or a 'tight fit'), then this scene demands attention not just for its lubricious comedy, but for the way in which this metonymic chain integrates, or inter-implicates, the two plots and the two couples. In Sedgwick's terms, the verbal play slides freely along the homosocial continuum.

After deconstruction

But who exactly is joking here? It's the question, more or less, that Roland Barthes asks to such far-reaching effect in 'The Death of the Author' (1967). And it's Barthes' post-structuralist assumptions that inform During's reading, as indeed the model of *S/Z*, with its intense ('*en detail*') investigation of atomised fragments or *lexia*, stands behind his disentangling of certain congested moments in the story without ever presuming to reassemble them into a single coherent reading.[60] Nothing could be further from During's mind than the question of Sargeson's *intention*, that bogey banished once by the New Critics (who nonetheless still assumed that the text amounted to what they called an 'organic unity') and then, with several more turns of the interpretive screw, by the deconstructive regime inspired by Barthes and Derrida. In post-structuralist hands, the text bleeds out into a field of meanings without origin or boundaries: a 'multi-dimensional space' (writes Barthes) 'in which a variety of writings, none of them original, blend and clash.'[61] To the question of who speaks, who writes, who jokes, the answer is a given: 'We shall never know, for the good reason that writing is the destruction of every voice, of every point of origin.'[62]

During, who has since made a distinguished career in Australia and beyond, is a critic always on the move. The deconstructive voice of this early Sargeson essay is not characteristic. However, in this particular moment it answers to his strategic ambitions, releasing the text (Sargeson's text, and by extension 'New Zealand literature') from the critical orthodoxy at which nationalism had arrived. The more fragmentary and irresolvable the outcome, the more effective (that is, disturbing) the intervention would prove. And disturb it did. During initially delivered the paper to a seminar in the University of Auckland English Department. The following morning (the story comes from Bill Pearson), an anonymous squib appeared on the Common Room noticeboard:

> Little Jack Horner sat in the corner
> Deconstructing a pie.
> He put in his thumb and pulled out a plum
> And said, 'What a clever boy am I.'[63]

Our own local version of the 'theory wars' had officially begun. For those of us just learning our trade, nothing would ever be quite the same. The reading and teaching of 'N.Z. Lit' was for us to be conducted under the 'clever' sign of Theory.

If I seem to be digressing, it's because there's something I need to get off my chest: namely, how counter-intuitive it feels to be reintroducing now the question of Sargeson's intent. It feels like a kind of apostasy. But for a gay-affirmative reading, the question, however forbidding, is of crucial importance—not, of course, as an ultimate 'answer' ('the "message" of the Author-God')[64] but as one indispensable datum in a dense tangle of historical effects. For During it doesn't matter—it's most productively left open: 'It is impossible finally to distinguish between what belongs to the narrator's unconscious and what belongs to the text's unconscious. Assigning repressed textual elements to various levels remains a provisional activity, a matter of tact, open to debate.'[65] But to understand how Sargeson negotiates his context, we are obliged to run this gauntlet of intentions and levels of consciousness. To appreciate the game he's playing, we need to ask: What does he *think he's saying*, and to whom?

About 15 years ago, in an essay in *Landfall*, I approached the same question, and answered it according to the mood (or certainly my own mood) of the time.[66] Reading for gay heroics, I was looking to find in Sargeson a subversion of the nationalist programme. That sportive semantic undercurrent of lubricants and encoded anal sex makes such a reading happily available. It's a reading which answers both to the ceremonious textualism (or 'language' orientation) of deconstruction, and to the transgressive sentiments of gay affirmation. It also responds to the scepticism about the orthodoxies of nationalism which at the time seemed so imperative. Sargeson emerges as a writer intent on subverting the assumptions of nationalist realism, even (with delicious irony) in the very act of patenting its definitive prose idiom ('the Sargeson style'). In this light the writer knows exactly what he's doing. Sargeson is allowed his joke. He knows that homosocial realism is oblivious to the continuity between mateship and eroticism, and that its literal-minded reading habits (specimen texts: Baxter and Rhodes) will enable a 'disguised poetry' to explore that continuity and yet pass unnoticed. Ultimately realism is recast as satire. As During reminds us, Sargeson's classic stories imply a sharing of perspective between a (naïve) narrator and an implied (educated) reader.[67] While the reader brings to the text his high-cultural sophistication, he aspires nonetheless to a cultural ideal informed by and sympathetic to the narrator's vernacular life-world. In a textualist 'gay' reading, that alliance of perspective remains, but the bond between narrator and reader is now their common deafness. The story's verbal playfulness secretes an erotic discourse at a level where neither the naïve narrator nor the literal-minded and homophobic nationalist reader has the wit to detect it.

A heroics of language, a heroics of the closet, a planned obsolescence encoded in the nationalist house style: Sargeson becomes the writer *present without leave*, a spy in the house of homophobic mateship. It's a gratifying scenario. Regretfully, however, I am forced to conclude that it doesn't make sense. It cannot be a conscious undertaking. Unless it's a strategy whose only conceivable reward would be the discovery, the 'outing' it so fears—unless it's a game whose recognition would bring the whole structure down on the writer's head, and cancel the freedom that masculine realism gives him to celebrate his loves and affiliations—if these are not the outcomes the strategy solicits, then there must be another implied reader. There must be someone to share the joke. In a deconstructive reading the question doesn't arise. The reader is an abstraction, a *possibility* of reading, an ideal 'space' where 'all the quotations that make up a writing are inscribed without any of them being lost'.[68] But if we're trying to understand Sargeson's role in the development of mid-century writing, then we need to be able to posit an historical reader by whom a flesh-and-blood author might potentially, and confidentially, be heard.

When I first addressed this problem in the essay that I've referred to, I left this question of a 'real' reader open. The archive, I was happy to say, might yet supply a forensic solution. In the meantime I allowed myself a dollar each way and invoked the textualist alibi of the author speaking *to us*. But what I really hoped for was a voice from the archival record, most likely, I assumed, from among Sargeson's many gay contemporaries (McCormick, Pearson, Cresswell, Brasch, Rodney Kennedy, John Lehmann, William Plomer: there are metres of correspondence between Sargeson and his gay friends) that might attest to a shared understanding of how to read these stories at the expense of nationalist realism. Sargeson was a sociable man: he liked to share food and jokes and gossip. If he was aiming a joke at realism, there must have been someone to enjoy it with. But after weeks spent combing the Sargeson archive, I am forced to conclude that no such reader existed. There is no one whom Sargeson digs in the ribs, no reader whom we hear him check in with in order to alert them to the subtext and to make sure they're getting it. And moreover—for this is the implication that follows—nor was Sargeson himself that reader. The richest, most scandalous verbal effects in Sargeson's stories operate unconsciously. I don't mean of course that there is no conscious homoerotic dimension to 'That Summer' or 'The Hole that Jack Dug' (or 'The Making of a New Zealander', or *I Saw in My Dream*). Plainly there is. But I don't believe that sex has been knowingly inscribed at the level of covert semantic resonance. When we read about Jack and his deep-thrusting shovel, or the tight fit managed in Bill's narrow bed, we're not asked to smile at the double entendre, because Sargeson can't hear it himself.

But what does it mean to call this semantic under-song *unconscious*? Is this to say that it speaks out of *Sargeson's* unconscious—that it voices an unconscious desire of the man who wrote the story? Prudently, one reaches for the deconstructive catechism: the question is 'undecidable'. To ascribe these sexual figures to the story's unconscious is to argue that Sargeson himself cannot hear them; however, the weightiest implications point not towards his sexual desires and practices, but towards his practices as a writer. The hidden truth betrayed by these stories—the blockage, the pathology, the compromising secret, the great 'reveal' about Sargeson's project and the way it shapes our mid-century fiction—is more scandalous than sex. It is that *Sargeson can't read.*

Legacies

My combing of the archives was in this sense wasted labour. Sargeson is never going to make this kind of joke because his literary mind doesn't work this way. Effects like these presuppose the verbal consciousness of modernism, and the collaboration of modernist complexity with academic close reading. The world of the university aroused Sargeson's deepest suspicions. Scholars who approached him ran the risk of a verbal hazing, and he was apt to regard overly attentive criticism as a breach of both privacy and good taste (he would undoubtedly have applauded the 'Little Jack Horner' put-down).[69] When it came to the modern novel, he had certainly covered the ground. He particularly admired Proust and Stein; and we know that he read *Ulysses* at least twice.[70] Nonetheless, his loyalties in fiction were centred a generation or two earlier: with Twain and Anderson, Lawson, Olive Schreiner and (from a slighter later period in his life) Henry James. Like Fairburn and Glover, he engages with modernism only as far as it suits his limited purposes: he embraces its compact with masculinity, its minimalist aspect, and its anti-didacticism. But despite his enthusiasm for Joyce, he has no apparent use for the dimension of modern fiction that develops out of psychoanalysis and Symbolism.

On modernism's recondite interiority, and on the close-grained transactions with poetic language that are the vehicle of that inward migration, Sargeson turns his back. We only need to think about the way he reads Mansfield. For a reader acculturated to modernist close reading, with its psychoanalytically informed alertness to the verbal operations of interior consciousness, a story like 'Prelude' opens into a labyrinth of subjective complexity. For Sargeson, 'It is mainly about children' and possibly owes a debt to Chekhov. End of story.[71] More arresting still is Sargeson's indifference to 'Bliss'. Surely, one would think, a reader with Sargeson's investment in the slippage between the homosocial and the homoerotic couldn't fail to be engaged by its crosscurrents of unconscious identification and inchoate same-sex desire. Could he? Not a bit of it: 'And again you have a young woman who experiences a few hours of intense happiness for no particular reason. She is just happy to be alive, that is all. But it all ends with the discovery that her husband is engaged in a love affair.'[72]

Sargeson's consistent reproach is that Mansfield left no workable legacy: 'Schreiner really started something in SA, and one can't say that Mansfield did anything like the same thing in NZ';[73] 'Katherine Mansfield was our Henry Lawson, but what context can we point to?'[74] It is, of course, a maddeningly circular complaint; in order for Mansfield to create a 'context', her successors had to *read her*, and Sargeson didn't, or couldn't.

For Sargeson the rewards lay elsewhere: not with modernism's heroics of consciousness, but with a homosocial humanism that privileged tenderness, loyalty, other-directedness, love. To this extent, the Sargeson of the 30s and 40s does bring a softness and warmth to mid-century fiction. It's a purely masculine experience, of course; the viewpoint is bracingly misogynistic. And it leaves in abeyance that inheritance from modernism that puts in play the agency of language in interior consciousness. While refining the use of the naïve narrator, Sargeson's iconic fictions abdicate both from psychological complexity, and from linguistic density. These are values we have to seek at a level of his writing that he himself isn't listening to. Sargeson himself plainly *does* bequeath a context. But for post-war inheritors like Maurice Duggan and Janet Frame, the challenge will be to reactivate a poetic complexity gone underground in nationalist realism.

Afterword

'ascetic Charles & the hefty Able Seaman'

Denis Glover's experience in the navy may well have been the high point of his life. Beyond doubt he had what was known as a 'good' war; he withstood the punishing Arctic convoys, and won a DSC for his heroics during the D-Day landings.[1] His time on shore was important as well. In London on leave he met Dorée Elkind, whom Ogilvie describes as 'the grand passion of his life'.[2] But it's a second key relationship that concerns us here, the friendship that arose in London between Glover and Charles Brasch. On his first two London leaves, Glover stayed with (who else?) D'Arcy Cresswell—'all very well in his way, but a moody sort of a fellow & apt to be too petulantly feminine.'[3] Better in all respects, it turned out, was Brasch's hospitality at the Lawn Road flats in Hampstead:

> What a fine chap he is—so quiet & sensitive & balanced. We are complete opposites, the ascetic Charles & the hefty Able

> Seaman, but yet get on extremely well. And of course one lives in a simple & restrained luxury chez lui.[4]

They are, as Glover says, an incongruous couple; but in the alliance forged between them—and in the tensions between them—we can discern the shape of New Zealand writing after World War II.

It's not just that Brasch is different from Glover; he stands apart from all of them, from Fairburn, from Curnow, even from Sargeson. If Glover is the epitome of hard frost masculinity—and never more confidently so than in uniform—then Brasch is surely the anti-type of that same nationalist brand. In contrast to the exclusively WASP origins of his Caxton colleagues, Brasch's family were Jewish on both sides. Where the rest were modest shades of middle class, his Hallenstein progenitors were wealthy enough to supply him with private means. Nor was it merely material wealth; he also inherited cultural capital. For Brasch, the refinements of European taste were already internalised: he grew up among books; he spoke French, Italian and German.[5] Out of this matrix came a sensibility entirely at odds with the black-singlet masculinism of Glover or Fairburn. However uncertainly and hesitantly, Brasch was gay. He 'abominated' drinking culture.[6] He was studious, shy and habitually introspective. When Glover goes in search of more riotous companionship, Brasch, quietly wounded, can only reproach himself: 'I am such bad company, so self-enclosed, walled up [. . .] that I can scarcely communicate.'[7] And yet one senses he would not have it any other way: 'The only thing I really want is for my inner world to be consistently more important to me than the outer world.'[8]

A manifestation of this inwardness is Brasch's copious journal writing (predictably, he's alone in this—none of his male colleagues confides his private thoughts to paper). So while we don't yet have a Brasch biography, we have a more than useful account of what was going on in his head.[9] Increasingly as the war drags on he broods on the problem of returning to New Zealand. By the conflict's end he will have spent the best part of 18 years, and virtually his entire adult life, in Europe. Yet he knows that as a poet he is at his best with New Zealand material;[10] and the thought of returning 'haunts' him, he writes, 'part vision, part nightmare, so insistently that I know it will be impossible for me not to try'.[11] By the end of 1942 this much is 'pretty well settled'.[12] But it doesn't resolve the accompanying anxieties. How is he to cope with the familiar limitations: the provincialism, the suspicion of difference, the absence of his London friends and of the amenities of high culture? And what is he actually going to *do*? Though money is not an issue, he has too many doubts about himself as a writer to anticipate being content without a day-to-day occupation. But what kind of occupation can New Zealand offer him? It is these anxieties that furnish the backdrop to Brasch's incisive portrait of Glover. His house guest will help solve one part of the puzzle. Equally, though, his presence will reinforce Brasch's intimations of how much there is to fear.

The need to establish a new journal, a 'mature & professional' successor to *Phoenix*, had been a subject of discussion for the best part of a decade—ever since 1933, in fact, when the first version folded under the weight of Bob Lowry's debts.[13] At the heart of the 'literary' iteration of *Phoenix*—that is, numbers 1 and 2, before Mason took over for 3 and 4—were the three Waitaki Old Boys, James Bertram (as editor), Brasch and Ian Milner, who between them, Brasch records, had written 'a good deal of [the] first number' over a weekend at the Milners' family bach at Waianakarua.[14] All three would then be in Britain in the 30s, as would another close friend and *Phoenix* contributor, Jack Bennett. These are the four names that Brasch singles out, though Bertram's elder brother also expresses interest in the task (a prospect at which Brasch is quietly appalled).[15] Finally, though, what starts to give the project a more definite shape is the appearance of Glover. Having contemplated starting such a journal himself, Glover clearly 'gets' the project; and of course he brings his printing skills and the capacity of the Caxton Press. The pair discuss the enterprise at length, even while Glover lounges in the bath, 'a large pink almost hairless octopus', and his host plies his way back and forth to the kitchen preparing breakfast.[16] Glover makes the idea concrete. He also seems to help bolster Brasch's self-belief. From initially proposing that the journal be run by a committee, the latter progresses quickly to imagining himself in charge. And so by April 1944 he is working on 'the book which Denis is to publish after the war' (*Disputed Ground*, 1948), as well as plotting 'the revived Phoenix [. . .] assuming that the planning of it will be mine'.[17]

When he returns to New Zealand, then, it's now much clearer what Brasch will be doing. But in Glover's company he can't help fretting about the intellectual climate he's going to be doing it in:

> It struck me today that Denis, in common with many NZers, sets more store by kindness or common humanity than by the qualities of a person's beliefs or intellect, while the opposite is true in general of intellectuals here [. . .] A country of course needs both of these; either alone is fatal. Denis appears to have no sense of truth as something to be pursued & gradually to be revealed, no sense of ends and of purpose in life. Or do I wrong him? Is there an eagerness I am not aware of under his comfortable exterior, the solid figure beginning to round out, the enormously strong thrusting jaw & his one cauliflower ear, and the aggressively matter-of-fact tone of his talk with

> its no-nonsense good humour & impatience and touch of whimsicality? Could I work with him without all this—there is something provincial about it—jarring on me?[18]

While Brasch could see the positive side of Glover's masculine habitus, he could see just as plainly the costs that came with it. Scratch the demotic humanism and beneath it was indifference to intellectual nuance. The 'impatience' that went with the suspicion of cant and ceremony was too much like the impatience that shied away from sustained inquiry. Glover confirmed something that Brasch had noticed in his friend James Courage—in many ways so different from Glover (gay, and a permanent expatriate) and yet similarly uninterested in abstract thought.[19] Brasch liked to dwell on the large imponderables: pacificism, community, aesthetic values, spirituality (he insists that the projected journal 'take its stand as definitely theist, at the least').[20] But New Zealanders seemed to care more for personalities and for striking the right kind of 'no-nonsense' attitude. The country's intellectuals, he feared, were setting their sights too low: 'The lack of ideals of Denis & his circle, which is typical of so many intelligent NZers—Curnow, Mason, Fairburn all show this lack; [. . .] their lives and aims, as I see them through Denis's eyes when he talks about Chch & Curnow, are of a spiritual barrenness which terrifies me'.[21]

It's important to remember how long Brasch has been away; this helps explain the puzzling comments about Curnow. Brasch doesn't know these emerging players well; Curnow he won't meet till 1946.[22] And when he makes these observations, in 1943, he has not yet had the chance to read the Caxton anthology and so to appreciate the force of Curnow's critical thought; when he reads Curnow's poetry (which so far leaves him cold) it is framed for him, not by Curnow's prose, but by the rough-and-ready partisanship of Glover. Imagined in this light—'through Denis's eyes'—the scene that awaits him appears more frightening than it needs to. Curnow is not another version of Glover. He might baulk at Brasch's spiritualism, but he isn't afraid of difficult thought, any more than he lacks for high ambition. When Brasch finally meets him he will find himself readjusting: 'He looked more set and mature than I expected [. . .] very much the type of an English intellectual and man of the world [. . .] I was reminded of Priestley, of Day Lewis.'[23]

That said, however, it wasn't for nothing that Curnow and Glover had formed such a tight bond. There is certainly a Curnow with whom Glover identifies, a poet and critic who can be as 'aggressively matter-of-fact', and in some respects as cynical, as Glover himself. And it's true that the qualities that Brasch fears in Glover are ingrained in the nationalist movement at large: the macho assertiveness, the faith in common sense, the adherence to inhibiting vernacular protocols. What Brasch himself prefers, and idealises, is the culture he remembers around Bethell at Rise Cottage. Her death in 1945 will leave him feeling even more exposed: 'I had felt her my main support there; without her I will fear far more deeply to go back.'[24] Brasch will return to the country of his birth with the trepidations of a desert missionary. His long poem 'The Estate', in a routine nationalist conceit, will imagine the balm of European culture mellowing 'blunt hard natures / Of farmer and rabbiter, driver, storekeeper, orchardman.'[25] But in Britain, as he nervously plots his re-entry, he's thinking less about the raw sensibilities of the rural working man than about the mission of trying to Hellenise his fellow 'intellectuals'.

In fairness to Glover, he recognises that the end of the war will bring a mood for change, and that this stands to displace the regime with which he himself has been comfortable. This is the message he delivers to Sargeson, as Sargeson recalls in the middle volume of his autobiography:

> The war was officially over; and by my writer friend Denis Glover [. . .] I had been plainly told to forget I had ever put pen to paper: I was pre-war: the thirties and all that was over [. . .] all would be new, a new generation with different interests, brushing aside the one before [. . .][26]

For Sargeson this post-war break ushers in a period of creative perplexity. Throughout the 1950s he will publish very little; only after a prolonged struggle will he complete the transition from his realist mode of the 30s and 40s to the longer, more wordy, more mandarin fictions of what Lawrence Jones calls his 'second' career.[27] The pattern is similar with Curnow: the casting about for a new direction from the mid 1940s and into the 50s, followed by a decade or more of silence, leading to a major reinvention in a 'second', and perhaps in Curnow's case even a 'third', career. As much as their achievements in the period between the wars, it's their ability to remake their practice in the post-war period that marks out Sargeson and Curnow as the twin pillars of literary nationalism. It's a distinction that they share with two other 'greats' of the wider nationalist movement, Lilburn and McCahon. Each of these four will have to reconceive his project; each will take his work in a more difficult direction, challenging and extending the programme established in the 30s and 40s.[28] Others, though, won't make the same transition. Hyde and Mulgan won't get the chance. Glover and Fairburn will not survive either. Glover's masterpiece 'Sings Harry' appears complete in 1951. But it has been arriving in bits and pieces for a decade, and by the time of its publication—within weeks of Glover's sacking from the press that he himself had founded—it will read, as I have argued, like an elegy for his own career. Fairburn, similarly, will lose his way, writing nothing of significance between 1949 and his early death in 1957.

Then there's the question of Brasch himself, who 'bookends' this book without being strictly 'in' it. This in itself is not a value judgement (Mulgan isn't in this book either, though plainly he belongs here). However, one or two iconic early poems notwithstanding, Brasch for me is primarily a figure of the post-war. He will find his true calling as nurturer of the writing that emerges out of the break foreseen by Glover. The energy in post-war nationalist culture will come from a new confederation. The rowdiest contribution will be that of a second generation, born in the decade after World War I, which in the 1950s, in the now familiar manner, 'is beginning to articulate its structure of feeling'. But the situation is messier than the one proposed by Williams. For alongside these ambitious thirty-somethings are the ambitious forty-or-fifty-somethings, Curnow and Sargeson. And then woven through the mix is a third demographic, the influx of European refugees who arrive here either side of the war to contribute their vital injection of Old World intellectualism. The relationships among these three elements are intricate and variegated; but between them they make up the new post-war vanguard, whose journal will be *Landfall*, and whose editor and patron will be Charles Brasch.

In August 1944 Brasch takes the step that he's been agonising over. He puts down his name for a passage home. Although it won't come through until the following November, even this will be 'much sooner than I had been expecting; frighteningly near'.[29] In New Zealand he waits for the go-ahead from Glover. Lawrence Baigent suggests the name.[30] Finally, in March 1947, the first issue of *Landfall* rolls off the

Caxton Press. For a project with such a long gestation, and with such weighty expectations riding on it—particularly Brasch's own—the reception, as Ogilvie records, was distinctly underwhelming. Oliver Duff, in his *Listener* review, doubted it would outlast the year; another reviewer remarked that there had been school magazines 'which for vitality, originality and humour would wipe the floor with this first number.'[31] Glover was as unenthusiastic as anyone, introducing what would be an ongoing theme as the high solemnity of Brasch's vision drove the no-nonsense businessman and printer to despair. 'The first thing is to get the paper *read*,' exhorted Glover after the first issue: 'As it stands this is fine reading for a retired canon.' And in advance of the next: 'I wish to hell there was some way of jazzing up the second number . . . even the lino operator says it's duller than the first.' When a precious subscriber passed away, Glover could not resist the obvious 'joke': 'I suppose you had better send a 15 shilling refund to the estate of Anges Webb. I *thought* No. 2 might be a bit dull, but I never dreamed it would actually *kill* subscribers!'[32]

But Brasch, as we've seen, had anticipated this: Glover's 'impatience' wasn't news. *Landfall* was there to put a stake in the ground, and Brasch refused to relax his standards. His seriousness of purpose made an easy target for mockery. And it's true that the early issues felt solemn and monochrome, and that much of the non-fiction in particular was unexciting. Nonetheless, by refusing to give ground, Brasch was able to keep open a space in which better but still equally serious writing could appear: not only criticism and social theory (Robert Chapman, Bill Pearson), but more complex and demanding fiction. Indeed, the authors who would owe most to *Landfall*, and who would enjoy the most exposure in its pages under Brasch's editorship, would be writers trying to modernise the realist tradition in prose, namely Sargeson and Duggan. A fiction as ambitious as Duggan's novella *Riley's Handbook* was simply inconceivable without the scope that *Landfall* provided. The journal stood firm as a site of resistance against the anti-intellectualism that Brasch so feared. If it never really made much progress in the spiritual direction that he had initally proposed, it nonetheless ranged far beyond the aggressive matter-of-factness that had dismayed him in Glover.

Brasch, then, will prove to be just the right person to preside over nationalist literature in this second period, and it's greatly to his and *Landfall*'s credit that post-war New Zealand writing is able to grow in more complex directions. Not that the mood-change in post-war writing emerges simply out of Brasch's head. It is part of a broader adjustment in feeling that brings a loosening of at least some of the inhibitions of the 30s. Post-war intellectuals will become less defensive, less nervous about elitism, more willing to ignore vernacular prohibitions. More strenuous versions of modernism will appear, greater psychological complexity, deeper interiority. Hairline cracks will begin to show in the edifice of Kiwi monoculturalism. But while the 50s will bring a softening, it won't be a comprehensive thaw. Unlike the rupture of the early 30s, or the rupture to follow towards the end of the 60s, this post-war shift in the structure of feeling will not see a dramatic reordering of sex and gender. The writing will become more sophisticated but it won't become noticeably warmer. The depiction of complex adult relations will remain a rarity in local fiction, while for women writers of the 50s and 60s the going will be almost as difficult as it was for Robin Hyde.

Notes

Introduction
What was New Zealand Literature?

1. Charles Brasch, *Indirections: A Memoir 1909–1947* (Wellington: Oxford University Press, 1980), 391.
2. Sean Matthews, 'Change and Theory in Raymond Williams's Structure of Feeling', in *Pretexts: Literary and Cultural Studies* 10, no. 2 (2001), 181–82.
3. Raymond Williams, *Politics and Letters: Interviews with New Left Review* (London: New Left Books, 1979), 159.
4. David Simpson, 'Raymond Williams: Feeling for Structures, Voicing "History"', in *Cultural Materialism: On Raymond Williams*, ed. Christopher Prendergast (Minneapolis: University of Minnesota Press, 1995), 36.
5. Raymond Williams, *The Long Revolution* (London: Chatto & Windus, 1961), 48.
6. Ibid., 65.
7. Raymond Williams and Michael Orrom, *A Preface to Film* (London: Film Drama, 1954), 21.
8. Raymond Williams, *Marxism and Literature* (Oxford: Oxford University Press, 1977), 131.
9. Williams, *Politics and Letters*, 157.
10. Williams, *Marxism and Literature*, 132.
11. Raymond Williams, *The Raymond Williams Reader*, ed. John Higgins (Oxford: Blackwell, 2001), 35.
12. Cf. Roger Horrocks, 'Douglas Lilburn: Nationalism Now', in *Re-inventing New Zealand: Essays on the Arts and the Media* (Pokeno: Atuanui Press, 2016), 411.
13. Ralph Waldo Emerson, *Nature*, in *The Collected Works of Ralph Waldo Emerson, vol. 1: Nature, Addresses and Lectures,* ed. Robert E. Spiller and Alfred R. Ferguson (Cambridge, MA: Belknap Press, 1971), 7.
14. 'We are stunted emotionally because we have not dealt direct with

life, but through intermediaries.' Allen Curnow, *Look Back Harder: Critical Writings 1935–1984*, ed. Peter Simpson (Auckland: Auckland University Press, 1987), 56.

15. Walt Whitman (anonymously), 'Walt Whitman and his Poems' [1855], in *Walt Whitman*, ed. Francis Murphy (Harmondsworth: Penguin, 1969), 30.
16. Ibid., 31.
17. David Carter, 'Critics, Writers, Intellectuals: Australian Literature and its Criticism', in *The Cambridge Companion to Australian Literature*, ed. Elizabeth Webby (Cambridge: Cambridge University Press, 2006), 264.
18. *Angry Penguins* was a self-consciously avant-garde journal edited by Max Harris. In 1943 McAuley and Stewart faked up 16 pretentiously 'modernist' poems, and invented as their author Ern Malley, a garage mechanic who had supposedly died in obscurity in Melbourne at the age of 25. Harris fell for the hoax and published the work enthusiastically. The outcome of its subsequent exposure is summed up by David Lehman: 'high hilarity at the expense of the Angry Penguins, the humiliation of Max Harris, a colossal setback for modernism in Australia.' 'The Ern Malley Hoax—Introduction', *Jacket* 17 (June 2002), jacketmagazine.com/17/ern-dl.html. For a complete account, see Michael Heyward, *The Ern Malley Affair* (London: Faber & Faber, 1993). The Jindyworobak Club was established in Adelaide in 1937 by Rex Ingamells. The *Jindyworobak Anthology* appeared annually 1938–53.
19. Alex Calder, 'Unsettling Settlement: Poetry and Nationalism in Aotearoa / New Zealand', *REAL: Yearbook of Research in English and American Literature* 14 (1998), 169–71.
20. Christine Stansell, *American Moderns: Bohemian New York and the Creation of a New Century* (2000; New York: Henry Holt and Company, 2001), 225 ff.
21. Rita Felski, *The Limits of Critique* (Chicago and London: Chicago University Press, 2015), 1.
22. Leigh Davis, 'Set Up', *And* 1 (October 1983), 7.
23. Horrocks, 411.
24. Felski, 52–69.
25. Horrocks, 410.

26. Felski, 175–80.
27. Ibid., 158–59.
28. Derek Attridge, 'Context, Idioculture, Invention', *New Literary History* 42, no. 4 (2011), 682–83; cited by Felski, 172.
29. Felski, 48.

Chapter 1
'Nothing can ever be the same': Mansfield's new worlds

1. Rachel Barrowman, *Mason: The Life of R.A.K. Mason* (Wellington: Victoria University Press, 2003), 166.
2. James K. Baxter, 'Aspects of Poetry in New Zealand', in *Complete Prose*, vol. 2, ed. John Weir (Wellington: Victoria University Press, 2015), 330.
3. Barrowman, 165.
4. Ibid.
5. Frank Sargeson, *Conversation in a Train and Other Critical Writings*, ed. Kevin Cunningham (Auckland: Auckland University Press / Oxford University Press, 1983), 32.
6. Ibid.
7. Ibid.
8. Antony Alpers, *The Life of Katherine Mansfield* (New York: Viking Press, 1980), 373.
9. See Kai Jensen, *Whole Men: The Masculine Tradition in New Zealand Literature* (Auckland: Auckland University Press, 1996), 56–64.
10. Vincent O'Sullivan, *Finding the Pattern, Solving the Problem* (Wellington: Victoria University Press, 1989), 7–8.
11. Ibid.
12. Sydney Janet Kaplan, *Katherine Mansfield and the Origins of Modernist Fiction* (Ithaca, NY: Cornell University Press, 1991), 65.
13. Curnow, *Look Back Harder*, 244. I examine the origin of the term 'anti-myth', and its applications, on 162–66, below.
14. Alpers, 252.
15. Douglas W. Orr, *Psychoanalysis and the Bloomsbury Group* (Clemson, SC: Clemson University Digital Press, 2004), 4.
16. Alpers, 252.

17. Orr, 9–10, 12–13, 18–19, 24–25.
18. Alix Strachey, in *Recollections of Virginia Woolf*, ed. Joan Russell Noble (London: Owen, 1972), 116.
19. Orr, 9–10, 37 n.13.
20. Claire Tomalin, *Katherine Mansfield: A Secret Life* (1987; London: Penguin, 1988), 128.
21. Katherine Mansfield, *The Letters and Journals of Katherine Mansfield: A Selection*, ed. C.K. Stead (Harmondsworth: Penguin, 1977), 76–77.
22. Kaplan, 106.
23. Lyndall Gordon, *Eliot's Early Years* (Oxford: Oxford University Press, 1977), 28–29. See also Kaplan, 76.
24. Kaplan, 76.
25. Clare Hanson and Andrew Gurr, *Katherine Mansfield* (London: Macmillan, 1981), 21–22.
26. Arthur Symons, *The Symbolist Movement in Literature* (London: Archibald Constable & Co., 1908), 10, 17.
27. Ibid., 2.
28. Ezra Pound, *Literary Essays of Ezra Pound* (London: Faber & Faber, 1954), 4.
29. M.H. Abrams, *A Glossary of Literary Terms* (Orlando: Harcourt Brace, 1999), 311.
30. Ibid.
31. Mansfield to John Middleton Murry, 11 January 1918, in Katherine Mansfield, *Letters and Journals*, 93; *The Katherine Mansfield Notebooks*, vol. 2., ed. Margaret Scott (Canterbury and Wellington: Lincoln University Press / Daphne Brasell Associates, 1997), 153–54.
32. O'Sullivan, *Finding the Pattern*, 10.
33. Kaplan, 103.
34. Mansfield, *Notebooks*, vol. 2, 204.
35. Katherine Mansfield, *Katherine Mansfield's Selected Stories*, ed. Vincent O'Sullivan (New York: Norton, 2006), 97.
36. Ibid.
37. Ibid., 107.
38. Ibid.
39. Ibid., 89.

40. Vincent O'Sullivan, 'The Magnetic Chain: Notes and Approaches to Katherine Mansfield', *Landfall* 114 (June 1975), 124.
41. Mansfield, *Selected Stories*, 91.
42. Dorrit Cohn, *Transparent Minds: Narrative Modes for Presenting Consciousness in Fiction* (Princeton, NJ: Princeton University Press, 1983), 494. See also Gerald Prince, *A Dictionary of Narratology* (Lincoln and London: University of Nebraska Press, 1987), 34–35.
43. Mansfield, *Selected Stories*, 90.
44. Ibid., 111.
45. Ibid., 97.
46. Ibid., 90.
47. C.K. Stead, *In the Glass Case: Essays on New Zealand Literature* (Auckland: Auckland University Press / Oxford University Press, 1981), 40.
48. Henry James, *The Portrait of a Lady*, ed. Nicola Bradbury (1881; Oxford: Oxford University Press: 1998), 129.
49. Stead, 43–44.
50. Katherine Mansfield, *Katherine Mansfield's Short Stories* (Auckland: Random House, 2008), 607. This story is not included in O'Sullivan's Norton edition.
51. Ibid., 610.
52. Ibid., 611.
53. Stead, 45.
54. Mansfield, *Selected Stories*, 279.
55. Ibid., 145.
56. Ibid., 147.
57. Ibid., 151.
58. Ibid., 154.
59. Ibid., 153.
60. Ibid., 152.
61. Angela Smith, *Katherine Mansfield: A Literary Life* (Basingstoke: Palgrave, 2000), 118–19.
62. T.S. Eliot, 'The Love Song of J. Alfred Prufrock', in *Collected Poems 1909–1962* (London: Faber and Faber, 1963), 15.
63. Mansfield, *Selected Stories*, 159.
64. Sylvia Lynd, quoted in Tomalin, 241.
65. Unpublished letter, Humanities Research Centre, Texas. Quoted

in Sandra Jobson Darroch, *Ottoline: The Life of Lady Ottoline Morrell* (London: Chatto & Windus, 1976), 258.

66. Katherine Anne Porter, 'The Art of Katherine Mansfield', in *The Critical Response to Katherine Mansfield*, ed. Jan Pilditch (Westport, CN: Greenwood Press, 1996), 45–48.
67. Kaplan, 1–2.
68. Eliot, *The Waste Land*, in *Collected Poems 1909–1962*, 79.
69. Mansfield, *Notebooks*, vol. 2, 32.
70. 'Subjective epic': a conventional generic label for Romantic autobiography in the tradition of Wordsworth and Whitman.
71. Lydia Wevers, '"The Sod Under My Feet": Katherine Mansfield', in *Opening the Book: New Essays on New Zealand Writing*, ed. Mark Williams and Michele Leggott (Auckland: Auckland University Press, 1995), 37.
72. Ibid. Into this category would fall 'Bliss', 'A Married Man's Story', 'Je Ne Parle Pas Français', 'The Daughters of the Later Colonel', and so on.
73. Mansfield to Dorothy Brett, September 1921, *Letters and Journals*, 232; quoted in Wevers, 37.
74. Mansfield, *Selected Stories*, 255.
75. Ibid., 111.
76. Ibid., 112.
77. Wevers, 41.
78. Mansfield, *Selected Stories*, 97.
79. Ibid.
80. V.S. Pritchett, '[Who Are These People?]', in Mansfield, *Selected Stories*, 344.
81. Mansfield, *Selected Stories*, 97.
82. Wevers, 45.
83. Allen Curnow, 'To M.H. Holcroft', in *Collected Poems*, ed. Elizabeth Caffin and Terry Sturm (Auckland: Auckland University Press, 2017), 89.
84. O.N. Gillespie, 'New Zealanders in Literature. A Fine Record of Achievement', *The New Zealand Railways Magazine* 11, no. 2 (May 1936), 14.
85. Heather Murray, 'Celebrating Our Writers: 1936, 1951. Part 1: 1936', *Journal of New Zealand Literatur*e 10 (September 1992),

100; Chris Hilliard, *The Bookmen's Dominion: Cultural Life in New Zealand 1920–1950* (Auckland: Auckland University Press, 2006), 4–6, 13.

86. Hilliard, 5.

Chapter 2
Predecessors: Baughan, Bethell, Mason

1. Charles Brasch, 'R.A.K. Mason 1905–71: Some Tributes', *Landfall* 99 (September 1971), 236.
2. Nancy Harris, 'Making It New: "Modernism" in B.E. Baughan's New Zealand Poetry' (PhD thesis, University of Canterbury, 1992), core.ac.uk/display/35464528. Information in this paragraph and the next is from Harris, 1–31.
3. For details of Baughan's involvement in Vedanta and in prison reform, see Emma Bond, 'Colloquy and Continuity: The Integrated Dialogues of Blanche Edith Baughan' (MA thesis, University of Canterbury, 1998), core.ac.uk/download/pdf/35468043.pdf
4. Curnow, *Look Back Harder*, 151–52.
5. Blanche Baughan, 'A Bush Section', in *The Penguin Book of New Zealand Verse*, ed. Allen Curnow (Harmondsworth: Penguin, 1960), 104–05.
6. Curnow, 151.
7. Baughan, 107.
8. Quoted in Harris, 15.
9. Harris, 11.
10. Quoted in Harris, 14.
11. Emerson, *Nature*, in *The Collected Works of Ralph Waldo Emerson, vol. 1*, 10.
12. Blanche Baughan, *Studies in New Zealand Scenery* (Christchurch: Whitcombe & Tombs, 1916), 101.
13. Harris, 15.
14. Baughan, 'A Bush Section', 105.
15. Ibid., 106–07.
16. Ibid., 109.
17. Ibid., 110.

18. Ibid., 109.
19. Walt Whitman, 'Song of Myself', in *Complete Poems and Collected Prose*, ed. Justin Kaplan (New York: Viking Press, 1982), 200–03.
20. Baughan, 111.
21. Baughan to Miss Higgins, 8 April 1909, quoted in Bond, 68.
22. W.F. Alexander and A.E. Currie, eds., *A Treasury of New Zealand Verse* (Christchurch: Whitcombe & Tombs, 1926); M.H. Holcroft, *Discovered Isles: A Trilogy* (Christchurch: Caxton Press, 1950); Robert Chapman and Jonathan Bennett, eds., *An Anthology of New Zealand Verse* (London and Wellington: Oxford University Press, 1956); Eric McCormick, *New Zealand Literature: A Survey* (London: Oxford University Press, 1959). On Holcroft's transcendentalism, see 156–59, below.
23. Holcroft notes that there were also two 'flimsy' vanity press publications in London. M.H. Holcroft, *Ursula Bethell* (Wellington: Oxford University Press, 1975), 8. Biographical information in this paragraph is from Holcroft, 3–11.
24. Ursula Bethell, *Collected Poems*, ed. Vincent O'Sullivan (Wellington: Victoria University Press, 1997), 5.
25. Ezra Pound, *Gaudier-Brezska: A Memoir* (New York: New Directions, 1970), 89.
26. The best guide to Bethell's reading is Rosemary Brewer, 'A Pilgrim in the Library: The Private Letters and Public Poetry of Mary Ursula Bethell' (MA thesis, University of Auckland, 1995), 117–39. On the basis of correspondence, memoirs and personal library collections, Brewer assembles a checklist of titles 'read and/or owned' covering a period 'between about 1930 and 1945' (121). Indicative, inevitably, rather than comprehensive, it is nonetheless a very helpful document.
27. Brewer doesn't record any reference to Waley. The assumption, of course, is that Bethell would have read him earlier. But she doesn't appear to own his works, or to allude to them after 1930.
28. Holcroft, *Ursula Bethell*, 14–15.
29. H.C.D. Somerset, 'Ursula Bethell: Some Personal Memories', *Landfall* 8 (December 1948), 279.
30. Quoted in O'Sullivan, introduction to *Collected Poems* by Ursula Bethell, xvi.

31. 'I have told you, Ruth, in plain words / The pleasures of my occupation': Foreword to *Collected Poems*, 1. O'Sullivan identifies the addressee as Lady Ruth Head. 'Notes to the Poems', 103.
32. Bethell, *Collected Poems*, 10.
33. Ibid., 1.
34. Ibid., 14-15.
35. Lawrence Baigent, 'The Poetry of Ursula Bethell', *Landfall* 17 (March 1951), 24.
36. Curnow, *Look Back Harder*, 71.
37. Bethell, 2.
38. Ibid., 7.
39. Curnow, 35.
40. O'Sullivan, introduction, xvi.
41. Curnow, 69.
42. Bethell, 2, 3, 11, 12, 13,15, 17, 20, 24.
43. O'Sullivan, introduction, xx.
44. Bethell, 18.
45. Bethell to Holcroft, quoted in Holcroft, *Ursula Bethell*, 39.
46. Bethell, 81.
47. Curnow, 243.
48. Bethell, 83.
49. Quoted in Brewer, 56.
50. Curnow, 51–52.
51. Chapman and Bennett allow Cresswell three pages in 1956. But he is overlooked entirely in subsequent national anthologies: Vincent O'Sullivan, ed., *An Anthology of Twentieth Century New Zealand Poetry* (London: Oxford University Press, 1970), Ian Wedde and Harvey McQueen, eds., *The Penguin Book of New Zealand Verse* (Auckland: Penguin, 1985), Jenny Bornholdt, Gregory O'Brien and Mark Williams, eds., *An Anthology of New Zealand Poetry in English* (Auckland: Oxford University Press, 1997), Jane Stafford and Mark Williams, eds., *The Auckland University Press Anthology of New Zealand Literature* (Auckland: Auckland University Press, 2012).
52. Curnow, 70.
53. Virtually all of Mason's best known poems appear in *The Beggar* (1924) and *No New Thing* (1934), though the date of the latter is

deceptive: the volume bears the subtitle 'Poems 1924–29'. There were five new pieces in *End of Day* (1936), and a further five in the Caxton portfolio volume *Recent Poems* (1941). Of these 30s texts, however, only 'Prelude' and perhaps 'Flow at Full Moon' could be thought of as indispensable. Three later uncollected poems, of marginal interest, are added in R.A.K. Mason, *Collected Poems*, ed. Allen Curnow (Christchurch: Caxton Press, 1962).

54. Mason, *Collected Poems*, 81.
55. Ibid., 40.
56. Curnow, 156. See also J.E. Weir, *R.A.K. Mason* (Wellington: Oxford University Press, 1977), 39; Barrowman, *Mason*, 200.
57. Curnow, 52–53; Mason, 35; Barrowman, 299.
58. Curnow, 156–57. For an earlier (1941) version of this argument, see Curnow, 29.
59. The poem itself, according to Curnow, was written by 1929 (see Curnow, 187).
60. Mason, 53.
61. Stephen Spender, *The Struggle of the Modern* (London: Hamish Hamilton, 1963), 159.
62. Mason, 32.
63. Barrowman, 57.
64. Curnow, 56.
65. Ibid., 27, 155.
66. Ibid., 55.
67. Ibid., 74.
68. Barrowman, 55.
69. Ibid., 96.
70. Ibid., 97.
71. C.K. Stead, 'R.A.K. Mason: Bringing Disorder to Life', in *In the Glass Case*, 182–83.
72. Stead makes this point initially in 'Bringing Disorder to Life', first published as a review of Mason's *Collected Poems* in 1963. He then develops his argument in detail in *The New Poetic: Yeats to Eliot* (1964; Harmondsworth: Penguin, 1967), 57–59, 81–94.
73. Harold Monro, quoted in Myram Simon, *The Georgian Poetic* (Berkeley, CA: University of California Press, 1978), 82.
74. On Mason's enthusiasm for Housman, see Barrowman, 61–62.

75. T.S. Eliot, 'The Metaphysical Poets', in *Selected Essays* (London: Faber and Faber, 1932), 289.
76. Quoted in Barrowman, 173.
77. Curnow, 167.
78. Curnow, 'New Zealand City', in *Enemies: Poems 1934–67* (Christchurch: Caxton Press, 1937), 1. This is one of a number of Curnow's earlier poems that he alters in minor ways at a later date. Because of this study's emphasis on historical context, original versions are usually preferred.
79. Barrowman, 235–36.
80 See n. 50.
81. Quoted in Barrowman, 264.
82. Michele Leggott, 'Opening the Archive: Robin Hyde, Eileen Duggan and the Persistence of Record', in *Opening the Book*, 272.
83. Mason, 82.
84. Barrowman, 216.
85. Ibid., 13.
86. A.R.D. Fairburn, 'A New Zealand Poet', in *The Woman Problem & other prose* (Auckland: Blackwood and Janet Paul, 1967), 109; Curnow, *Look Back Harder*, 186.
87. Barrowman, 15.
88. Ibid., 364.
89. Quoted in Barrowman, 21.

Chapter 3

'Stridently sex-conscious': Writing and gender (and mountaineering) c. 1928

1. Williams, *Politics and Letters*, 157.
2. Holcroft, *Discovered Isles*, 159–60.
3. For a comprehensive survey, see Lawrence Jones, *Picking Up the Traces: The Making of a New Zealand Literary Culture, 1932–1945* (Wellington: Victoria University Press, 2003), 297–313.
4. Quoted in Jones, 299.
5. Jones, 300–02.
6. Quoted in Jones, 299.
7. Holcroft, 160–62; Brasch, quoted in Jones, 298.

8. Curnow, *Look Back Harder*, 160.
9. Leggott, 'Opening the Archive', 272.
10. Jensen, 101.
11. For an account of negotiations between Duggan and Curnow over her representation in his 1945 and 1960 anthologies, see Terry Sturm, *Simply by Sailing in a New Direction. Allen Curnow: A Biography* (Auckland: Auckland University Press, 2017), 193–94, 345–47.
12. Virginia Woolf, *A Room of One's Own* (1929; London: Hogarth Press, 1935), 129.
13. Ibid., 149.
14. Ibid., 147–48.
15. Ibid., 152–53.
16. Julia Briggs, *Virginia Woolf: An Inner Life* (London: Allen Lane, 2005), 218–19; Hermione Lee, *Virginia Woolf* (London: Chatto & Windus, 1996), 564.
17. Kaplan, *Katherine Mansfield and the Origins of Modernist Fiction*, 6–10.
18. Baughan, *Studies in New Zealand Scenery*, 9.
19. Ibid., 267.
20. Sally Irwin, *Between Heaven and Earth: The Life of a Mountaineer, Freda Du Faur* (Hawthorn, Victoria: White Crane Press, 2000), 152–53.
21. Baughan, *Studies in New Zealand Scenery*, 83.
22. Graham Langton, 'A History of Mountain Climbing in New Zealand to 1953' (PhD thesis, University of Canterbury, 1996), 139, ir.canterbury.ac.nz/handle/10092/3549
23. Ibid., 168.
24. Philip Temple, ed., *Castles in the Air: Men and Mountains in New Zealand* (Dunedin: John McIndoe, 1973), 54.
25. Porter climbed for several seasons in New Zealand. Langton gives the date of the crucial season with Kurz as 1926–27 (246–47), Andrew Anderson as 1925–26 (*Castles in the Air*, 100).
26. Philip Temple, *The World at their Feet: The Story of New Zealand Mountaineers in the Great Ranges of the World* (Christchurch: Whitcombe & Tombs, 1969), 28–34.
27. The argument is Temple's: *The World at their Feet*, 48–117.

28. Langton, 240.
29. Ibid., 239.
30. Ibid., 269.
31. Ibid., 288.
32. Ibid., 230; Chris Maclean, *John Pascoe* (Nelson: Craig Potton Publishing, 2013), 48.
33. Langton, 229–30.
34. Leggott, 'Opening the Archive', 266.
35. Mary Louise Pratt, *Imperial Eyes: Travel Writing and Transculturation* (London and New York: Routledge, 1992), 7.
36. Maclean, 210.
37. Barbara Caine, *English Feminism 1780–1980* (Oxford: Oxford University Press, 1997), 180–81.
38. Susan Kingsley Kent, *Gender and Power in Britain, 1640–1990* (London and New York: Routledge, 1999), 290–95.
39. Francis Ronsin, 'Heterosexuality', in *A Cultural History of Sexuality, vol. 6: In the Modern Age*, ed. Gert Hekma (Oxford and New York: Berg, 2011), 33; Stephen Garton, *Histories of Sexuality: Antiquity to Sexual Revolution* (London: Equinox Publishing, 2004), 171–78.
40. Ellen Chesler, *Woman of Valor: Margaret Sanger and the Birth Control Movement in America* (New York: Simon and Schuster, 1992), 150; Stansell, 234–41.
41. Museum of Contraception and Abortion, 'Ernst Graefenberg (1881–1957)', en.muvs.org/topic/ernst-graefenberg-1881-1957-en/
42. Stansell, *American Moderns*, 255 ff.
43. Anne-Marie Sohn, 'Between the Wars in France and England', in *A History of Women in the West, vol. V: Toward a Cultural Identity in the Twentieth Century*, ed. Françoise Thébaud (Cambridge, MA and London: Belknap Press, 1994), 118; Elaine Showalter, ed., *These Modern Women: Autobiographical Essays from the Twenties* (New York: The Feminist Press, 1978), 9–14.
44. Stansell, 227.
45. Nancy Cott, *The Grounding of Modern Feminism* (New Haven and London: Yale University Press, 1987), 156–58.
46. Ibid., 148–49. Comparable figures were reported in France. See Sohn, 108.
47. Cott, 147–48.

48. Ibid., 166–70.
49. Sohn, 92; Sheila Jeffreys, *The Spinster and Her Enemies* (London: Pandora Press, 1985), 149.
50. Showalter, 10.
51. Caroline Daley, 'Puritans and Pleasure Seekers', in *Sexuality Down Under: Social and Historical Perspectives*, ed. Allison Kirkman and Pat Moloney (Dunedin: University of Otago Press, 2005), 62.
52. Jane Tolerton, *Ettie: A Life of Ettie Rout* (Auckland: Penguin, 1992), 13.
53. Ibid., 28–30.
54. Ibid., 31.
55. Ibid., 90.
56. Ibid., 209–11, 246–48.
57. Ibid., 216–17.
58. Barbara Brookes, *A History of New Zealand Women* (Wellington: Bridget Williams, 2016), 234.
59. Ibid., 225.
60. For a discussion, see Cott, 170–74.
61. Robin Hyde, *The Godwits Fly* (1938; Auckland: Auckland University Press, 2001), 140.
62. Tolerton, 38.
63. Irwin, 128–29.
64. Ibid., 136.
65. Ibid., 288.
66. Ibid., 301.
67. Ibid., 298, 302, 333.
68. Lucy Bland, *Banishing the Beast: English Feminism and Sexual Morality 1885–1914* (London: Penguin, 1995), 290–96.
69. Nancy Cott, 'The Modern Woman of the 1920s, American Style', in Thébaud, 81; see also Lillian Faderman, *Surpassing the Love of Men: Romantic Friendship and Love Between Women from the Renaissance to the Present* (1981; London: The Women's Press, 1985), 297ff.
70. For a full account see Rebecca Jennings, *A Lesbian History of Britain: Love and Sex Between Women Since 1500* (Oxford: Greenwood World Publishing, 2007), 109–14.
71. James King, *Virginia Woolf* (London: Hamish Hamilton, 1994),

426–27; Virginia Woolf to Quentin Bell, 1 Nov. 1928, *The Letters of Virginia Woolf, vol. III: 1923–1928*, ed. Nigel Nicolson and Joanne Trautmann (London: Hogarth Press, 1977), 555.
72. Kent, 301.
73. Harris, 2–4.
74. Rae McGregor, *The Story of a New Zealand Writer: Jane Mander* (Dunedin: University of Otago Press, 1998), 69–70.
75. Ida Baker, *Katherine Mansfield: The Memories of LM.* (London: Joseph, 1971), 203.
76. Leggott, 'Opening the Archive', 267.
77. Holcroft, 19; H.C.D. Somerset, 'Ursula Bethell: Some Personal Memories', *Landfall* 8 (December 1948), 279.
78. Quoted in Rosemary Brewer, 'A Pilgrim in the Library: The Private Letters and Public Poetry of Mary Ursula Bethell' (MA thesis, University of Auckland, 1995), 63.
79. Brewer, 82.
80. Curnow, *Look Back Harder*, 51.
81. Williams, *The Raymond Williams Reader*, 35.

Chapter 4
'All the history that did not happen': Curnow's critical nationalism

1. Curnow, *Look Back Harder*, 49.
2. Curnow to Peter Simpson, quoted in Sturm, *Simply by Sailing in a New Direction*, 581.
3. Barrowman, *Mason*, 171; Sturm, 62.
4. Sturm, *Simply by Sailing*, 86. 'MacSpaunday' is a portmanteau nickname for the quartet of Louis MacNiece, Stephen Spender, W.H. Auden and Cecil Day-Lewis.
5. Allen Curnow, *Collected Poems*, ed. Elizabeth Caffin and Terry Sturm (Auckland University Press, 2017), 357.
6. Ibid., 39. Curnow also quotes this passage in his review of Fairburn's *Dominion*, 'Rata Blossom or Reality' (1938), and in 'Aspects of New Zealand Poetry' (1941). *Look Back Harder*, 10, 41.
7. Curnow, 'Second Song', in *Collected Poems*, 77. In a similar spirit Curnow writes to Lilburn: 'It's still my belief, though the hope is

daily more tenuous, that NZ may at least fill some historic mission, i.e. in that it is a people without a nation; that it may be in the forefront of the certain revolution against the nation-idea, the beginnings of which I fancy I see.' Sturm, 139.

8. Curnow, *Collected Poems*, 80–81.
9. I discuss Curnow's debt to refugee culture in 'Allen Curnow at Joachim Kahn's', *Landfall* 220 (November 2011), 16–30.
10. Curnow, 'Dialogue of Island and Time', in *Collected Poems*, 79.
11. For a witty and acerbic tour of the Centennial celebrations, see Patrick Evans, *The Penguin History of New Zealand Literature* (Auckland: Penguin, 1990), 92. See also Stuart Murray, *Never a Soul at Home* (Wellington: Victoria University Press, 1998), 20–47.
12. Sturm, 115.
13. Ibid., 139.
14. Curnow to Peter Simpson, quoted in Sturm, 581.
15. Curnow, *Look Back Harder*, 12.
16. Sturm highlights the importance of this pair of essays, 153.
17. Curnow, 40–41.
18. Not that his personal temperament helps. Cf. Sturm, 108.
19. Ibid., 155–56.
20. Curnow to Fairburn, 9.9.45, MS Papers 1128–080, Alexander Turnbull Library.
21. W.S. Broughton makes this argument. 'Curnow's Anthologies and the Strange Case of Walter D'Arcy Cresswell', *Journal of New Zealand Literature* 15 (1997), 38. See also Jones, *Picking Up the Traces*, 113–14.
22 Sturm, 83.
23. D'Arcy Cresswell, *Present Without Leave* (London: Cassell, 1939), 6.
24. Peter Simpson, in Curnow, 31. Simpson also helpfully supplies a checklist of Curnow's citations of the passage.
25. Curnow, 56.
26. Holcroft, *Discovered Isles*, 148, 281.
27. Ibid., 34, 151.
28. Ibid., 172; quoted in Curnow, 68.
29. Curnow, 124. Charles Brasch, *Journals 1945–1957*, ed. Peter Simpson (Dunedin: Otago University Press, 2017), 186.

30. Curnow, 123.
31. Holcroft, 21, 33.
32. For a more sanguine account of teaching Curnow, see Alex Calder, 'Blood and Water: Teaching Allen Curnow', in *Teaching Australian and New Zealand Literature*, ed. Nicholas Birns, Nicole Moore and Sarah Shieff (New York: Modern Language Association, 2017), 122–32.
33. Curnow, *Enemies*, 1.
34. Curnow, *Collected Poems*, 65.
35. Eliot, 'The Metaphysical Poets', 289.
36. Curnow, *Look Back Harder*, 50–51.
37. Ibid., 47.
38. Ibid., 50.
39. Mason, *Collected Poems*, 53.
40. Curnow, 27.
41. Ibid., 52.
42. Ibid., 35.
43. Ibid., 55, 68.
44. Ibid., 74.
45. George Barker, 'Therefore All Poems Are Elegies', quoted in Curnow, *Look Back Harder*, 55.
46. Curnow, 55.
47. Ibid., 136. This variation on the theme dates from 1960. But its 1945 equivalent makes the same point: 'the shock of their translation produced a communal repression which has persisted in the failure of their descendants to *realize* their Pacific habitation.' Curnow, *Look Back Harder*, 26.
48. Ibid., 47.
49. Ibid., 26.
50. Curnow, *Collected Poems*, 357.
51. See, for example, Jones, 173–293; Jane Stafford and Mark Williams, eds., *The Auckland University Press Anthology of New Zealand Literature* (Auckland: Auckland University Press, 2012), 331–41.
52. Curnow, *Look Back Harder*, 47.
53. Ibid., 136, 147.
54. Ibid., 141.

55. Ibid., 146.
56. Ibid., 74.
57. Curnow made minor revisions to this poem from 1962. I am quoting the final version. Curnow, *Collected Poems*, 56–57.
58. Ibid., 58.
59. Curnow, 'Mementos of an Occasion', in *Collected Poems*, 130.
60. Curnow, *Look Back Harder*, 49.
61. On Curnow and modernist Time, see Sturm's discussion of the influence of Henri Bergson, in Sturm, 140–45.
62. Curnow, 49.
63. Ibid., 74.
64. Ibid., 77.
65. Ibid., 44.
66. Curnow, *Collected Poems*, 142.
67. Glover, 'Songs (1)', in *Selected Poems* (Wellington: Victoria University Press, 1995), 40.
68. Walt Whitman, 'Song of Myself', 190.
69. Curnow, *Collected Poems*, 358.
70. Robin Hyde, *Young Knowledge: The Poems of Robin Hyde*, ed. Michele Leggott (Auckland: Auckland University Press, 2003), 312.
71. Jones reaches the same conclusion, 208.
72. Hyde, *Young Knowledge*, 314.
73. Cresswell, *Present Without Leave*, 1.
74. Ibid., 6.
75. Quoted in Curnow, *Look Back Harder*, 32, 36.
76. Ibid., 32.
77. Cresswell, 1.
78. James Belich, *Making Peoples: A History of the New Zealanders from Polynesian Settlement to the end of the Nineteenth Century* (Auckland: Allen Lane / Penguin, 1996), 163, 254–57.
79. Roland Barthes, *Mythologies*, trans. Annette Lavers (London: Paladin, 1973), 140.
80. Pratt, 7.
81. Ibid.
82. Curnow, *Look Back Harder*, 124; see also 253.
83. Curnow, *Island and Time*, dustjacket note; *Collected Poems*, 358.

84. Curnow, *Look Back Harder*, 71.
85. Charles Brasch, 'The Silent Land', in *Selected Poems*, ed. Alan Roddick (Dunedin: Otago University Press, 2015), 218; 'The Islands (3)', in *Selected Poems*, 17.
86. Curnow, 'The Scene', in *Collected Poems*, 67.
87. Ibid.
88. Curnow, *Look Back Harder*, 73.
89. Ibid., 146, 149.
90. Curnow, 'The Unhistoric Story', in *Collected Poems*, 57.
91. 'Unhistory' is the poet's own term. See 'Author's Note' in Curnow, *Selected Poems* (Auckland: Penguin, 1982), x.
92. Curnow, *Collected Poems 1933–1973* (Wellington: A.H. & A.W. Reed, 1974), 57.
93. Ibid., 58.
94. Ibid., 74.
95. Calder, 'Unsettling Settlement', 169.
96. In *Selected Poems* (1982) the stanza reads: '*And eke a shrowding sheet:* / For the brown singing people / Lift nobody off from Te Reinga, / So heavy, alone and late.' Curnow, in *Selected Poems*, 25.
97. Curnow, 'To M.H. Holcroft', in *Collected Poems* (2017), 89.
98. Curnow, 'Landfall in Unknown Seas', in *Collected Poems*, 96.
99. Curnow, 'Polynesia', in *Collected Poems*, 86.
100. Brasch, 'Forerunners', in *Collected Poems*, 16. Brasch records preparing the volume in Britain in 1944 (see 304, below).
101. Allen Curnow, *Not in Narrow Seas* (Wellington: The Progressive Publishing Society, 1943), 26. 'And Eliot cactuses' is later amended to 'And waste land botany', *Collected Poems*, 98.
102. Curnow, *Collected Poems*, 99.
103. Curnow, *Island and Time*, 28.
104. Roger Duff, *Pyramid Valley: The Story of New Zealand's Greatest Moa Swamp* (Christchurch: Pegasus Press, 1952), 29. According to Duff it was reconstructed out of 200 fragments by Edgar Stead.
105. Quinn Berentson, *Moa: The Life and Death of New Zealand's Legendary Bird* (Nelson: Potton and Burton, 2012), 194.
106. Ibid., 244.
107. Ibid., 235.
108. Roger Duff, *Moas and Moa-Hunters* (Wellington: Government

Printer, 1951), 23–25; Berentson, 237. After a 50-year rāhui, archaeologists have recently returned to the site under the supervision of Rangitāne o Wairau. Koiwi have been reinterred, although taonga uplifted by Eyles and Roger Duff remain in the Canterbury Museum. Berentson, 236; Blundell, 'Where it all Began', *New Zealand Listener* (1 June 2013), 18–24.

109. Curnow, 'The Unhistoric Story', in *Collected Poems*, 57–58.
110. Barthes, *The Pleasure of the Text*, trans. Richard Miller with a note on the text by Richard Howard (New York: Farrar, Straus and Giroux), 31.
111. Curnow, *Collected Poems*, 98. The poem was commissioned in 1943 to mark the tercentenary of Tasman's 'discovery'.

Chapter 5

Taking poetry seriously? Manliness in Fairburn and Glover

1. Richard Ellman, *James Joyce* (1959; Oxford: Oxford University Press, 1982), 495.
2. Ezra Pound, 'A Retrospect', in *Literary Essays of Ezra Pound*, 1, 3, 4, 5.
3. Ibid., 12.
4. In an interview in 1973 Curnow remembers the process of 'catching up [. . .] forty years ago.' Curnow, *Look Back Harder*, 264; see also 292.
5. Pound, 'A Retrospect', 7.
6. Curnow, 68, 151, 168.
7. Ibid., 79; Pound, 'A Retrospect', 1.
8. Ibid., 165.
9. Ibid., 33.
10. For an account of Glover's contribution as printer, see Peter Simpson, *Bloomsbury South: The Arts in Christchurch 1933–1953* (Auckland: Auckland University Press, 2016), 41–71, 167–93.
11. Whitman, 'Song of Myself', 27.
12. Frank Sargeson, *The Letters of Frank Sargeson*, ed. Sarah Shieff (Auckland: Vintage, 2012), 7, 159.
13. Michael Roberts, preface to *New Country*, ed. Michael Roberts

(London: Hogarth Press, 1933), 18.
14. Unsigned foreword, *Verse Alive* 2 (Christchurch: Caxton Press, 1937), unpaged.
15. Once again, my debt to Kai Jensen will be self-evident.
16. I'm talking here about Glover's poetry. A different case could be made about his printing.
17. Jones, *Picking Up the Traces*, 148–50.
18. Ezra Pound, *Selected Poems* (New York: New Directions, 1957), 26.
19. Denis Glover, *Selected Poems*, ed. Bill Manhire (Wellington: Victoria University Press, 1995), 33–34.
20. Curnow, 144.
21. William Wordsworth, preface to *Lyrical Ballads* (1802), in *Romantic Poetry and Prose*, ed. Harold Bloom and Lionel Trilling (New York: Oxford University Press, 1973), 595, 599.
22. Pound to Harriet Monro, January 1915, in *The Letters of Ezra Pound 1907–1941* (London: Faber, 1951), 91.
23. Pound, 'A Retrospect', 7.
24. Ibid., 12.
25. Walt Whitman (anonymously), 'Walt Whitman and his Poems', *Walt Whitman*, ed. Francis Murphy (Harmondsworth: Penguin, 1969), 31.
26. Holcroft, *Discovered Isles*, 65, 72.
27. Curnow, 60.
28. Barrowman, *Mason*, 223, 227–28.
29. A.R.D. Fairburn, *The Letters of A.R.D. Fairburn*, ed. Lauris Edmond (Auckland: Oxford University Press, 1981), 131.
30. Curnow, 170.
31. Ibid., 93.
32. Jensen, 51–61.
33. Curnow, 50.
34. For a particularly telling account, see Roger Horrocks, 'No Theory Permitted on these Premises', *And* 2 (1984), 119–37.
35. Denys Trussell, *Fairburn* (Auckland: Auckland University Press / Oxford University Press, 1983), 142.
36. Curnow, 51–52.
37. Ibid., 93.
38. A.R.D. Fairburn, *Collected Poems* (Christchurch: Pegasus, 1966),

220.

39. Curnow, 37.
40. Ibid., 58.
41. Ibid., 59.
42. The best guide to the poem—the process of its composition, and its structure and argument—is Trussell, 154–66.
43. Fairburn, 18; Trussell, 130–31.
44. Curnow, 58.
45. Trussell, 164.
46. Eliot, *Selected Essays*, 290; Fairburn, *Letters*, 131.
47. Trussell, 166.
48. Fairburn, 21.
49. Ibid., 27.
50. Ibid.
51. Ibid., 29.
52. Trussell, 242.
53. Ibid.
54. Fairburn, 'The Cave', in *Collected Poems*, 82.
55. Ibid., 104.
56. There is at least one love poem in *Enemies*, perhaps two; another in *Poems 1949–57*. 'Spectacular Blossom' has been described as a love poem (though, personally, I find the idea disturbing). Among the sonnets of the late 40s there may be one or two candidates, but their manner is so unforthcoming that it's difficult to tell.
57. Glover, *Selected Poems*, 77; Curnow, 295.
58. Trussell, 168.
59. Fairburn, *Dominion*, in *Collected Poems*, 26.
60. Trussell, 277.
61. Ibid., 261.
62. Dinah Holman, introduction to *Fairburn and Friends*, ed. Dinah Holman and Christine Cole Catley (Cape Catley, 2004), 23.
63. Trussell, 218.
64. Ibid., 217.
65. Fairburn, *The Woman Problem*, 24.
66. Ibid.
67. John Newton, *Family Songbook* (Wellington: Victoria University Press, 2013), 23–24.

68. Glover to Sargeson, 2.9.73, MS Papers 4261–068, Alexander Turnbull Library.
69. Jill McCracken, 'Full Houses for Four', *New Zealand Listener* (31 May 1975), 17.
70. Gordon Ogilvie, *Denis Glover: His Life* (Auckland: Godwit, 1999), 262.
71. W.B. Yeats, '*Anima Hominis*' [1917], in *Selected Criticism*, ed. A. Norman Jeffares (London: MacMillan & Co, 1964), 170.
72. Glover, *Selected Poems*, 37.
73. Curnow, 62, 294.
74. Glover, 53.
75. Ogilvie, 238.
76. Quoted in Jones, 149.
77. Denis Glover, *The Wind and the Sand: Poems 1934–44* (Christchurch: Caxton Press, 1945), 19.
78. Glover, *Selected Poems*, 29.
79. Ibid.
80. Bill Manhire, introduction to *Selected Poems* by Denis Glover, 17.
81. Glover, *Selected Poems*, 42–43.
82. Barry Barclay, 'The Other Eye' (extract), in *Te Ao Mārama* 2, ed. Witi Ihimaera (Auckland: Reed, 1993), 323.
83. Brasch, in *Collected Poems*, 17.
84. Bill Manhire, 'Notes', in *Selected Poems* by Denis Glover, 133.
85. Glover, *Selected Poems*, 43.
86. Ibid., 32–33.
87. Manhire, introduction, 12.

Chapter 6

'Caught on the hinge of an opening door': Hyde and heterosexuality

1. Robin Hyde, 'The Beaches', in *Young Knowledge*, 374–75.
2. For years I read this poem and mistook it for free verse; it's easy not to notice either its rhymes or its decasyllabic scansion. Leggott's restoration from manuscript of Hyde's original version makes the formal regularity slightly more obvious. See Michele Leggott, 'Notes on Young Knowledge: The Poems of Robin Hyde',

nzepc.auckland.ac.nz/authors/hyde/yk.pdf
3. Curnow, *Look Back Harder*, 59.
4. James Bertram, 'Robin Hyde: A Reassessment', in *Flight of the Phoenix: Critical Notes on New Zealand Writers* (Wellington: Victoria University Press, 1985), 15–27.
5. Jacques Lacan, *The Four Fundamental Concepts of Psychoanalysis*, ed. Jacques-Alain Miller, trans. Alan Sheridan (1973, 1977; Harmondsworth: Penguin, 1979), 70.
6. Robin Hyde, *A Home in This World* (Auckland: Longman Paul, 1984), 28–29.
7. Mary Edmond-Paul, 'Introduction: Dark Torch', in *Lighted Windows: Critical Essays on Robin Hyde* (Dunedin: Otago University Press, 2008), 20.
8. Stephen Danby, quoted in Edmond-Paul, 21.
9. Robyn Hyde to J.H.E. Schroder, quoted in Derek Challis and Gloria Rawlinson, *The Book of Iris: A Life of Robin Hyde* (Auckland: Auckland University Press, 2002), 691.
10. Leggott, 'Opening the Archive', 268.
11. Ibid., 266.
12. Ibid., 269.
13. Ibid., 266.
14. Michele Leggott, *DIA* (Auckland: Auckland University Press, 1994), 92.
15. Quoted in Murray, *Never a Soul at Home*, 197.
16. Curnow, 54.
17. Hyde, quoted in Challis and Rawlinson, 732.
18. Alex Calder, *The Settler's Plot: How Stories Take Place in New Zealand* (Auckland: Auckland University Press, 2011), 195.
19. Challis and Rawlinson, 360.
20. Ibid., 344.
21. Robin Hyde, *Passport to Hell* (London: Hurst and Blackett, 1936), 235.
22. Ibid., 97–101.
23. Ibid., 249–50.
24. Ibid., 86.
25. Ibid., 255.
26. Robin Hyde, *Nor the Years Condemn* (1938; Dunedin: Otago

University Press, 1995), 25.
27. Hyde, 'The People', in *Young Knowledge*, 380.
28. Ibid., 25, 132.
29. Hyde, *Passport to Hell*, 81.
30. Hyde, *Nor the Years Condemn*, 89–90.
31. Robin Hyde, *Your Unselfish Kindness: Robin Hyde's Autobiographical Writings*, ed. Mary Edmond-Paul (Dunedin: Otago University Press, 2011), 235.
32. Ibid., 236.
33. Hyde, *A Home in This World*, 55.
34. Leggott, 'Opening the Archive', 267; and see above, 145.
35. Hyde, *Your Unselfish Kindness*, 236.
36. Robin Hyde, *The Godwits Fly* (1938; Auckland: Auckland University Press, 2001), 99.
37. Challis and Rawlinson, 207.
38. On gendered rates of pay, see Hyde, *A Home in This World*, 32.
39. Challis and Rawlinson, 256.
40. Ibid., 116.
41. This belief appears to have been unfounded. See Challis and Rawlinson, 483–84.
42. Sargeson to Glover, 9.8 [1937?], Denis Glover Papers, MS Papers 418, Folder 18, Alexander Turnbull Library.
43. Sargeson to Glover, 2.2.38, *The Letters of Frank Sargeson*, ed. Sarah Shieff (Auckland: Vintage, 2012), 20.
44. Challis and Rawlinson, 683.
45. Ibid., 681. Hyde was suffering from sprue, contracted in China.
46. Ibid., 288, 339, 688; Brasch, *Indirections*, 337.
47. Challis and Rawlinson, 701.
48. Bertram, 16.
49. Brasch, *Indirections*, 337.
50. Ibid., 84; see also Brasch's poem, 'To JB at Forty', in *Selected Poems*, 53–54.
51. Brasch, *Indirections*, 338.
52. Ibid., 340.
53. Challis and Rawlinson, 738–39.
54. Ibid., 737.
55. Ibid., 738–39.

56. Ibid., 742.
57. Ibid., 740–41.
58. Woolf, *A Room of One's Own*, 99.
59. Showalter, 10.
60. Murray, *Never a Soul at Home*, 189ff.
61. O'Sullivan, *Finding the Pattern*, 5.
62. Challis and Rawlinson, 476.
63. Ibid., 313.
64. Ibid.
65. Hyde, *Your Unselfish Kindness*, 66.
66. Challis and Rawlinson, 698.
67. Hyde, *Your Unselfish Kindness*, 227.
68. Hyde, *Wednesday's Children* (1937; Dunedin: Otago University Press, 1979), 57.
69. Roberts, preface to *New Country*, 18.
70. Challis and Rawlinson, 448–49.
71. Hyde, *Your Unselfish Kindness*, 176.
72. Hyde, *A Home in This World*, 51; see also Hyde, *Your Unselfish Kindness*, 246.
73. Hyde, *Young Knowledge*, 296.
74. Ibid., 292.
75. Ibid.
76. Robin Hyde to J.H.E. Schroder, quoted in Challis and Rawlinson, 102.
77. Hyde, *Your Unselfish Kindness*, 266.
78. Hyde, *Passport to Hell*, 176–77.
79. Vincent O'Sullivan, *Finding the Pattern*, 8.
80. Quoted in Challis and Rawlinson, 328.
81. Robin Hyde to John A.Lee, Lisa Docherty, '"Do I Speak Well?" A Selection of Letters by Robin Hyde 1927–1939' (PhD thesis, University of Auckland, 2000), 199, researchspace.auckland.ac.nz/handle/2292/735
82. Ibid., 198.
83. Hyde to Schroder, quoted in Challis and Rawlinson, 182.
84. Hyde, *A Home in This World*, 10.
85. Quoted in Leggott, introduction to *Young Knowledge*, 19.
86. Hyde, *Young Knowledge*, 293.

87. Leggott, introduction, 9, 29.
88. Hyde, *Your Unselfish Kindness*, 212.
89. Megan Clayton, 'Thoroughly Modern Malory: Robin Hyde's Poetic Ciphers and Camelot Codes', in *Lighted Windows*, ed. Edmond-Paul, 107–18.
90. Curnow, *Look Back Harder*, 168.
91. Brasch, *Indirections*, 339.
92. Leggott, introduction, 19, 24.
93. Leggott, introduction to *The Book of Nadath*, xxxiv; see also ix.
94. Hyde, *Young Knowledge*, 245.
95. See introductory notes to *Prometheus Unbound*, in Bloom and Trilling, 421.
96. Curnow, *Collected Poems*, 130–31.
97. I have expanded on this in 'Running with the Fast Pack', *Ka Mate Ka Ora* 14 (July 2016), 24–25.
98. Curnow, *Look Back Harder*, 44.

Chapter 7
Calling a spade a shovel: Sargeson's 'disguised poetry'

1. Sargeson, *Sargeson*, 11.
2. Frank Sargeson, 'D'Arcy Cresswell by His Friends', *Landfall* 56 (December 1960), 350.
3. Sargeson, *Conversation in a Train and Other Critical Writings*, 34.
4. Quoted in Michael King, *Frank Sargeson: A Life* (Auckland: Viking Press, 1995), 293. Ray Copland records a similar shock of recognition on discovering 'That Summer' in 1944: 'To a New Zealander serving in England at the time, to hear one's own native dialect coming straight off the page [. . .] was an astonishment never to be forgotten.' Ray Copland, *Frank Sargeson* (Wellington: Oxford University Press, 1976), 17.
5. King, 94–95, 111–12.
6. Sargeson, *Sargeson*, 211.
7. King, 161–62. See also Phil Parkinson, 'The Wanganui Affair of 1920', *Pink Triangle* 56, 1985, 10–11; Peter Wells and Rex Pilgrim,

introduction to *Best Mates: Gay Writing in Aotearoa New Zealand* (Auckland: Reed, 1997), 16; Chris Brickell, *Mates and Lovers: A History of Gay New Zealand* (Auckland: Godwit, 2008), 115–16.
8. John Newton, 'Poetry and Other Marvels: D'Arcy Cresswell on His Own Terms', *Journal of New Zealand Literature* 21 (July 2003), 14–31.
9. Brickell comments that Cresswell 'is widely presumed to have taken money' (116), although he doesn't bring any new evidence to the discussion.
10. Curnow makes this point about Cresswell in the 1945 introduction. Curnow, *Look Back Harder*, 54.
11. Sargeson, *Sargeson*, 210.
12. Ibid, 214–15.
13. Ibid, 214.
14. Sargeson to Glover, 26.9.37, *Letters*, 16.
15. Sargeson, *Sargeson*, 207, 261. See also Janet Frame, *An Angel at My Table* (Auckland: Hutchinson, 1984), 143–51.
16. Sargeson, *Sargeson*, 222.
17. Ibid.
18. Eve Kosofsky Sedgwick, *Epistemology of the Closet* (Berkeley, CA: University of California Press, 1990), 11.
19. Michel Foucault, *The History of Sexuality, vol. 1: An Introduction* (New York: Vintage, 1980), 42–43.
20. Sedgwick, 11.
21. Eve Kosofsky Sedgwick, *Between Men: English Literature and Male Homosocial Desire* (New York: Columbia University Press, 1985), 88.
22. Sargeson, *Sargeson*, 266.
23. Sargeson himself treasured the story, in exactly these terms. Sargeson to John Ower, 24.8. 80, *Letters*, 599–600.
24. Frank Sargeson, *The Stories of Frank Sargeson* (1964; Auckland: Penguin, 1982), 227.
25. Sargeson to Alec Pickard [A.P. Gaskell], 1.4.44, *Letters*, 63.
26. Bill Pearson, letter to the author, 23.3.00.
27. McCormick, 133.
28. Baxter, 221, 222.
29. Ibid.

30. Sedgwick, *Between Men*, 1–2.
31. Baxter, 222.
32. H. Winston Rhodes, 'The Moral Climate of Sargeson's Stories', *Landfall* 33 (March 1955), 34.
33. Ibid., 35.
34. King, 94–95. King's account, which I'm paraphrasing here, has been queried by Brickell, 119–22. Brickell points to King's reliance on the memories of Sargeson's elderly sister, whose testimony is not confirmed by the surviving court record (itself incomplete). Sargeson/Davey's behaviour may have been less treacherous than King believes. However, the fact remains that it was Hollobon who was sentenced to hard labour, and the younger man who escaped with probation.
35. Sargeson confirms this explicitly in correspondence. Sargeson to John Ower, 24.8.80, *Letters*, 599–600.
36. Sargeson, *Stories*, 226.
37. Ibid., 170.
38. Ibid., 177.
39. H. Winston Rhodes, *Frank Sargeson* (New York: Twayne, 1969), 87.
40. Sargeson, *Stories*, 223.
41. Ibid, 225.
42. King, 215.
43. Sargeson, *Stories*, 243.
44. Ibid, 248.
45. Ibid, 250.
46. Ibid, 244; Simon During, 'Towards a Revision of Local Critical Habits', *And* 1 (August 1983), 81.
47. Ibid.
48. Ibid, 79–80.
49. Jensen, 126.
50. Baxter, 222.
51. Rhodes, *Frank Sargeson*, 85.
52. Baxter, 222.
53. Sargeson, *Stories*, 198–99.
54. Ibid, 173.
55. Ibid, 171.

56. Ibid, 219.
57. Ibid.
58. Ibid.
59. Ibid.
60. During, 79.
61. Roland Barthes, 'The Death of the Author', in *Image Music Text,* trans. Stephen Heath (London: Fontana, 1977), 146.
62. Ibid, 142.
63. Bill Pearson, letter to the author, 23.3.00.
64. Barthes, 146.
65. During, 83.
66. John Newton, 'Homophobia and the Social Pattern: Sargeson's Queer Nation', *Landfall* 199 (March 2000), 91–107.
67. During, 80.
67. Barthes, 148.
69. See, for example, Sargeson, *Letters*, 383, 387, 428, 518–19, 552.
70. Sargeson to Glover, 2.2.38, *Letters*, 20.
71. Sargeson, *Conversation on a Train*, 32.
72. Ibid.
73. Sargeson to William Plomer, 5.6.56, *Letters*, 226.
74. Sargeson to M.I. Alfred, 29.9.74, *Letters*, 527.

Afterword
'ascetic Charles & the hefty Able Seaman'

1. Ogilvie, *Denis Glover*, 210.
2. Ogilvie, unpaged, caption between 288–89.
3. Glover to Mary Glover 26.6.42; quoted in Ogilvie, 147.
4. Glover to Mary Glover 1.12.42; quoted in Ogilvie, 164.
5. Rachel Barrowman, 'Finding "A Home For The Spirit": Charles Brasch, 1909–1973', in Charles Brasch, *Journals 1938–1945* (Dunedin: Otago University Press, 2013), 26.
6. Brasch, *Journals 1938–1945*, 457.
7. Ibid., 446.
8. Ibid., 41.
9. At the time of writing, two volumes have been published (1938–1945, 1945–1957), with a third forthcoming.

10. Brasch, *Journals 1938–1945*, 410.
11. Ibid., 334.
12. Ibid., 353.
13. Barrowman, *Mason*, 188; Brasch, *Indirections*, 187.
14. Brasch, *Indirections*, 185.
15. 'No man who can talk of the girl he loves and is engaged to as "the wench"—the only way he ever speaks of her—could have real taste.' Brasch, *Journals 1938–1945*, 86.
16. Ibid., 388.
17. Ibid., 474.
18. Ibid., 326.
19. Ibid., 147.
20. Ibid., 385.
21. Ibid., 403.
22. Brasch, *Indirections*, 409.
23. Ibid.
24. Brasch, *Journals 1938–1945*, 486.
25. Brasch, *Selected Poems*, 68.
26. Sargeson, *Sargeson*, 242–43.
27. Lawrence Jones, *Barbed Wire and Mirrors: Essays on New Zealand Prose* (Dunedin: Otago University Press, 1990), 44–45.
28. I have extended this argument, in preliminary fashion, in two essays: 'Surviving the War', *Journal of New Zealand Literature* 31 (November 2013), 84–106; 'Running With the Fast Pack', *Ka Mate Ka Ora* 14 (July 2016), 4–29.

29 Brasch, *Journals 1938–1945*, 572.

30 Ogilvie, 237; Simpson, 199.

31 Ogilvie, 237.

32 Ibid., 237–38.

Bibliography

Abrams, M.H. *A Glossary of Literary Terms*. Orlando, FL: Harcourt Brace, 1999.

Alexander, W.F. and A.E. Currie, eds. *A Treasury of New Zealand Verse*. Christchurch: Whitcombe & Tombs, 1926.

Alpers, Antony. *The Life of Katherine Mansfield*. New York: Viking Press, 1980.

Anderson, Andrew. 'The Mountaineer as Explorer'. In *Castles in the Air: Men and Mountains in New Zealand*, edited by Philip Temple, 79–107. Dunedin: John McIndoe, 1973.

Attridge, Derek. 'Context, Idioculture, Invention'. *New Literary History* 42, no. 4 (2011): 681–99.

Baigent, Lawrence. 'The Poetry of Ursula Bethell'. *Landfall* 17 (March 1951), 23–30.

Baker, Ida. *Katherine Mansfield: The Memories of L.M.* London: Joseph, 1971.

Barclay, Barry. 'The Other Eye' (extract). In *Te Ao Mārama* 2, edited by Witi Ihimaera, 322–29. Auckland: Reed, 1993.

Barrowman, Rachel. *A Popular Vision: Arts and the Left in New Zealand 1930–1950*. Wellington: Victoria University Press, 1991.

—. *Mason: The Life of R.A.K. Mason*. Wellington: Victoria University Press, 2003.

—. 'Finding "A Home For the Spirit": Charles Brasch, 1909–1973'. Introduction to *Journals, 1938–1945* by Charles Brasch, 23–34. Dunedin: Otago University Press, 2013.

Barthes, Roland. *Mythologies*. Translated by Annette Lavers. London: Paladin, 1973.

—. *The Pleasure of the Text*. Translated by Richard Miller with a note on the text by Richard Howard. New York: Farrar, Straus and Giroux, 1975.

—. 'The Death of the Author'. In *Image Music Text*, translated by Stephen Heath, 142–48. London: Fontana, 1977.

Baughan, Blanche. *Studies in New Zealand Scenery*. Christchurch: Whitcombe & Tombs, 1916.

Belich, James. *Making Peoples: A History of the New Zealanders from Polynesian Settlement to the End of the Nineteenth Century*. Auckland: Allen Lane / Penguin, 1996.

Bethell, Ursula. *Collected Poems*. Edited by Vincent O'Sullivan. Wellington: Victoria University Press, 1997.

Berentson, Quinn. *Moa: The Life and Death of New Zealand's Legendary Bird*. Nelson: Potton and Burton, 2012.

Bertram, James. *Flight of the Phoenix: Critical Notes on New Zealand Writers*. Wellington: Victoria University Press, 1985.

Bland, Lucy. *Banishing the Beast: English Feminism and Sexual Morality 1885–1914*. London: Penguin, 1995.

Bond, Emma. 'Colloquy and Continuity: The Integrated Dialogues of Blanche Edith Baughan'. MA thesis, University of Canterbury, 1998. core.ac.uk/download/pdf/35468043.pdf

Bornholdt, Jenny, Gregory O'Brien and Mark Williams, eds. *An Anthology of New Zealand Poetry in English*. Auckland: Oxford University Press, 1997.

Brasch, Charles. 'R.A.K. Mason 1905–71: Some Tributes'. *Landfall* 99 (September 1971): 236–37.

—. *Indirections: A Memoir 1909–1947*. Wellington: Oxford University Press, 1980.

—. *Journals 1938–1945*. Dunedin: Otago University Press, 2013.

—. *Collected Poems*. Edited by Alan Roddick. Dunedin: Otago University Press, 2015.

—. *Journals 1945–1957*. Edited by Peter Simpson. Dunedin: Otago University Press, 2017.

Brewer, Rosemary. 'A Pilgrim in the Library: The Private Letters and Public Poetry of Mary Ursula Bethell'. MA thesis, University of Auckland, 1995.

Brickell, Chris. *Mates and Lovers: A History of Gay New Zealand*. Auckland: Godwit, 2008.

Briggs, Julia. *Virginia Woolf: An Inner Life*. London: Allen Lane, 2005.

Brookes, Barbara. *A History of New Zealand Women*. Wellington: Bridget Williams, 2016.

Broughton, W.S. 'Curnow's Anthologies and the Strange Case of Walter D'Arcy Cresswell'. *Journal of New Zealand Literature* 15 (1997): 26–39.

Caine, Barbara. *English Feminism 1780–1980*. Oxford: Oxford University Press, 1997.

Calder, Alex. 'Unsettling Settlement: Poetry and Nationalism in Aotearoa / New Zealand'. *REAL: Yearbook of Research in English and American Literature 14* (1998): 165–82.

—. *The Settler's Plot: How Stories Take Place in New Zealand.* Auckland: Auckland University Press, 2011.

—. 'Blood and Water: Teaching Allen Curnow'. In *Teaching Australian and New Zealand Literature*, edited by Nicholas Birns, Nicole Moore and Sarah Shieff, 122–32. New York: Modern Language Association, 2017.

Carter, David. 'Critics, Writers, Intellectuals: Australian Literature and its Criticism'. In *The Cambridge Companion to Australian Literature*, edited by Elizabeth Webby, 258–93. Cambridge: Cambridge University Press, 2006.

Challis, Derek, and Gloria Rawlinson. *The Book of Iris: A Life of Robin Hyde*. Auckland: Auckland University Press, 2002.

Chapman, Robert, and Jonathan Bennett, eds. *An Anthology of New Zealand Verse*. London and Wellington: Oxford University Press, 1956.

Chesler, Ellen. *Woman of Valor: Margaret Sanger and the Birth Control Movement in America*. New York: Simon and Schuster, 1992.

Cohn, Dorrit. *Transparent Minds: Narrative Modes for Presenting Consciousness in Fiction*. Princeton, NJ: Princeton University Press, 1983.

Copland, Ray. *Frank Sargeson*. Wellington: Oxford University Press, 1976.

Cott, Nancy. *The Grounding of Modern Feminism*. New Haven, CN and London: Yale University Press, 1987.

—. 'The Modern Woman of the 1920s, American Style'. In Françoise Thébaud, ed., *A History of Women in the West, vol. V: Toward a Cultural Identity in the Twentieth Century*, 76–91. Cambridge, MA and London: Belknap Press, 1994.

Cresswell, D'Arcy. 'The Poet's Progress: Part Two' [extract]. The *Press*, 9 April 1932.

—. *Present Without Leave*. London: Cassell, 1939.

—. *The Letters of D'Arcy Cresswell*. Edited by Helen Shaw. Christchurch:

University of Canterbury Press, 1971.

Curnow, Allen. *Enemies: Poems 1934–67*. Christchurch: Caxton Press, 1937.

—. *Not in Narrow Seas*. Wellington: The Progressive Publishing Society, 1943.

—, ed. *The Penguin Book of New Zealand Verse*. Harmondsworth: Penguin, 1960.

—. *Collected Poems 1933–1973*. Wellington: A.H. & A.W. Reed, 1974.

—. *Selected Poems*. Auckland: Penguin, 1982.

—. *Look Back Harder: Critical Writings 1935–1984*. Edited by Peter Simpson. Auckland: Auckland University Press, 1987.

—. *Collected Poems*. Edited by Elizabeth Caffin and Terry Sturm. Auckland: Auckland University Press, 2017.

Daley, Caroline. 'Puritans and Pleasure Seekers'. In *Sexuality Down Under: Social and Historical Perspectives*, edited by Allison Kirkman and Pat Moloney, 47–62. Dunedin: University of Otago Press, 2005.

Darroch, Sandra Jobson. *Ottoline: The Life of Lady Ottoline Morrell*. London: Chatto & Windus, 1976.

Davis, Leigh. 'Set Up'. *And* 1 (1983): 1–8.

de Montalk, Geoffrey. *Recollections of My Fellow Poets*. Auckland: Prometheus Press, 1983.

Docherty, Lisa. '"Do I Speak Well?" A Selection of Letters by Robin Hyde 1927–1939'. PhD thesis, University of Auckland, 2000. researchspace.auckland.ac.nz/handle/2292/735

Duff, Roger. *Pyramid Valley: The Story of New Zealand's Greatest Moa Swamp*. Christchurch: Pegasus Press, 1952.

During, Simon. 'Towards a Revision of Local Critical Habits'. *And* 1 (1983): 75–92.

Edmond-Paul, Mary, ed. *Lighted Windows: Critical Essays on Robin Hyde*. Dunedin: Otago University Press, 2008.

Eliot, T.S. *Selected Essays*. London: Faber and Faber, 1932.

—. *Collected Poems 1909–1962*. London: Faber and Faber, 1963.

Ellmann, Richard. *James Joyce* [1959]. Oxford: Oxford University Press, 1982.

Emerson, Ralph Waldo. *The Collected Works of Ralph Waldo Emerson, vol. 1: Nature, Addresses, and Lectures*. Edited by Robert E. Spiller and Alfred R. Ferguson. Cambridge, MA: Belknap Press, 1971.

Evans, Patrick. *The Penguin History of New Zealand Literature.* Auckland: Penguin, 1990.

—. *Gifted.* Wellington: Victoria University Press, 2010.

Faderman, Lillian. *Surpassing the Love of Men: Romantic Friendship and Love Between Women from the Renaissance to the Present* [1981]. London: The Women's Press, 1985.

Fairburn, A.R.D. *Collected Poems.* Christchurch: Pegasus, 1966.

—. *The Woman Problem & Other Prose.* Auckland: Blackwood and Janet Paul, 1967.

—. *The Letters of A.R.D. Fairburn.* Edited by Lauris Edmond. Auckland: Oxford University Press, 1981.

Felski, Rita. *The Limits of Critique.* Chicago, IL and London: University of Chicago Press, 2015.

Foucault, Michel. *The History of Sexuality, vol. 1: An Introduction* [1978]. New York: Vintage, 1980.

Frame, Janet. *An Angel at my Table.* Auckland: Hutchinson, 1984.

Garton, Stephen. *Histories of Sexuality.* London: Equinox Publishing, 2004.

Gillespie, O.N. 'New Zealanders in Literature. A Fine Record of Achievement'. *The New Zealand Railways Magazine* 112 (1 May 1936): 9–11, 14.

Glover, Denis. *The Wind and the Sand: Poems 1934–1944.* Christchurch: Caxton Press, 1945.

—. *Selected Poems.* Edited by Bill Manhire. Wellington: Victoria University Press, 1995).

Gordon, Lyndall. *Eliot's Early Years.* Oxford: Oxford University Press, 1977.

Haeberle, Erwin J. 'Chronology of Sex Research'. Archive for Sexology, sexarchive.info/GESUND/ARCHIV/CHR06.HTM.

Hamilton, S.D. 'New Zealand English language periodicals of literary interest active 1920s–1960s'. PhD thesis, University of Auckland, 1996. researchspace.auckland.ac.nz/bitstream/handle/2292/1146/Hamilton_1996-v2.pdf?sequence=14

Hanson, Clare, and Andrew Gurr, *Katherine Mansfield.* London: Macmillan, 1981.

Harris, Nancy. 'Making It New: "Modernism" in B.E. Baughan's New Zealand Poetry'. PhD thesis, University of Canterbury, 1992.

core.ac.uk/display/35464528

Heyward, Michael. *The Ern Malley Affair*. London: Faber & Faber, 1993.

Hilliard, Chris. *The Bookmen's Dominion: Cultural Life in New Zealand 1920–1950*. Auckland: Auckland University Press, 2006.

Holcroft, M.H. *Discovered Isles: A Trilogy*. Christchurch: Caxton Press, 1950.

—. *Mary Ursula Bethell*. Wellington: Oxford University Press, 1975.

Holman, Dinah, and Christine Cole Catley, eds. *Fairburn and Friends*, Auckland: Cape Catley, 2004.

Horrocks, Roger. 'No Theory Permitted on these Premises'. *And* 2 (1984): 119–37.

—. *Re-inventing New Zealand: Essays on the Arts and the Media*. Pokeno: Atuanui Press, 2016.

Hyde, Robin. *Passport to Hell*. London: Hurst and Blackett, 1936.

—. *Wednesday's Children* [1937]. Dunedin: Otago University Press, 1979.

—. *A Home in This World*. Auckland: Longman Paul, 1984.

—. *Nor the Years Condemn* [1938]. Dunedin: Otago University Press, 1995.

—. *The Book of Nadath*. Auckland: Auckland University Press, 1999.

—. *The Godwits Fly* [1938]. Auckland: Auckland University Press, 2001.

—. *Young Knowledge: The Poems of Robin Hyde*. Edited by Michele Leggott. Auckland: Auckland University Press, 2003.

—. *Your Unselfish Kindness: Robin Hyde's Autobiographical Writings*. Edited by Mary Edmond-Paul. Dunedin: Otago University Press, 2011.

Irwin, Sally. *Between Heaven and Earth: The Life of a Mountaineer, Freda Du Faur*. Hawthorn, Victoria: White Crane Press, 2000.

James, Henry. *The Portrait of a Lady* [1881]. London: David Campbell Publishers, 1991.

Jeffreys, Sheila. *The Spinster and Her Enemies*. London: Pandora Press, 1985.

Jensen, Kai. *Whole Men: The Masculine Tradition in New Zealand Literature*. Auckland: Auckland University Press, 1996.

Jennings, *Rebecca. A Lesbian History of Britain: Love and Sex Between Women Since 1500*. Oxford: Greenwood World Publishing, 2007.

Jones, Lawrence. *Barbed Wire and Mirrors: Essays on New Zealand Prose*. Dunedin: Otago University Press, 1990.

—. *Picking Up the Traces: The Making of a New Zealand Literary Culture, 1932–1945*. Wellington: Victoria University Press, 2003.

Kaplan, Sydney Janet. *Katherine Mansfield and the Origins of Modernist Fiction*. Ithaca, NY: Cornell University Press, 1991.

Kent, Susan Kingsley. *Gender and Power in Britain, 1640–1990*. London and New York: Routledge, 1999.

King, James. *Virginia Woolf*. London: Hamish Hamilton, 1994.

King, Michael. *Frank Sargeson: A Life*. Auckland: Viking Press, 1995.

Lacan, Jacques. *The Four Fundamental Concepts of Psychoanalysis*. Edited by Jacques-Alain Miller, translated by Alan Sheridan. Harmondsworth: Penguin, 1979.

Langton, Graham. 'A History of Mountain Climbing in New Zealand to 1953'. PhD thesis, University of Canterbury, 1996, ir.canterbury.ac.nz/handle/10092/3549

Lee, Hermione. *Virginia Woolf*. London: Chatto & Windus, 1996.

Leggott, Michele. *DIA*. Auckland: Auckland University Press, 1994.

—. 'Opening the Archive: Robin Hyde, Eileen Duggan and the Persistence of Record'. In *Opening the Book: New Essays on New Zealand Writing*, edited by Mark Williams and Michele Leggott, 266–93. Auckland: Auckland University Press, 1995.

—. 'Notes on *Young Knowledge: The Poems of Robin Hyde*', nzepc.auckland.ac.nz/authors/hyde/yk.pdf

Lehman, David. 'The Ern Malley Hoax—Introduction'. *Jacket* 17 (June 2002), jacketmagazine.com/17/ern-dl.html

Maclean, Chris. *John Pascoe*. Nelson: Craig Potton Publishing, 2013.

Mansfield, Katherine. *The Letters and Journals of Katherine Mansfield: A Selection*. Edited by C.K. Stead. Harmondsworth: Penguin, 1977.

—. *The Katherine Mansfield Notebooks*. Edited by Margaret Scott. Canterbury and Wellington: Lincoln University Press / Daphne Brasell Associates, 1997.

—. *Katherine Mansfield's Selected Stories*. Edited by Vincent O'Sullivan. New York: Norton, 2006.

—. *Katherine Mansfield's Short Stories*. Auckland: Random House, 2008.

Mason, R.A.K. *Collected Poems* [1962]. Wellington: Victoria University Press, 1971.

Matthews, Sean. 'Change and Theory in Raymond Williams's Structure of Feeling'. *Pretexts: Literary and Cultural Studies* 10, no. 2 (2001): 179–94.

McCormick, E.H. *New Zealand Literature: A Survey*. London: Oxford University Press, 1959.

McCracken, Jill. 'Full Houses for Four'. *New Zealand Listener* (31 May 1975): 17.

McGregor, Rae. *The Story of a New Zealand Writer: Jane Mander*. Dunedin: University of Otago Press, 1998.

Murray, Heather. 'Celebrating Our Writers: 1936, 1951. Part 1: 1936'. *Journal of New Zealand Literature* 10 (September 1992): 99–114.

Murray, Stuart. *Never a Soul at Home: New Zealand Literary Nationalism and the 1930s*. Wellington: Victoria University Press, 1998.

Newton, John. 'Homophobia and the Social Pattern: Sargeson's Queer Nation'. *Landfall* 199 (March 2000): 91–107.

—. 'Poetry and Other Marvels: D'Arcy Cresswell on His Own Terms'. *Journal of New Zealand Literature* 21 (July 2003): 14–31.

—. 'Allen Curnow at Joachim Kahn's'. *Landfall* 220 (November 2011): 16–30.

—. 'Surviving the War'. *Journal of New Zealand Literature* 31 (November 2013): 84–106.

—. *Family Songbook*. Wellington: Victoria University Press, 2013.

—. 'Running with the Fast Pack'. *Ka Mate Ka Ora* 14 (July 2016): 4–29.

Noble, Joan Russell, ed. *Recollections of Virginia Woolf*. London: Owen, 1972.

Ogilvie, Gordon. *Denis Glover: His Life*. Auckland: Godwit, 1999.

Orr, Douglas W. *Psychoanalysis and the Bloomsbury Group*. Clemson, SC: Clemson University Digital Press, 2004.

O'Sullivan, Vincent, ed. *An Anthology of Twentieth Century New Zealand Poetry*. London: Oxford University Press, 1970.

—. 'The Magnetic Chain: Notes and Approaches to Katherine Mansfield'. *Landfall* 114 (June 1975): 95–131.

—. *Finding the Pattern, Solving the Problem*. Wellington: Victoria University Press, 1989.

Pilditch, Jan, ed. *The Critical Response to Katherine Mansfield*. Westport, CN: Greenwood Press, 1996.

Pound, Ezra. *The Letters of Ezra Pound 1907–1941*. London: Faber and Faber, 1951.

—. *Literary Essays of Ezra Pound*. Edited by T.S. Eliot. London: Faber and Faber, 1954.

—. *Selected Poems*. New York: New Directions, 1957.

—. *Gaudier-Brezska: A Memoir*. New York: New Directions, 1970.

Pound, Francis. *The Invention of New Zealand: Art and National Identity, 1930–1970*. Auckland: Auckland University Press, 2009.

Pratt, Mary Louise. *Imperial Eyes: Travel Writing and Transculturation*. London and New York: Routledge, 1992.

Prince, Gerald. *A Dictionary of Narratology*. Lincoln and London: University of Nebraska Press, 1987.

Roberts, Michael, ed. *New Country*. London: Hogarth Press, 1933.

Rhodes, H. Winston. *Frank Sargeson*. New York: Twayne, 1969.

—.'The Moral Climate of Sargeson's Stories'. *Landfall* 33 (March 1955): 25–41.

Ronsin, Francis. 'Heterosexuality'. In *A Cultural History of Sexuality in the Modern Age*, edited by Gert Hekma, 27–47. Oxford and New York: Berg, 2011.

Ross, Andrew. *No Respect: Intellectuals and Popular Culture*. London and New York: Routledge, 1989.

Sargeson, Frank. *I Saw in My Dream* [1949]. Auckland: Auckland University Press / Oxford University Press, 1974.

—. 'D'Arcy Cresswell, by His Friends'. *Landfall* 56 (December 1960): 349–50.

—. *Sargeson*. Auckland: Penguin, 1977.

—. *The Stories of Frank Sargeson*. Auckland: Penguin, 1982.

—.*Conversation in a Train and Other Critical Writings*. Edited by Kevin Cunningham. Auckland: Auckland University Press / Oxford University Press, 1983.

—. *The Letters of Frank Sargeson*. Edited by Sarah Shieff. Auckland: Vintage, 2012.

Sedgwick, Eve Kosofsky. *Between Men: English Literature and Male Homosocial Desire*. New York: Columbia University Press, 1985.

—. *Epistemology of the Closet*. Berkeley, CA: University of California Press, 1990.

Showalter, Elaine, ed. *These Modern Women: Autobiographical Essays from the Twenties*. New York: The Feminist Press, 1978.

Simon, Myron. *The Georgian Poetic*. Berkeley, CA: University of

California Press, 1978.

Simpson, David. 'Raymond Williams: Feeling for Structures, Voicing "History"'. In *Cultural Materialism: On Raymond Williams*, edited by Christopher Prendergast, 29–50. Minneapolis, MN: University of Minnesota Press, 1995.

Simpson, Peter. *Bloomsbury South: The Arts in Christchurch 1933–1953*. Auckland: Auckland University Press, 2016.

Smith, Angela. *Katherine Mansfield: A Literary Life*. Basingstoke, UK: Palgrave, 2000.

Sohn, Anne-Marie. 'Between the Wars in France and England'. In Thébaud, 93–118.

Somerset, H.C.D. et al. 'Ursula Bethell: Some Personal Memories'. *Landfall* 8 (December 1948): 275–96.

Spender, Stephen. *The Struggle of the Modern*. London: Hamish Hamilton, 1963.

Stafford, Jane, and Mark Williams, eds. *The Auckland University Press Anthology of New Zealand Literature*. Auckland: Auckland University Press, 2012.

Stansell, Christine. *American Moderns: Bohemian New York and the Creation of a New Century* [2000]. New York: Henry Holt and Company, 2001.

Stead, C.K. *The New Poetic: Yeats to Eliot* [1964]. Harmondsworth: Penguin, 1967.

—. *In the Glass Case: Essays on New Zealand Literature*. Auckland: Auckland University Press / Oxford University Press, 1981.

Sturm, Terry. *Simply by Sailing in a New Direction. Allen Curnow: A Biography*. Auckland: Auckland University Press, 2017.

Symons, Arthur. *The Symbolist Movement in Literature*. London: Archibald Constable & Co., 1908.

Temple, Philip. *The World at their Feet: The Story of New Zealand Mountaineers in the Great Ranges of the World*. Christchurch: Whitcombe & Tombs, 1969.

—, ed. *Castles in the Air: Men and Mountains in New Zealand*. Dunedin: John McIndoe, 1973.

Thébaud, Françoise, ed. *A History of Women in the West, vol. V: Toward a Cultural Identity in the Twentieth Century*. Cambridge, MA and London: Belknap Press, 1994.

Tolerton, Jane. *Ettie: A Life of Ettie Rout*. Auckland: Penguin, 1992.

Tomalin, Claire. *Katherine Mansfield: A Secret Life*. London: Penguin, 1988.

Trussell, Denys. *Fairburn*. Auckland: Auckland University Press / Oxford University Press, 1984.

Wedde, Ian, and Harvey McQueen, eds. *The Penguin Book of New Zealand Verse*. Auckland: Penguin, 1985.

Weir, J.E. *R.A.K. Mason*. Wellington: Oxford University Press, 1977.

Wells, Peter, and Rex Pilgrim, eds. *Best Mates: Gay Writing in Aotearoa New Zealand*. Auckland: Reed, 1991.

Wevers, Lydia. '"The Sod Under My Feet": Katherine Mansfield'. In Williams and Leggott, 31–48.

Whitman, Walt (anonymously). 'Walt Whitman and his Poems' [1855]. In *Walt Whitman*, edited by Francis Murphy, 29–37. Harmondsworth: Penguin, 1969.

Whitman, Walt. *Complete Poems and Collected Prose*. Edited by Justin Kaplan. New York: Viking Press, 1982.

Williams, Mark, and Michele Leggott, eds. *Opening the Book: New Essays on New Zealand Writing*. Auckland: Auckland University Press, 1995.

Williams, Raymond. *The Long Revolution*. London: Chatto & Windus, 1961.

—. *Marxism and Literature*. Oxford: Oxford University Press, 1977.

—. *Politics and Letters: Interviews with New Left Review*. London: New Left Books, 1979.

—. *The Raymond Williams Reader*. Edited by John Higgins. Oxford: Blackwell, 2001.

Williams, Raymond, and Michael Orrom. *A Preface to Film*. London: Film Drama, 1954.

Woolf, Virginia. *A Room of One's Own* [1929]. London: Hogarth Press, 1935.

—. *A Change of Perspective: The Letters of Virginia Woolf, vol. III, 1923-1928*. Edited by Nigel Nicolson and Joanne Trautmann. London: Hogarth Press, 1977.

Yeats, W. B. *Selected Criticism*. Edited by A. Norman Jeffares. London: MacMillan & Co, 1964.

Illustrations

Index